The Case For Religious Naturalism

The Case For Religious Naturalism

A Philosophy for the Modern Jew

by JACK J. COHEN

The Reconstructionist Press • New York

Designed by Harvey Satenstein
Manufactured in the United States of America by
Book Craftsmen Associates, Inc., New York

„ויאהב יעקב את רחל"

Acknowledgments

The author acknowledges with appreciation the courtesy of the following publishers in permitting him to quote passages from these publications:

American Zionist Council, for an excerpt from *The Jewish State* by Theodor Herzl, New York, 1946.

Beacon Press, for the passage from *Reflections of a Wondering Jew* by Morris R. Cohen, 1950.

Cornell University Press, for the quote from *The Liberal Spirit* by Horace Kallen, 1948.

Doubleday & Co. Inc., for the selection from *Protestant, Catholic, Jew* by Will Herberg, 1955.

E. P. Dutton & Co. Inc., for the excerpt from *The Guide for the Perplexed* by Moses Maimonides, Tr. by M. Friedlander, 1923.

Farrar, Straus & Cudahy, Inc. for the quotations from *Judaism and the Modern Man* by Will Herberg, copyright 1951 by Will Herberg.

Harper & Brothers, for the selection from *Moral Principles of Action*, edited by Ruth Nanda Anshen, 1952.

Henry Holt & Co. Inc., for the passages from *The Faith of a Liberal* by Morris R. Cohen, copyright 1946.

International Publishers, for the passages from *History of the Communist Party of the Soviet Union*, 1931.

Jewish Publication Society, for the selection from *Sefer Ha'Ikkarim* by Joseph Albo, translated by Isaac Husik, 1946.

Lippincott, for the passage from *The Art of Making Sense* by Lionel Ruby, 1954.

The Macmillan Company, for the passages from *Religion in the Making* by Alfred N. Whitehead, 1926; *Process and Reality* by Alfred N. Whitehead, 1926; *Space, Time and Deity* by Samuel Alexander, 1927; *The Future of the American Jew* by Mordecai M. Kaplan, 1948.

New American Library, for the quotations from *Science and the Moral Life* by Max Otto, 1949.

W. W. Norton & Co. for the passage from *Concord and Liberty* by Jose Ortega y Gasset, 1946.

Public Affairs Pamphlet, for the passage from *Races of Mankind* by Ruth Benedict and Gene Weltfish, 1943.

Random House, Inc., for the extensive quotes from *The Wisdom of Laotse,* translated and edited by Lin Yutang, 1948.

Rinehart & Co. for the passage from *Man for Himself* by Erich Fromm, 1947.

Schocken Books, for the excerpt from Gershom G. Scholem, *Major Trends in Jewish Mysticism,* New York, 1946, p. 11.

Charles Scribner's Sons, for the selections from *Christianity and Civilisation* by Emil Brunner, 1948; *History of Religions* by George Foot Moore, 1937; *Reason in Society* by George Santayana, 1930.

Simon & Schuster, for the excerpt from *I Believe,* ed. by Clifton Fadiman, 1939.

Yale University Press, for the quotations from *The Problem of Knowledge* by Ernst Cassirer, 1950; *A Common Faith* by John Dewey, 1934; *Psychoanalysis and Religion* by Erich Fromm, 1950; *The Meaning of Evolution* by George Gaylord Simpson, 1950; *The Social Systems of American Ethnic Groups* by H. Lloyd Warner & Leo Srole, 1945.

The passage from *Language, Truth and Logic* by A. J. Ayer was reprinted by permission of Dover Publications, Inc., New York 10, N. Y. ($1.25).

PREFACE

In the summer of 1947, my wife and I went to Eretz Yisrael, she to study and I to carry out a long cherished desire to observe the grapplings of the Yishuv with the problems of Jewish tradition. I had been deeply impressed over the years with what I had heard and read about the way in which the Jewish pioneers of what was then Palestine were seeking to create for themselves new forms of Jewish spiritual life.

I had just settled down to research in the literature of the *kibbutzim*, in the work of the Cultural Department of the Histadrut and in the educational programs of the various religious and nonreligious trends, when the Arab-Israeli conflict broke out. My research, to all intents and purposes, came to an end. I had learned enough, however, to realize that the problem of religion in Israel must be understood as part of a larger issue which concerns religion everywhere. That issue is the question as to whether or not religion can any longer be tied to a supernaturalist view of life. It was this question which led to the writing of this volume.

I have been helped immeasurably by the thinking and criticism of teachers, friends, and colleagues, and I want now to express to them my deep appreciation and to absolve them of responsibility for any errors of logic, weakness of argumentation, or narrowness of vision. I can only hope that those who were kind enough to read earlier drafts of my manuscript will feel that the time and thought they so generously gave to constructive criticism were well spent.

First, I wish to acknowledge my indebtedness to my teacher Dr. Mordecai M. Kaplan, the inspiration of whose thought drew me into the rabbinate. I consider myself one of the most fortunate members of the American rabbinate in having been privileged to work intimately with him since 1945. It will be obvious to any reader that the pages which follow could not have been written without his influence.

Dr. Eugene Kohn made his first impact on me many years ago when he took the trouble to befriend an eager young contributor to *The Reconstructionist* and to discuss word by word the first article I ever offered to any magazine. I have never forgotten the kindly criticism of thought and wording which finally made that article on the role of Hebrew in American Jewish life fit for publication. Dr. Kohn has been a friend and influence ever since.

To Rabbis Harold Weisberg and Harold Schulweis I express the hope that their faith in this work will be sustained. They both contributed pages of criticisms, many of which I have tried to meet. Dr. Sidney Morgenbesser, than whom there is no more perceptive critic, disclosed to me a number of pages loosely argued. I hope they have been tightened to his satisfaction. Rabbi Ludwig Nadelmann also read the manuscript and offered several cogent suggestions which are incorporated in the text.

The publication of this book was made possible by the generosity of my dear friends, Mr. and Mrs. Maurice Linder. I am deeply grateful to them.

Finally, no author has ever been blessed with an editor like Mrs. Ruth Eisenstein. But I can say no more in praise of her. She would simply edit my glowing words right out of this page.

New York, November 1957

TABLE OF CONTENTS

INTRODUCTION

Among the many questions that trouble American Jews in our time is the place of religion in their lives. The question is a twofold one. There is the curious fact that Jews continue to identify themselves as Jews, and to be so identified by others, long after they have abandoned the beliefs and practices of their religion. In the American scheme of things Jews are commonly classified as members of a religious communion. In what category, then, are "nonreligious" Jews to be placed? If they do not fit neatly into the category of religion, neither do they fit into any of the familiar sociological classifications like race, nation or state.

The sociological aspect of the problem is perplexing enough. But it is probably not so serious as the philosophical and theological challenge with which Jewish religion, along with all other historic faiths, is confronted. Whether or not there is any real conflict between science and religion, the effects of scientific discovery and scientific method on the traditional religions have been devastating. Efforts currently being made to restore faith in a personal God by stressing the limitations of science are an indication of the decline in the sense of security that has accompanied the revelations of science about the nature of the universe. These efforts, however, can hardly be said to be crowned with success. They neither restore faith nor stand the test of logical analysis.

Religion cannot be confined to the limited realm of theological speculation. Some religionists try to divide human thinking into hermetically sealed compartments. They hope to have religion by establishing it as the source of a distinct kind of knowledge, unlike that conveyed by science. But they lose sight of one thing: they weaken religion by depriving it of a potential ally. For is not one of religion's age-old purposes to lead man to an understanding of cosmic unity? And how can such an understanding be achieved without an organic conception of human knowledge?

The mistake made by such theologically directed religionists arises out of their failure to see the close relationship between ideas and experience, between systems of thought and the social conditions under which they grow. If the present-day revival of religion is to be genuine and lasting, we must treat the sociological factors of religion as seriously as the theological. Religion, even in the limited sense of a theological system, is subject to all the periodic adjustments in thinking that result from the advancement of knowledge and the changing institutions of society.

Thus the study of Jewish religion today involves investigation into the meaning of religion in general and its manifestation in the life of groups and individuals. Until recently, Jewish religion had either been studied as an isolated phenomenon or viewed through the lenses of the dominant civilization surrounding the Jewish group at a particular time and place. The great Jewish philosophers of the Middle Ages, for example, committed as they were to the doctrine of revelation, could not take advantage of their occasional insights into comparative religion. They had to treat Jewish religion from the starting point of its supposed supernatural and unique origin. That origin made it understandable only in terms of the Torah, which by definition was unassailable from outside the tradition. This approach to the study of Jewish religion has been characteristic of those scholars, in are said to be ways of knowing, each with its own legitimate frame of reference. Science deals with the material, religion with the spiritual. Kaplan's remarks are directed against this epistemological dualism.

What is Kaplan's basic point? It is not, as some recent critics have held, to declare that the laboratory procedures of science are the only ways to attain knowledge. It is not a priori to place the hypotheses of revelation and intuition on a level below that of critical intelligence. It is not even to deny theology intellectual respectability. It is to place our hopes for the establishment of the "Kingdom of God on earth" in concepts and practices that are recognized as valid within their historical setting, rather than in theoretical absolutes which stand beyond any reference to time, place, or consequence. This is all that is to be inferred from insisting that religion be subject to the same methods of verification as are applied in other realms of human experience.

The events of the past two decades have not rendered easier the application of Kaplan's method to the problems of Jewish religion. A cataclysmic war and the annihilation of a third of the Jewish people have caused many of us to despair of the power of reason. We hesitate to buckle down to the hard chore of analyzing our problems and experimenting with proximate solutions. Like most people, we want security and "peace of mind," and we want them in a form that will silence all doubts and obviate the need for constant reappraisal of our situation. Our refusal to face reality accounts for the superficial solutions that have been offered for the spiritual malaise that is prevalent among modern Jews. The first corollary that follows from the sociological approach to religion is the recognition of its changing (which does not always mean "progressive") character. Since the conditions under which any religion functions are subject to change, the religion itself—its beliefs and practices—must undergo change. The problem which then presents itself is— what is the element of continuity or sameness in Jewish religion? What, in other words, makes Jewish religion Jewish? And what can make Jewish religion of universal worth to mankind?

This essay points the way to a naturalistic reconstruction of Jewish religion. I shall try to do justice to that which Jewish religion shares with all other religious experiences and at the same time to hold up to examination that which is unique in it. It is within this perspective, I believe, that the religious problems of American Jews can best be solved.

This book, then, is addressed, in the main, to Jews. But if it conveys some idea of the spiritual problems which confront them, it should prove of more than passing interest to non-Jews. For Jews share in the universal problems of human existence.

To be understood, Jews must be studied primarily as men and women engaged in the eternal human endeavor to savor life to the fullest. They do so, of course, within the framework of the group and the heritage into which they are born or with which, in an act of conversion, they affiliate. But their behavior follows, too, from the human needs and characteristics which they share with the rest of mankind. Understanding the Jews, therefore, might help non-Jews to understand themselves, just as the study of other groups is indispensable to an adequate appreciation of Jewish experience.

The Case For
Religious
Naturalism

ing of the words. He may well feel that the views and experience of heretics like Spinoza have superior value. But the dignity and value of such experience of cosmic emotion does not depend on its being called religious. It seems to have been felt by those who, like Lucretius and Shelley, frankly called themselves, and were called by others, irreligious. The current fashion of attaching an honorific value to the word "religion" has caused it to be stretched so that it no longer has any definite meaning.[4]

It is true that anthropomorphism was characteristic of most early religion, but the humanistic emphasis of Confucianism, the naturalistic elements of early Taoism, and the profound rejection of anthropomorphism of much of biblical Judaism are among the numerous exceptions that contradict this aspect of Cohen's sweeping remarks. But even if we were to accept as fact the assumption that religion has been associated, in the mind of "mankind as a whole," with anthropomorphism, this is no reason to assert that the association need be permanent.

Since the heresies of today often become the orthodoxies of tomorrow, it may be that an objective study of the significance of religion would reveal that the designations religious and irreligious* tell us more about the people who use them than about the phenomena they purport to describe. The reader is reminded at this point that we are considering fallacious ideas about religion that stem from prejudices of one sort or another. As regards Cohen's views, one is tempted to judge them to be those of a man who, intellectually outraged by the orthodoxy in which he was raised, built a

---

*"Irreligious" as used by Cohen in the passage cited means "antireligious." Some writers, however, use it as a synonym for "nonreligious." It is precisely this kind of semantic looseness that often beclouds the discussion of religion.

structure of opinions about religion and had no intention of rebuilding it—even if it should be shown to be shaky. Obviously Cohen had decided early in his intellectual career that religion was to be irrevocably condemned to intellectual ignominy, from which it should not and could not be redeemed. But what is the justification for associating religion solely with anthropomorphism, supernaturalism, dogmatism, authoritarianism, and various other far from honorific isms, as Cohen and others have done? One can only conclude that the reconstruction of religion would have made Cohen intellectually unhappy. It is almost as if he had a personal stake in preventing religion from becoming acceptable to philosophical naturalists like himself.

The fact is that numerous religious individuals and some religious groups no longer accept the theology of the traditions, yet frankly call themselves, and are called by others, religious. The Unitarians, the Universalists, and many Reform and Conservative Jews are in this category, and there are millions of churchgoing men and women whose conception of the universe would be acceptable to even the most skeptical members of the American Philosophical Association. It has been charged, as is implicit in Cohen's remarks, that these millions are really secularists in religious disguise, but those who make the charge must be prepared to defend the view that religion and traditional theology are synonymous.

The same fallacy, which aims at freezing religion in the mold of the past, is well exemplified by the following lines from the pen of a young Jewish thinker, Irving Kristol:

> For religion, we live under the jurisdiction of the past. The truth is in the revelation on Sinai, and in Scripture, which fully comprehends us while we are powerless to fully comprehend it. God's word, spoken in the

remote past and now hardly audible, is ever more
true than the persistent chatter of men. Religion informs us that our ancestors were wiser and holier than
we; that they were therefore more normal because
they lived by divine law, while our laws are driftwood
in the streams of time; that no matter how mightily we
strive, we shall probably never see with their clarity
into the fundamental constitution of existence and
shall always be of little worth compared with them;
and that, indeed the virtue we inherit by reason of
being descendants of Abraham, Isaac and Jacob is far
greater than any we can hope to claim to have merited.[5]

According to Kristol, religion relies on the authority of
an ancient revelation and an authoritative past: an outlook
based on contemporary experience or on a naturalistic view
of history is not religion. Reinterpretation of revelation as
the progressive disclosure of moral and natural law cannot
be considered religion; to believe, as many avowed religionists do, that modern man possesses more knowledge than his
ancestors and is potentially wiser, is irreligion.

It must be admitted that the kind of religion described by
Cohen and Kristol is widely prevalent. It must also be con·
ceded that reliance on supernaturalism has been characteristic of religion throughout the ages. But the religionist who
thinks religion should and can be freed from supernaturalism
simply cannot be dismissed as one who is confusing the issue.
How can the modern liberal, who accepts change as a basic
ingredient of the universe, deny that religion is fully capable of living up to the demands of an evolving universe,
and indeed must necessarily rise to them? Only on the assumption that religion has ceased to grow or has no right
to grow can one agree to embalm religion in the mummy
case of antiquity.

A fourth common fallacy is the use of "religion" honorifically and the use of "secularism" derogatorily. To illustrate this fallacy I quote from a letter which appeared in the *New York Times* of July 9, 1950:

> I submit that this nation was founded on Christian principles, and that the blueprint for democracy grew from the seeds planted by Plato and nourished by Augustine, Thomas Aquinas and many other philosophical realists. A logical understanding of the term secularism can lead us only to the inescapable conclusion that our nation today is fighting for certain basic spiritual values; and that its enemies are secularists who practice a philosophy of life which allows no room for religious creeds or for the institutions of worship.
>
> The Platonic principle, repeated by Augustine and his successors, that "an unjust law is no law" is the guiding principle of all true revolutions. It is the concept that made America a nation.
>
> Either we believe in the principles upon which this nation was founded, in the dignity of man, in honesty, truth, justice and honor, or we have become so confused that we have been caught in the maelstrom, unable to identify our own cause and confused to a point where we accept the philosophy of the totalitarian. This nation is not and will not be opposed to public schools, but I fervently hope it will always be opposed to a secular, materialistic philosophy.

There is no point in dealing here with the philosophical confusions of the correspondent. What concerns me is his ambiguous use of the term secular and its derivatives. Is a secularist one who rejects the principles of the dignity of man, honesty, truth, justice, and honor? Then there should be very few secularists in the United States—for these are the values which our public schools have been inculcating

for many years. And who are the secularist enemies of
America? If they are the Communists, whose ideological
leaders in Russia now permit public worship, with many
restrictions, are they not also the Catholics, whose brethren
in Spain place severe limitations on non-Catholic worship?
Even a cursory analysis of this remarkable letter demonstrates
that the correspondent's use of "secularism" is emotive
rather than analytic. He is not alone. "Secularism" has become the battle cry of all those who fear the implications,
for traditional religion, of the naturalistic leanings in modern thought.

What the correspondent and the many who think in the
same vein want to affirm as religious is Christianity in its
institutionalized form. For they agree with Emil Brunner,
who asserts that "only Christianity is capable of furnishing
the basis of a civilization which can rightly be described as
human."[6] According to this view, all social theories and institutions that are not Christian must be secular. But even
the most devout Christian is forced to concede that there are
other expressions of humane religiousness—however mis-
guided, in his opinion, these expressions may be. He is prepared to grant Judaism, Hinduism, Buddhism, and other
organized religions the right to classification as religions.
In other words, religion, in the eyes of the average Christian
—and, indeed, of most other religionists—must be institutionalized. Whatever is sponsored by a religion so institutionalized, whether in the form of church, synagogue, or mosque,
is considered religious. All other expressions are secular,
and those persons who feel no need for expressing their
spiritual yearnings within the four walls of a house of worship are secularists.

If all religionists and all nonreligionists would base their definition of secularism on this institutional criterion, they would render a great service to the cause of clarity. Unfortunately, that is not the case. For some religionists apply the term secularism in a derogatory sense to the concept of naturalism. They consider anyone who does not accept belief in a supernatural God or in some Absolute a secularist. But what about the countless men and women within the churches whose theological beliefs are no different in their naturalist bent from those of spiritual-minded persons who do not attend formal worship? Are the naturalist churchgoers, too, to be called secularists? On the other hand, when a nonreligionist (who, not being a member of any religious communion, is therefore a secularist in the eyes of the formally affiliated) declares, "I have my own private religion,"[7] he makes the problem much more complex for religionists. For according to religionists, such a person has no right logically to speak of his beliefs as religion.

What, then, is the distinction in common usage between the sacred and the profane, the religious and the secular, the religionist and the secularist? There is no clear distinction. The student of religion, therefore, must be aware of the purpose in the mind of the writer or speaker who uses these terms. Thus for those who seek to introduce the doctrine of one of the historic religious sects into the public school, any theory of education which omits that doctrine is secular. But the theory of education that is secular to them may be religious in the judgment of another person. Evidently, then, words like secular and religious are more likely to be evaluative than descriptive.

Because these terms have largely lost their objective reference, linguistic ethics requires that I stipulate their meaning in my own system of thought. I distinguish between the sacred and the profane and the religious and the secular in terms of a scale of values. "Sacred" and "religious" are terms properly attached to those ideas, institutions, and activities which bear on the supreme concerns of individual and group life, those very concerns—expressed in our society in the concepts of the dignity of man, honesty, truth, etc.—which the avowed secularist wants to dissociate from formal religion. Profane and secular are those everyday experiences which are unrelated (except remotely) to the supreme concerns. Playing golf, buying furniture, reading the newspaper, etc., are all secular activities. But the dividing line can never be an absolute one. Where freedom of the press is abridged, reading an underground newspaper might be viewed as a religious duty, as would any other act of defiance against tyranny. "Rebellion to tyrants is obedience to God." Eating is normally a secular act, but a table ritual expressing a sense of gratitude for the labor and sacrifices that have gone into bringing a meal to the dining table raises the act to the level of a religious experience. Secular acts are thus capable of becoming vehicles of religious expression, an idea convincingly expounded in the writings of Paul Tillich[8] and Abraham J. Heschel.[9]

To distinguish between the religionist and the secularist is perhaps more difficult. For if a man insists he is a secularist, why should anyone want to dispute his claim and declare that he is actually a religionist? In common parlance, as previously shown, the religionist is a church member, while the secularist insists that church affiliation is unnecessary for the achievement of the ethical goals that both he and the religionist desire. However, if it was this ethical and educational objective, rather than the means to this end, which was to differentiate the religionist from the secularist, it would be almost impossible to make the distinction. For most nonchurchgoers accept the same basic ethical values that are held by churchgoers.

Nor can belief in God be the determining factor. The religionist is popularly held to be a man who believes in God, even though he may have only a vague idea of the nature of his God. The secularist claims that he has no need for such a belief; in other words, he is an avowed agnostic or atheist. However mistaken he may be philosophically in his definition of atheism, his avowed attitude is one of renouncing the religious approach to life. Again, however, the reader should be warned of the ambiguity of words. The word God covers so many varying interpretations of reality that it is altogether possible for a secularist who never uses the term to hold a more theistic position than a religionist whose every other sentence contains the divine Name. I am reminded of one Jew who perceives no meaning in life but nevertheless asserts that the Jew must rigidly observe the Torah. He prays regularly according to the demands of tradition, but he believes, or says he believes, that life is a matter of chance. Few theists would consider his a religious point of view. This man is actually an atheist, and his religiousness is either a psychological aberration or a matter of social habit. Many atheists might be called religious and many religionists atheistic if we could get beneath the slogans and discover what they actually believe.

Thus the complex nature of religion makes it difficult to discern a clear-cut philosophical distinction between the secularist and the religionist. We are forced to conclude that, to all intents and purposes, the actual difference between them is an organizational one. The religionist sees his world outlook as religious because he is attached to some group or institution which calls itself religious and is generally recognized as such. The secularist has no such attachment and denies its essentiality.

2

People are more dogmatic about religion than about any other subject. This in itself impedes communication. Furthermore, when people try to express their religious views to one another, they often use the same terms for entirely different, and sometimes conflicting, ideas. That is why discussions on religion are so often fruitless, whether the discussants are all religionists, all antireligionists, or some of each.

We have seen that analysis of the religious phenomenon is made difficult by some common fallacies rooted in prejudice. These fallacies cause us not only to misread the history and evolution of religion but to lose sight of its very character. If we are to understand religion, we must be prepared to keep it in sight in all environments and in all times. Like the detective shadowing a suspect, we must keep our eyes on our subject no matter how it is dressed or in what company it appears. Above all, we must know what it is we are looking for.

Definitions are not the simple matters they appear to be on the surface. For ordinary discourse the dictionary suffices, and any dispute about the meaning of a word can be settled by resort to it. But dictionaries have to undergo constant revision, because reality changes and the symbols which refer to it must keep pace. Particularly is this true where normative terms or social institutions are involved.

The fluid character of terminology has led some thinkers to assert that the essential factor for logical and significant discourse is the stipulation by the writer or speaker of his own particular meaning. (Where common words bear several meanings, such stipulation is obviously necessary.) More-over, these thinkers say one has a right to create one's own symbols so long as one is consistent in applying them. Thus it makes no difference whether there is any important con-nection between the definition and the actual subject matter under consideration. For example, a person who defines re-ligion as belief in a Creator cannot be required to prove the truth or falsity of his definition; he can be held to account only for any deviation from this usage or for any fallacies that he falls prey to in handling the term. The only control that the public can have is that of social pressure—to insist that definitions conform as closely as possible to prevailing usage. "Readers and audiences find it difficult to follow a speaker who uses words in unfamiliar ways, and the speaker's freedom is limited by his desire to hold his audience."[10]

It should be apparent, however, that there is a vast differ-ence between the semantic device represented by "Define your terms," which makes real communication possible, and the semantic trick represented by the creation of definitions to suit special purposes. For what we are after is not only logical consistency but truth—and, equally important, rele-vance. Once we accept the assumption that religion promotes fear, that it belongs to the past alone, or that it is reactionary, then it follows logically that anything which frees man's minds from fear, awakens him to the constant revelation of new truths, or drives him to seek social reform cannot be religion. I say that definitions based on these assumptions are neat tricks, because they are actually designed to conceal something. That something is the particular bias with which their authors enter discourse. Let me illustrate this point by citing again the common fallacy of identifying religion with the supernaturalism of the traditional creeds.

Starting with the premise, let us say, that religion is based on the beliefs and practices revealed by God to a particular person or group of people at a particular time and place, we can build, as Aquinas did, a logical and self-contained system of thought. In such a system, of course, only the traditional ideas will be deemed worthy of being given a religious status; all contradictory notions will be excluded as antireligious or nonreligious. Thus the beliefs of the traditional saints are religious; the beliefs of a modern, "secular" saint are nonreligious—unless they can be made to fit into the traditional mold. Suppose, however, that religion be defined as "affirmation of life." With such a definition, one might include under religion both orthodox and heterodox attitudes toward a revealed tradition. In actuality, then, definition depends on the bias that precedes the start of inquiry. To know this bias, in its manifold expressions, is of greater importance in an investigation of religion than to understand the internal logical development of a particular religious philosophy.

If, therefore, we treat religion from the standpoint of both meaning, in the symbolic sense, and significance, in terms of its emotional, intellectual, and social references, we shall undoubtedly be able to penetrate more deeply into its actual, objective status in human affairs. We must learn to observe how "religion" is used in propositions. Is the term applied clearly, in accordance with the consensus of usage? To what does the word refer in real life?

To get at the significance of religion, we must guard against two other sources of error, besides the arbitrary limiting by definition of the area of belief and action covered by religion. One is to ignore the context in which religion appears; the other is to conceive of religion solely in structural terms and to ignore its function. Many thinkers remove religion from its context of time and place and speak of it in isolation from its social setting. John Dewey emphasizes the danger of this kind of isolation when he makes the point that the noun religion can be properly applied only to the religious orientation of a particular group. To speak of religion in general is to lump together so many varied and conflicting experiences and viewpoints as to render the term meaningless. The thought-worlds of Christianity, Judaism, and Buddhism, for example, are poles apart. Each is a religion, but "religion" cannot be defined in terms of any one of them. The best that we can do, says Dewey, is to seek out the common spiritual experience, if there be such, of these and other religions and apply the adjective religious to it. The noun we can legitimately apply only to the religious experience of a particular group.

I feel that Dewey overstates the case and that it is possible to use "religion" in a more general sense. I shall try to substantiate this later in the text; here I wish only to concur in his opposition to lumping all religions, in all times and places, into a single category. The most common example of such arbitrary categorization is the association of all religions with supernaturalism.

Religionists and nonreligionists alike are guilty of this fallacy. The State of Israel today supplies an instance. There is a sharp cleavage between the religious Israelis and those who are nonreligious or antireligious. The religious are all taken to accept the traditional, supernatural approach. Any other world view is not considered religious. The many Israelis who do not accept supernaturalism must consider themselves to be nonreligious. By sharing the common view that religion must be identified with supernaturalism the nonreligious Israelis subscribe to the same fallacy as the religionists. Thus religion in Israel, having grown up in a universe of discourse in which supernaturalism was predominant, is held to be constitutionally incapable of throwing off the shackles of an ancient approach to reality. Religion, in a word, is equated with supernaturalism.

"Naturalism" and "supernaturalism" are key words in any discussion of religion. They are also among the most difficult concepts to free of semantic confusion. They are overloaded with prejudices. To illustrate, when the Catholic speaks of "natural law," he posits along with it a conception of nature in which the suspension of that law by a supernatural deity is possible. For him, since naturalism cannot possibly mean a renunciation of miracle, there is no clear demarcation between it and supernaturalism. Yet a distinction between naturalism and supernaturalism is essential if rational communication is to be a possibility. Naturalism cannot be made to mean supernaturalism and vice versa. Let us examine some of the ramifications of these terms.

3

By naturalism I mean the disposition to believe that any phenomenon can be explained by appeal to general laws confirmable either by observation or by inference from observation. The term disposition is used advisedly, since it is perfectly clear that even the most ardent supporter of the scientific method cannot in any "ultimate" sense disprove "miracles." But it is inherent in the naturalist disposition to accept any discontinuities in the affairs of the physical universe or of man as part of the "natural" scheme of things. This is not to say that everything that happens in the universe is necessarily explainable. Only extreme arrogance would lead men to believe they possessed the potentiality of omniscience. All the naturalist insists upon is that man has only one instrument of knowledge, his reason, and that any knowledge or "vision" purportedly received by man from sources beyond "nature" are products of that same rational faculty operating either in inspired fashion or mistakenly, as the case may be.

The main problem in any definition or description of naturalism is the fog surrounding "nature" itself. This is a concept which appears, in all likelihood, as frequently as any other in the literature of philosophy, science, and religion. It is, therefore, important to realize the great variety of meanings and shades of meanings conferred upon it by the leading thinkers of all ages. Nature is sometimes a designation for the physical universe exclusive of man. It is sometimes held to include man as well. Frequently nature is set off in contrast to man's spiritual qualities, much as the body is contrasted to the spirit. Nature is conceived of as created existence, in contrast to the absolute existence of God. It is the totality of all existence, and it is the orderly process which characterizes that part of reality which man can experience. It is the totality of physical reality, and it is the principle of its operation. Nature is substance, and it is function. And so it goes. Some of these usages contradict one another; some are complementary.

In these pages, nature will be conceived of as the totality of reality—its substance, functioning, and principles of operation—including man and his spiritual qualities. The naturalist thus tends to explore as deeply as possible the pattern of things as they lend themselves to human understanding and to deny the existence of any realm of human knowledge beyond that apprehensible through men's faculties of mind. He would deny that there is a realm of meaning "beyond" the process of life manifest to human investigation.

But to many thinkers human understanding is itself a problem. Are there not methods of arriving at truth, such as intuition and revelation, which are as valid as the scientific method of hypothetical reasoning and experimental verification? Assuming that such methods are different in character from that of science, what are their implications for the meaning of nature? Do they imply a spatial beyondness, such as that pictured in traditional accounts of heaven and hell? In this case would not some form of revelation be essential if man were ever to receive any inkling of that realm? Or is the beyondness an ontological dimension, a principle of explanation, without which nature itself is hardly understandable? If so, revelation might still be considered essential for man's grasp of nature to be more than a tenuous one.

It is a common assumption that there is a sharp cleavage between the methods of science and religion, that there are different roads to truth, and that there are, indeed, different kinds of truth, each apprehended by its own distinctive method. I take the view that all hypothetical thinking is a projection beyond the actually experienced, that all so-called revelations and intuitions are extensions of such imaginative constructions, and that the ultimate test of their validity must lie in experience. The key to the solution of the foregoing questions I find in the concept of transcendence. For this concept opens the door to harmonizing the so-termed scientific and nonscientific methods of arriving at truth.

The problem of thinking deserves the kind of extensive consideration which cannot be given to it here. I shall limit my discussion of thinking primarily to its connection with the idea of transcendence which is basic in religious terminology.

Transcendence is a necessary category of all human thinking; but it in no way requires going beyond nature. Consider, for a moment, scientific method. The scientist, faced with the problem of relating facts of observation in some pattern of cause and effect, or of analyzing the factors entering into a given phenomenon, must necessarily transcend a given situation in order to arrive at a new and more inclusive framework of explanation. Transcendence in this sense actually adds nothing to nature which is not inherently and essentially involved in a particular concatenation of events. In the realm of values, however, it is frequently asserted that transcendence involves an entirely new category of existence, one which is "beyond" nature and which can only be grasped by the human mind through intuition or revelation.

There is really only one method of arriving at knowledge about the universe. What intuitionists and revelationists do is to omit the final step in the process of thought, which is validation. For example, what happens when we try to understand the status of freedom? To say that man is free, in the sense that he *ought* to be free, is to transcend the present state of man and to project for him a new mode of existence. This kind of transcendence seems, on the surface, to add a new dimension to nature, a dimension that has been supplied only by man and that if absent would in no way affect man's understanding of nature. But to conclude that human values are not part of nature is superficial, for it ignores completely man's proneness to transcend his immediate experience. This human characteristic is as much an aspect of nature as an observed fact or the scientific context into which that fact is placed. Furthermore, the fact that man feels he ought to be free is not the final step in the process of value judgment, no matter how dogmatically certain religious theorists insist that we must accept this ideal as moral truth. There are a number of other serious questions that require investigation. What, really, do we mean by human freedom? How does this ideal relate to the other values we hold out for human life? What are the conditions of human intercourse essential to the achievement of freedom? Are not the answers to these questions prerequisites for the acceptance of freedom as an "ought"? And when we have undergone such a process of investigation, have we not at the same time validated our assumption that this "freedom" is part of the very existential framework within which the nature of man becomes more clearly apprehended?

All thinking, in other words, requires acts of imaginative vision about an infinite present and of equally imaginative projection into an always expanding future. The realm of the transcendent is thus the ever-present unknown, the source at one and the same time of intellectual and spiritual challenge and of our future knowledge. But it is all part of nature, for nature, too, has a future, as well as a past and a present.

Some naturalists, on the basis of scientific experience, include in the naturalist disposition a tendency to assume that the universe is an orderly process. But whether or not they make this admittedly unverifiable assumption, all naturalists believe that there is no conscious force outside the universe acting upon it. On the other hand, the assumption that the universe is orderly permits many generalizations about reality that take us far beyond the realm of mere observation. Naturalism is not a commitment to holding as real only those phenomena which are capable of mechanistic determination. Indeed, mechanism is no longer considered to be an adequate explanation of the behavior of even the physical universe. There is too much mystery, creativity, and uncertainty in life for us to countenance mechanism as a satisfactory explanation of reality. But disbelief in mechanism does not warrant belief in arbitrariness. It warrants only reserving judgment about the significance of a particular experience. Man has unraveled the answer to many mysteries, and there is no reason to assume that he will not unravel others. The naturalist believes that solutions can be found to the unsolved mysteries of life, because the still mysterious phenomena are subject to the same natural processes as those already understood.

It should be realized that naturalists do not deny their inability to answer questions like "Was the world created?" and "How was life initiated?" But although they find such questions, at least for the present, unanswerable, they do not posit a cause outside nature; to do this, they assert, would simply add to the mystery.

4

The difficulty with language is that we have to define words with words. I have been using "supernaturalism" in my discussion in connection with naturalism, and I suppose the reader has been wondering if I ever intended to define it. The time has come to do so.

By supernaturalism I mean the belief that there is a power (or powers) operating in the universe not subject to the same restraints as are imposed on natural phenomena. Whatever order does exist is present by virtue of an arbitrary, omnipotent will above nature and is subject to interference at any time. The world, according to this view, exists by the grace of a living God.*

---

*Making allowances for the mood of their thinking, we can classify both Reinhold Niebuhr and Paul Tillich in the naturalist camp as described in this volume. However, it seems to me that Niebuhr, in his profound work *The Nature and Destiny of Man,* introduces considerable confusion by setting up an arbitrary and restrictive definition of nature. By denying to nature elements of freedom and spirituality, he is able to refer to the self-transcending aspects of nature, such as freedom and creativity, as "supernatural." Tillich similarly denies to nature the quality of self-transcendence. Supernaturalism for him then becomes the ontological tool by means of which alone man can gain true perspective on himself and on the process of nature. For both these thinkers super-nature is the transcendent aspects of reality, not a realm of space and time beyond nature.

Both the assumption of a self-ordered universe, which is the view taken here, and of a God transcending (in the sense of "beyond") nature and capable of overturning it are acts of faith by which man tries to read meaning into his life. From the perspective of human values, there is perhaps as much evidence that the world is chaotic as that it is orderly. Earthquakes, tornadoes, floods are as real as night and day, summer and winter. Why, then, does not the naturalist posit either chaos or arbitrary rule from above? The answer, which is necessarily psychological rather than ontological, lies in the fact that the assumption of order is at least capable of validation. Every successful experiment points in this direction, and many of the admitted disorders in nature have gradually been explained in terms of natural causes. No such canons of validation have ever been worked out for the existence of an omnipotent God transcending nature.

In the spiritual realm, the struggle between naturalism and supernaturalism is centered in the problem of the source of values. Whence do we derive our ideals of justice, truth, equality? And once derived, how is their fulfillment to be guaranteed? The naturalist would assert, as we have seen, that it is the very nature of man, by virtue of his powers of thinking and willing, to establish values for himself. He would contend further that some values are more worthy than others, in the sense that the attainment of specific objectives is dependent on the integration of certain values rather than others into the life of the individual and society. For example, given the objective of peace, equality of opportunity is more likely than class stratification to lead a society toward this goal. The naturalist would concede also that there are certain values or spiritual objectives which are absolute in a given context. That is to say, while peace may not always be desirable—for instance, where freedom is at stake—this does not gainsay the fact that peace as an objective of mankind is a goal toward which all men should strive. Naturalism would stop at this point in the argument, claiming that the further question "Why is peace more desirable (or more 'good') as a value than war?" can be answered only by locating peace in the scheme of all values, the keystone of which is the affirmation of life itself.

Supernaturalism cannot be satisfied with this self-contained system of values. It seeks to break through the circle and locate the source of values and the guarantee of their fulfillment in a cause beyond man. Therefore God beyond nature is invoked once again, as in the case of the physical world. Otherwise by virtue of what standard, asks the supernaturalist, do democrats struggle for their system against that of the totalitarians? Unless democratic ethics are grounded in the will of God—and God is here interpreted as being a Power who communicates his values to man, who could never be certain of their truth without such revelation—they can make no legitimate claim on the conscience of man. For without such cosmic authority, it is held, one man's claim would be as valid as another's.

Naturalism and supernaturalism agree on the existence of moral order, but they differ in their understanding of that order. Naturalism holds this order, in the form that it is available to human awareness, to be a construct of the human mind, subject to all its weaknesses. The moral law, in other words, is for the naturalist a term applied to *man's* understanding of what is ethically valid. Supernaturalism, equally cognizant of human frailty, asserts the need for an absolute system of morality whose validity is dependent on its being equated with the will of God. Naturalism is satisfied to struggle for human betterment without any guarantee concerning the ultimate triumph of goodness (except the guar-

antee of potentiality) ; supernaturalism insists on the existence of God as man's assurance that evil will be banished
from the earth (or in the afterlife). In the search for such
certainty, supernaturalism has often involved itself in two
basic paradoxes: the first, that if God's absolute goodness
and omnipotence will necessarily produce an ethical world,
then man's conduct is actually of little moment in its
achievement; the second, that if God is absolutely good and
omnipotent, then evil should be impossible.

Naturalism is not a new approach to reality. But its early
formulations lacked the backing of scientific knowledge,
which has now been marshaled to support it. Thus, although
the Greeks developed a conception of nature and took the
first real steps toward the scientific method, their science,
being embryonic, scarcely touched the popular religion of
the time. Rather was it the dialectician who challenged the
traditional beliefs, in much the same way that thinkers and
religious geniuses (or virtuosos, to use a term of Max
Weber's) had effected changes in other religions in both
Eastern and Western Asia. It was not until the cumulative
effect of centuries of scientific discovery had swept away
the last hope of convincingly explaining the universe by
positing a conscious deity that the era of naturalism really
arrived.

When religion arose in society, its intellectual foundation
was neither supernatural nor natural. Primitive man had
only a vague conception of nature as a "self-operative" phenomenon; therefore, he could have no idea of the supernatural, in the refined sense in which we use the term
today. Cassirer, in summarizing Renan's views, declares:

> What we today call a miracle, what appears as such to
> the modern man, can be expressed only through a
> definite contrast and difference. A miracle is something

that falls outside the field of "natural" occurrences which is governed by fixed and universal laws, but for a consciousness that has not yet achieved such a view of nature and its complete subjection to causal order, this contrast has no meaning; the idea of a miracle escapes it. Hence our historical perspective is false when we transfer to primeval times an antithesis that is valid and decisive for us."[11]

For the ancients, literally everything that happened was caused by the activity of a god or gods. Whether for good or for evil, the final authority was not man's. Man could have a hand in his fate by keeping on good terms with his deity, but it was the deity who managed the world.

Ancient Jewish thinkers made the concept of God's rule more subtle by attributing to man freedom of the will. If everything was in the hands of God, then human behavior could have no independent status. Hence God created man with a peculiar nature of his own, a nature which included freedom. Man's freedom could have meaning only if the world in which he functioned was so orderly as to make sense of his power to choose. Miracles, in turn, were a deliberate and occasional intervention of God in the orderly affairs of His universe in pursuit of some divine purpose. This refinement of the more primitive concept, however, did not eliminate the idea that nature itself was a miracle. This view, as exemplified in the prayer "We will give thanks to Thee—for Thy miracles [the ordinary acts of nature] which are daily with us . . ." permeated the tradition.

The following passage from the writings of Joseph Albo, fifteenth-century Jewish philosopher, should counteract any tendency to credit premodern Judaism with a consistent view of an independent natural law: "Now the existence of rain cannot be ascribed to nature, because it is not a thing which occurs every year at the same time in the same way, like the other natural phenomena. Rain comes at different times, in different ways, in a wonderful manner, not uniformly and naturally."[12] The tradition, like many modern religionists who delight in the limitations of science, ascribed the slightest discontinuity in nature to the operation of a supernatural force. And since there are always areas of discontinuity, the belief in the supernatural continues to flourish.

During the many centuries of their progressive discovery of the laws of nature, scientists were unaware of the revolution they were helping to foster. Many of them were as devout as their religious leaders, and some of them were churchmen. Today, however, we realize fully what they wrought. They destroyed the entire intellectual foundation of the then existing Western civilization. That civilization rested on the assumption that since all of life depended on the actions of an omnipotent power, it was necessary for men to abide by the code of behavior which the deity had supposedly revealed to them. It was not only revealed religion that was undermined; every institution which rested on the assumption that the status quo was God-inspired was weakened. Monarchical governments, for example, even after the Reformation and the break-up of the temporal power of the Roman Church, found justification in the assumption that class distinctions were divinely approved.

The foregoing analysis should make it clear why authoritarian religionists insist on the supernaturalist view; it should also help to explain the usefulness of supernaturalism to a diametrically opposed group, the authoritarian antireligionists. The dogmatic religionist knows that to admit the legitimacy in religion of replacing the supernaturalist position by a naturalist one would be to weaken the authority of orthodoxy. The dogmatic antireligionist, of the Marxist type in particular, stands to gain equally from the pinning of the supernaturalist label on all religion. It helps support his own critique of religion as intellectually reactionary and unworthy of serious consideration as an option for intelligent men. For these two types of minds religion, by definition, includes the assumption that there is a conscious Power beyond nature which brought the universe into being and which ultimately determines its fate. No naturalistic belief can be religion in the eyes of the Marxist, any more than it can in the eyes of the fundamentalist.

The fact is that the identity of religion and supernaturalism that some thinkers try to establish is a historical judgment arising from the fact that religion, during a considerable portion of human history, could hardly have been grounded in any other view. Supernaturalism was for centuries convincing to mankind as a whole; the naturalism of the Greeks had its influence and its small following among the intellectuals, but it never came anywhere near achieving the popularity of supernaturalism. Today, however, given the context of scientific knowledge, it can be urgently argued that supernaturalism is a millstone around the neck of religion: with the spread of education supernaturalism becomes less and less appealing even to nonintellectuals.

Moreover, the identity of religion and supernaturalism can stand only when religion is treated without concern for its bearing on human needs. Taken as an institution which has an independent existence, religion could, of course, be defined as the embodiment of supernaturalism. This would be a structural definition. When viewed functionally, however, as an institution capable of fulfilling certain needs of man, religion cannot so easily be limited; it cannot be restricted in definition to one particular method of satisfying those needs. We see, then, that a structural definition of religion associates religion with some specific *Weltanschauung;* it follows that when the *Weltanschauung* changes, the religion is undermined. Indeed traditional religionists, who hold to the structural definition, to this day insist that the future of religion depends entirely on its ability to continue to inspire belief in revelation. Those who define religion functionally, on the other hand, take account of the fact that there are often many answers to a single problem and realize that there are thus many pathways in man's eternal quest for fulfillment.

The distinction between these two concepts of religion, the structural and the functional, also involves a presumption about the nature of religious development. Those who hold to the structural definition conceive of religion statically. The church is an end in itself; all other institutions must adapt themselves to its spiritual hegemony. The church never changes; it is eternal. Those who abandon it are sinners, deliberate or unwitting. The church never errs, since it operates on a mandate from God. Proponents of the structural definition of religion also posit certain basic doctrines that are unchangeable and eternal. Adaptation to new conditions is never necessary because the doctrines are assumed to have anticipated their own evolution and to have embodied a method of interpretation at the time of their revelation.

Those who interpret religion functionally, quite otherwise, discern unending change in the conditions of life, change that necessitates constant revision of the doctrines and institutions of religion. They must, then, find some identifying factor common to religion in all its varying forms. If no common factor could be found, then the term religion could justifiably be used only in the narrowest sense. Indeed, we should have to rewrite almost every book containing the word. For it is apparent that the particular sense in which "religion" is understood varies from author to author. This conclusion should show the absurdity of trying to pin "religion" down to a single theology or a single institutional form. An adequate definition, which would enable normal discourse about religion to continue without the necessity of the invention of a new term for each subtle nuance, must therefore provide a suitable generalization. It will perhaps shed light on the problem to use the concept of government as an analogy.

If we examine governments throughout the ages, we find a wide variety of forms, from the patriarchy of the early Hebrews to the republicanism of the United States. The functions of government as well have varied, beginning, among the primitives, with the rudimentary purposes of protection and the securing of food. These minimal needs obviously cannot account for the pyramiding of structure characteristic of subsequent governments. Initially established to care for the basic physical wants, governments were later called upon to answer additional needs, physical, intellectual, and spiritual, resulting from the growth of civilization—the need for internal law and order, for the development of agriculture and industry, for the maintenance (or eradication) of class distinctions, for education and culture, etc. To identify government with the satisfaction of just one of these needs would be an unwarranted circumscription of its function. If we were to apply to government the logic of those who define religion structurally and identify it with a particular response to a particular human need, we should have to eliminate the term government from our vocabulary as the designation for many of our present-day ruling authorities. In the United States the government was once conceived of as an instrument for ensuring the untrammeled exercise of free private enterprise. For some time now the government has been imposing limits on such freedom, yet no one in his right mind would declare that the term government, as applied to the ruling power of our country, has outlived its function and ought to be superseded by a new designation.

If I seem to labor this point, it is because so many liberal intellectuals try to read "religion" out of existence by denying that it can be legitimately employed as a designation for any other attitude than the supernaturalism of a bygone age.

Doubtless there are religions which originated, at least partially, as responses to fear, and doubtless there are a few religions in which fear still plays a significant role. But some religions today exhibit only normal concern with that emotion. Some orthodox churches seek power in order to force their conceptions of truth and salvation on the world, but there are others, for instance the Quakers, which have traditions of serving mankind. Some religions abound in ritual; others, like Unitarianism and Quakerism, are relatively devoid of it. I need not multiply examples. From the standpoint of specific function, there is as much (or as little) reason to provide a new term for every kind of religion as there is for every kind of government.

5

I have tried by semantic analysis to rescue religion from the vested interests, both intellectual and institutional, which would like to appropriate it for their own purposes. Semantics alone, however, cannot solve the problem. Whatever power religion retains as an institution, as an intellectual or emotional factor in modern society, is a mere vestige of past glory. Like the monarch of England, it reigns but does not rule. It is respectable but not respected. Its restoration to its former position of importance in the thinking and behavior of intelligent men and women depends on whether religious spokesmen will have the courage to abandon outmoded positions and strike out in new directions.

2

THE TWOFOLD NATURE
OF RELIGION

ONE OF THE OUTSTANDING PALEONTOL-
OGISTS of our time, George Gaylord Simpson, declares, "I
take it as now self-evident, requiring no further special discussion, that evolution and *true* religion are compatible. It
is also sufficiently clear that science, alone, does not reach
all truths, plumb all mysteries, or exhaust all values and
that the place and need for true religion are still very much
with us."[1] Contrast this view with that expressed by Morris
R. Cohen in the essay quoted above, the first section of which
is entitled "Religion Strengthens Superstition and Hinders

Science or the Spirit of Truth-Seeking." Cohen goes on to say, "To religion, agreement is a practical and emotional necessity, and doubt is a challenge and an offense."[2]

Simpson implies that there are at least two realms of truths and two methods of arriving at it. Cohen assumes, in his essay, that there is only one kind of truth and that science is the method by which it is disclosed. That method, he asserts, stands in direct opposition to the fallacious method of religion. Involved in this difference of opinion is more than a controversy over the worth of religion. Simpson and Cohen actually differ as to the meaning and status of truth. Cohen relates truth to the outcome of scientific inquiry; Simpson implies that there is a kind of truth, bound up with religion, about which science can tell us nothing, and he denies that there is any inherent conflict between scientific and religious truth. It is clearly evident that an understanding of religion must reckon with these conflicting views of the bearing that religion has on truth.

Religion and science, as methods of arriving at truth, are epitomized by Horace M. Kallen in the following way:

> Where religion takes its ground on revelation, science appeals to experience; where religion imposes authority and tradition, science invites free experimentation and testing; where religions assert the primacy and eternity of their respective revelations to the exclusion of all alternatives, science acknowledges the genuineness and validity of the alternatives, the reality of change, and keeps perfecting a technique for the progressive and fair testing of all alternatives. Religion, in sum, imposes a grammar of assent, while science invites participation in a logic of doubt and inquiry.[3]

It is not my purpose to try to resolve these conflicting viewpoints but to draw some implications from the prevalence of such radically different evaluations of religion.

Simpson is quite explicit in his book about his opposition to authoritarian religion, as his use of the phrase *"true religion"* in the passage cited indicates. For Simpson religion can accept the assumptions and methods of science and still logically remain religion. Not so for Kallen and Cohen. They assert an unbridgeable gap in methodology: modern man is asked to choose between the "enlightened" method of science and the "obscurantism" of religion. How are we to explain two such irreconcilable readings of religion? May it not be that the disagreement is really due to a difference in understanding of what it is that the term religion denotes? Kallen, for example, in the passage quoted above, ignores Dewey's admonition that religions have to be studied with the same objectivity that is applied to other social phenomena. Thus "religion [which means *all* religion] takes its ground on revelation." If this were true, then much of liberal religion would not be religion. Kallen should either prove his statement, qualify his assertion that religion takes its ground on revelation, or state that religion, by definition, is belief in revelation. He does none of these things, but merely assumes that when he speaks of religion as taking its ground on revelation all his readers understand his words as he does and agree with his usage. Critics of religion (and religionists too) speak of the spirit and method of religion as though they were identical with their institutional embodiments. It is true that there should be a relation between theory and practice. But just as it is possible for men to pervert science (as in the whole Michurin-Lysenko incident in Russia), so is it possible for men to pervert the spirit of religion in the institutions they set up in its name.

Many distinguished thinkers, like Cohen and Kallen, in extracting the dark aspects of religion, create the impression that such findings are universal or necessary adjuncts of religion. Yet these same thinkers are found to write glowingly about religion in other passages. Thus Cohen in his autobiography finds religion, stripped of supernaturalism, to be a necessary aspect of man's spiritual adventure.[4]

Apparently, even first-rate thinkers have difficulty in understanding the nature of religion. Cohen is, as I have just illustrated, self-contradictory. He and Kallen, on the one hand, and Simpson, on the other, can find no common ground on which they can join issue. They all accept the basic premises of scientific method, but they differ—at least in what they write—about the principles on which religion rests. Are they not, however, raising a false issue? Cannot the term religion be validly applied to contradictory ideas, just as "science" designates both sides of the as yet unresolved problem of relativity and quantum physics? If, then, religion is not to be limited to one ideological or theoretical response to the universe, we must find for it a context within which opposing views can be legitimately accommodated. That context is the social setting of religion.

There is an almost universal failure in writings about religion to differentiate between its social or institutional and its doctrinal aspects, and there is a strong tendency to speak of religion with a capital R. Just as objectionable as the unscholarly failure to differentiate between religion as doctrine and religion as social organization is the reluctance to draw the necessary conclusion from the existence of conflicting religious philosophies. Such diversity might suggest, at least, that religious theory, far from being opposed to science, might be brought into consonance with it. I might add, parenthetically, that adjustments to science made by religious philosophies should not be held against them as a sign that religion is abandoning its domain in favor of science. We ought to know enough about the interrelations between branches of knowledge and culture to realize that growth in one branch must have some corresponding effect on the others. Religion has to react to science, and vice versa.

It is to the elucidation of the twofold nature of religion, its doctrinal and social aspects, and their respective dynamics, that this chapter is devoted.

1

Religion antedates theology. Its social aspects had developed for centuries before the first theologian came upon the scene. In our own day there are religions in which the theological and doctrinal side predominates, but the time has come, if the phenomenon of religion is to be understood, to emphasize anew religion's social origins.

In the long history of philosophy, most systems of thought, until recently, have been formulated around a God-concept. It is often difficult to distinguish between philosophical and theological writing. True, there is a wide disparity in spirit between the Prime Mover of Aristotle and the living God of Maimonides and Aquinas. Aristotle had no recourse to a revealed scripture, whereas Aquinas and Maimonides, because of their theological convictions, would have accepted the existence of God even without the support of Aristotle. But even Aquinas and Maimonides, in their more speculative moments, wrote as true philosophers, whose ideas take them where their reason, rather than tradition, leads. Nevertheless, reliance on revealed authority was by no means the only difference between the Aristotelian and Scholastic philosophies of reality. Aristotle founded no religion; nor did his thinking affect Greek religion. Aquinas and Maimonides, on the other hand, made no fundamental philosophical innovations, but their synthesizing philosophies had profound effects on the development of Christianity and Judaism. Aristotle's metaphysical position was not related organically to Greek life, however much it may have been a product of Greek culture. It undoubtedly grew out of the Greek milieu, particularly out of the questions of appearance and reality that bothered the Greek mind, but so far as Greek religion was concerned, it had no effect. Aristotle was not interested in buttressing the popular cults of his day, unlike the Scholastic philosophers, who sought to provide a stronger ideological basis for the communion of which they were a part and to which they were committed. It was this intent that enabled them to borrow ideas formulated in an entirely foreign culture and transplant them into their own native soil. The success of their endeavor is to be seen in its lasting effects on Western religions.

When we ask ourselves why the philosophy of Aristotle, who, after all, exerted a tremendous influence on religion, did not lead to the founding of a religious sect, or have any effect on the Greek religion of his time, we come to realize that religion is not essentially a matter of metaphysical doctrine. It is not enough to say that Artistotle did not want to found a religion. In all likelihood, neither did Jesus, who considered himself a Jew to the day of his death. Nor is it enough to say that Aristotle's God is devoid of personality. So is the God of some Eastern religions whose communicants number in the millions. A more complete answer lies in the fact that Aristotle's philosophy of religion had no relation to any specific social setting. His ethics, for example, could easily be adapted to existing organized religions but were not, in themselves, a sufficient basis for organizing a new sect. Similarly, his idea of God could and did help numerous religions to refine their own theologies but had no socially compelling force behind it. Aristotle's thinking was for the sake of thought itself. It was curiosity, rather than the search for individual or social fulfillment, that motivated his philosophizing. Aristotle stands outside the pale of Greek religion.

From all this there emerges the premise that the proper starting point for an understanding of a religion is the study of the total civilization of the group which has produced it, and not solely of the theology or the religious philosophy of that group.

2

If we examine the history of religion, we find that there is hardly a group of people, granted a sufficiently differentiated common experience, who have not produced a religion or some of the ingredients of a religion. This involves us in what appears to be a bit of question begging. For if I describe religion, as I propose to do, some critics will accuse me of preparing a Procrustean bed for all the facts I can muster. My defense is that I am *describing religions* rather than *defining religion*. Before trying to understand a phenomenon whose designation is used as subjectively as "religion," it is necessary to discover if there is any common denominator in all the senses in which that designation is used. On this point Erich Fromm comments, "We simply have no word to denote religion as a general human phenomenon in such a way that some association with a specific type of religion does not creep in and color the concept."[5] Even if the following description fails to lead to a satisfactory definition of religion, it should, help the reader to see how his own religious position relates to the group phenomena and ideological systems that are commonly identified as religious.

Before embarking on this description, let us deal with

Dewey's semantic objection to the use of "religion" generally. He decries the use of the word as designating an identifiable human experience. There are, in his opinion, only *religions;* the various definitions of religion in the universal sense fail to win his approval. He quotes, as an example, the definition in the Oxford Dictionary, to the effect that religion is "recognition on the part of man of some higher unseen power as having control of his destiny, and as being entitled to obedience, reverence, and worship." As Dewey points out, while this definition is less explicit than others in its reference to belief in the supernatural, it veers in that direction. The definition itself is thus an object of controversy. When one begins to analyze the content of each of the components of the definition—unseen power, obedience, reverence, etc.—one enters upon an even more complicated sphere of disagreement, for each may be interpreted in manifold ways. In actuality, every religious group has given a different meaning to each word in the definition. Dewey concludes that "religion" has no generalized connotation that can be meaningfully applied to all the specific manifestations of the religious experience.

Despite this reasoning, Dewey seems to me to be pointlessly precise in his avoidance of the term religion as a general concept covering a universal human experience. For if his insistence on exact language were to prevail, it would remove from circulation a great many nouns which facilitate intercourse among scholars and lay people alike. Take "philosophy," for example. There are areas of philosophy that can scarcely be differentiated from the science, physical or normative. Unquestionably, too, philosophers have given such varied content to key philosophical concepts—quality, time, space, matter, idea, being, reality, and countless others—that each word has to be explicitly defined by each philosopher who uses it. Yet Dewey finds no fault with the use of the term philosophy as a universal.

Clear thinking on religious matters requires the ability to isolate the areas of experience by which, in whole or in part, all religions may be recognized. These areas, and not the particular forms which religions and religious ideologies take, constitute the substance of religion.

There is an important application of such an understanding of religion, related to the question as to whether or not Soviet Communism is a religion, which has been widely discussed in recent years.

Lenin once denounced a German scholar for attempting to adjust religion to the demands of a naturalist outlook on life. He called him "a straight-forward conscious reactionary, who is openly helping the exploiters to substitute new, viler and more despicable religious prejudices for old and rotten ones."[6] It was Lenin's contention (he was writing to Gorki at the time) , that the term religion could never be stretched to include the viewpoint of philosophical naturalism. "Religion," by definition, could be legitimately applied only to supernaturalism. To use it as a designation for a naturalist position would only confuse issues and would play into the hands of the reactionaries by rendering the idea of religion palatable in liberal and revolutionary circles. Lenin, who had to face the religio-political axis of church and state in Russia, insisted that the enemy always be kept in sharp focus. Religion, in his mind, was one of the ideological tools of the tsarist tyranny.

It is ironical, then, that the tide of history has swept the Soviet version of Marxism, in the opinion of many outstanding thinkers of our time, into the category of authoritarian religion. Some years ago Morris R. Cohen could write, "It must be admitted that the current sentimental use of the word 'religion' by sophisticated people, according to which atheistic communism is called a religion, breeds a scandalous confusion. It promotes obscurantism and hinders a perfect honesty of expression, on a most serious question."[7] Yet Richard Crossman, in 1950, could gather the testimony of an array of prominent ex-Communists into a volume of essays entitled *The God that Failed*. Crossman, like many other liberals, has recognized in Soviet Communism some of the trappings of an authoritarian religion. According to these thinkers, only the designation authoritarian religion can explain the strait-jacketing of science and art to fit a purely abstract theory of natural, social, and aesthetic development, the theory of dilectical materialism. The Soviet purges in science, politics, and art have all been justified by their perpetrators by appeal to Marxist theory as understood by Stalin and his successors. The closest analogy to what has happened in Russia periodically in the past few decades is the outlawing of the theories of Galileo and Copernicus by the Church on the ground that they contradicted the biblical view of the universe. Under what heading, if not "authoritarian religion," can we put the beatification of Lenin and the (now abandoned) glorification of Stalin? Certainly the hundreds of paeans of praise to Stalin that once appeared in Soviet newspapers read very much like prayers. One of the first of these to be translated into English reads in part:

> O leader of the peoples,
> Thou who broughtest man to birth,
> Thou who fructifiest the earth,
> Thou who restorest the centuries,
> Thou who makest bloom the spring,
> Thou makest vibrate the musical cords.
>
>   *   *   *   *   *
>
> Thou, splendor, of my spring, O Thou,
> Sun reflected by millions of hearts. . . .[8]

Is it legitimate to call Soviet Communism a religion? If so, why should a thinker as acute as Morris R. Cohen have considered the designation to be "obscurantism"? If Communism is not a religion, did not Crossman take undue advantage of poetic license in dubbing Communism the God that failed?

In our own American situation, an accurate description of the ingredients of religion might help us to see the struggle between church and state in a new light. It might clarify somewhat the current issues in the conflict over religion in the public schools.

Much of the controversy is over the definition of religion. Protagonists of religion in education differ in their conceptions of religion. Many of them belong to the school of thought which interprets religion on the basis of one of the historic Christian approaches, whereby belief in a supernatural God is a *sine qua non* of religion. They hold, too, to the idea that ethical values require grounding in a traditional theism, a grounding which must be taught to the children as part of the theory of democracy. These are the motivations, for example, of those who, a few years ago, precipitated a controversy in New York State by advocating starting the school day with a standard prayer. The recent statement of the Superintendents of the New York City schools in favor of introducing a theistic basis in the teaching of moral and spiritual values was similarly motivated.

Other protagonists of religion in education, however, believe that there is no single approach to theism. In this group, too, are many who hold that ethical values occupy a realm of their own, separable from a theistic background. Should not, then, the introduction of religion in public education, *on the grounds set forth by its most vociferous, traditionally theistic proponents*, be seen as a sectarian religious move? If religion is to be taught in the public schools, it will have to be freed from the limitations of the particular interpretations of the major American churches. Undoubtedly these interpretations are religious and should enter into any treatment of the subject of religion, but are they the only legitimate forms of religious expression? Perhaps, if the varieties of religious ideology were more widely appreciated, it would be found that what is needed in public education is not so much the teaching of doctrines and values already formulated by the historic religions, but a free inquiry into the relative merit of these doctrines and values for the good life in a democracy.

If we could be more objective about the makeup of religion, it might also help us to perceive the common strivings of men that have resulted in such markedly different forms of social organization as church and state, sect and nation. We would then see the organization of states as intimately connected with the same problems of human fulfilment that are the concern of religion. The state, as such, is not a "secular" institution. Sometimes it is the political arm of a church; sometimes it controls the church, even to the extent of dictating religious doctrine; sometimes it is an instrument that, among other things, acts as a mediator among conflicting religious claims to total control of the society. The state is never devoid of religious ideology. It always espouses a social ethic, it invariably organizes a ritual, and it may, at times acknowledge God to be the source of its ideals.

Such a broad understanding of religion might offer us some of the instruments of discrimination necessary for the making of the One World we all seek. It would enable us, for example, to acquire the patience essential to negotiation. It would help us to see why a united world, built upon a

common set of ethical standards, cannot be created overnight, and why we must try to open wider areas of interaction among the peoples of the world. Only after much
interaction, basic to the evolution of a world group feeling,
can we expect to begin to realize our hopes for the One
World ideal.

It is not the purpose of this volume to fill in the details of
these and other concrete implications of my description of
religion, but it should, at least, suggest them. Now to the
description.

3

There are two common responses to the mention of the
word religion. Some persons think immediately of a group;
for others the word brings to mind an individual and the
way he thinks or behaves. But this is not the end of the
confusion. The religion of a group is sometimes pictured as
a body of beliefs and doctrines and sometimes as the on-
going adjustment of that group to the ultimate problems of
existence. Similarly, what is called personal religion is
sometimes a philosophy of life and sometimes a characteristic
pattern of behavior which remains constant even in the face
of critical changes in philosophy.

This subjective tendency to narrow religion to one aspect
of what is really a larger perspective often misleads us in our
attempts to understand the phenomenon of religion. In
talking about group religions, for example, we frequently
refer to tradition as the distilled experience of a people's
history, as that people's religion. But what about contemporary experience? What about the new ideas and practices that
spring out of the present predicament? Moreover, are there
no differences between groups? Some groups seem to lay

great stress on dogma, others on practice. In my description of religion I shall try to encompass the total panorama.

It is a far cry from Whitehead's "Religion is what the individual does with his own solitariness"[9] to the concept of group religion. Nevertheless, as we shall see, the term religion can be applied to both.

When we examine the recognized religions—whether Judaism, Protestantism with its hundreds of divisions, Catholicism, Islam, Hinduism, or any other—we meet up with both doctrine and people. To ignore one or the other is to fail to encompass the whole panorama of religion. A religion, whatever else it may be, is meant to be lived; consequently it has to be rooted in the life of some group.

There are only two ways in which an idea or practice becomes part of the thinking or behavior of a group—that is, reaches the point where it is deemed essential to the welfare of the group as a collective entity and to the welfare of each of its members. One way is the process of gradual articulation by the group, of extraction from the group's own experience. The other is deliberate adoption by the group; in this case the idea or practice that is adopted may have been produced either by another group (or an individual in another group) or by an individual within the ingroup. The first way is largely an unconscious process which goes along unarticulated until its spiritual implications burst on the awareness of the people; the second way involves a conscious act of assent at the outset.

When most of the religious elements in the civilization of a society are the creations of its own historical development, that society can be said to have developed a group religion. As has been said, any people, given a sufficiently long period of historical experience, theoretically can develop its own religion. Whether it does so or not will depend on such factors as the nature and breadth of its experience, the strength of its inner ties, and the character of its culture.

The history of the group religions of the world reveals two main patterns. Some peoples have achieved group religion by consciously recognizing their heroes, their historic events, places, and occasions, their literature, art, and folkways as symbolizing the values and needs whose expression and satisfaction constitute self-fulfillment for their members. This pattern is characteristic of Judaism and some of the emerging national religions of the contemporary world. Other peoples have created group religions by borrowing an entire system of religion from some other cultural context and adapting it to their own local setting. This describes the rise of Christianity and applies also to religious development in the Orient. The universal faith, Buddhism, for example, which originated as a critical refinement of Hinduism, has entered into the fabric of life of many peoples in the Far East and in Southeast Asia. Ceylon, Burma, Thailand, China, Japan, and other countries have found Buddhism congenial to their indigenous civilizations. In each case, however, Buddhism has been transformed in the course of its integration into the native civilization, so that, to take one illustration, a wide disparity prevails between the pale ethicism of Japanese Buddhism and the intense ethical emphasis of the Burmese version.

Let me digress briefly at this point to clarify the meaning of "self-fulfillment." I use the term to denote the whole complex of felt needs, the satisfaction of which becomes the ultimate goal in life of a person or group of people. In traditional theology self-fulfillment is termed salvation; its connotation in Western religions of bliss in the afterlife should not blind us to the fact that the quest for that kind of salvation is merely an extension of the desire for fulfillment. The eternal happiness of the afterlife is the projection of the widespread hope for immortality. That hope, however, is not a prerequisite for belief in salvation. It is well known that eternal bliss was a late accretion to Jewish religion; the generations prior to the Babylonian exile (586-538-B.C.E) were content to live without hope of an afterlife. It goes without saying, then, that self-fulfillment is highly subjective, differing from person to person, from group to group, from place to place, and from time to time. Yet, because men have more or less the same physical endowments and because their similar environments beget similar needs, there are usually broad areas of agreement within which the expression of these human needs manifests itself. Thus the physical needs for food, shelter, clothing, and sexual gratification are universal. Of course, in the various schemes of self-fulfillment these needs are variously treated, sometimes being entirely suppressed. The ascetic subdues his appetite for food in order to discipline his body. The Catholic priest sublimates his sexual appetite in the service of what to him is primary in the scheme of salvation. Similar variations are to be found in the areas of the social, intellectual, aesthetic, moral, and spiritual needs of men. What is common to all men, however, is their desire to live life in response to such needs, which stem partly from biological endowment and partly from interaction with the environment. There may even be some inherent psychological needs which are universal. One writer thinks, for example, that all normal human beings feel a need for mastery, for succoring and protecting others in distress and sympathizing with them.[10] All humans, too, experience awe, wonder, and creativity under appropriate circumstances, which seems to indicate that there are deep-rooted spiritual needs to which these experiences are responses.

No one, in other words, simply lives. Everyone *lives for some purpose,* and that purpose in its broadest sense is self-fulfillment, or salvation. The "self" in "self-fulfillment" in no way implies that salvation is necessarily an egocentric concept. Indeed, all "advanced" concepts of salvation contain many elements of self-transcendence, altruism, and universalism. The "self" in the term implies merely that all schemes of fulfillment are subjective in character, with the individual himself the final determinant of what his purpose in life is to be. The self is that which transforms a need into a want, a physical impulse into purposive behavior. Since the purpose may involve all men, and even the cosmos itself, it is inaccurate to speak of salvation, as some critics do, as an egocentric weakness. Nor does the subjectiveness of the conceptions of salvation deprive them of objective validity. To say that a man wants to live in a world of peace and brotherhood in no way implies that these values are unrelated to man's nature. Erich Fromm has made a strong case of the idea that "our knowledge of human nature does not lead to ethical relativism but, on the contrary, to the conviction that the sources of norms for ethical conduct are to be found in man's nature itself."[11]

Now to return to my central theme of the dynamics of group religion. How, for example, does a group know its own ideals?

It is common for a group to act without being aware of the ideals implicit in its behavior. Thus in the course of its history every people comes to recognize the greatness of outstanding leaders, but it may take generations for those leaders to enter into the consciousness of the people as the human embodiments of all that is sacred to them. Frequently the leaders themselves reveal to the people what they ought to hold sacred; sometimes their words find ready acceptance, sometimes it takes generations.

In the same way, ideal motives are concretized in memorable days and places, portrayed in works of literature, and acted out in folkways that eventually become sanctified ritual. The ideal goals and standards by which all in life is measured themselves become part of the people's character, as a result of successive generations of indoctrination, education and conscious identification with the spirit of the people as it seeks to adjust itself to the circumstances of its existence.

Group religion is thus an inevitable outgrowth of the efforts of a people to enhance its corporate existence. Since, however, the experience of every people is unique, it is equally inevitable that every religion should evolve at a rate of speed and with qualities different from those of every other religion.

In some groups, ideals may predominate, rituals may be numerous and complex, but sacred literature may be relatively scarce. This is true of most primitive religions. In others, ritual may be simpler, as among the Quakers. Some religions, like Hinduism, Judaism, and Catholicism, abound in all elements. And so on. But where there is group religion, the various sancta will be present, potentially or in actuality, and in greater or lesser degree.

At this point the reader is probably asking himself, "If this is religion, what, then, is nationalism?" The question is in order. As described here, group religion and nationalism do sometimes overlap and may even be identical. Hans Kohn[12] and Salo Baron[13] have shown that nationalism has among its roots a religious one. In ancient times nationalism and religion were organically related, inasmuch as every nation was a religious entity. With the evolution of universal, doctrinal religions, however, national boundaries were crossed; religions often became transnational or super-national. Particularly in Europe, groups of people were set-tling down to corporate existence, developing national his-tories, and exhibiting common economic, social, and political needs, all of which found spiritual expression in language, literature, and art. Concurrently the Church was seeking to unify the world on the basis of a universal doctrine of sal-vation, and differences in local needs and patterns of be-havior were being accentuated everywhere. The Christian world view that sprang from ancient Israel and absorbed pagan and Greek ingredients failed to satisfy the spiritual needs of the European nations. Maurice Samuel[14] has sug-gested that Europe never digested Christian dogma and that it sought in both the Nazi and Bolshevik revolutions to eliminate the Christian philosophy of life and to substitute ideologies more closely related to the needs and spirit of its peoples. To this extent, modern nationalisms are em-bryonic religious movements.

It might also be said that the Church was a political force seeking to unify a variety of groups under its domain in order to achieve a universal society. From this stand-point, the struggle between the papal leaders of the Holy Roman Empire and the kings and princes of the embryonic nationalities of which it was constituted was a struggle not so much between church and state as between state and state. It can readily be seen that the border line between religion and nationalism is sometimes a very thin one.

Nationalism, of course, particularly in its modern form, includes at least two essential elements not requisite to most religions. In our day the idea of the state appears to be indispensable to nationalism. The world has not yet ac-cepted the concept of spiritual nationalism, in which the forms of polity are incidental to the ethical ideals for which the nation organizes its life. Under that concept, nationalism will more closely approximate those religions which seem able to dispense with the political forms of power. On the other hand, it is a moot question whether a religion like Catholicism, which seeks, and in some countries possesses, temporal power, may not also be classified as a nation or a federation of nations. Certainly the Vatican state is not to be understood solely as a religious society.

Another apparent essential of nationalism is land. Religions appear able to rise above geography, to take the whole worlds their terrain, although there are some group religions whose traditions are all but inseparable from particular lands. Judaism is the outstanding example, in its relation to Palestine, of the latter variety, but there are various denominations within Protestantism and Catholicism which derive much of their strength from their roots in a particular soil. The ties of Irish Catholics and Italian Catholics to their ancestral lands despite the fact that Catholicism was not native to these lands, are cases in point. Once imported, the religion evolved unique characteristics emanating from the national experiences of Ireland and Italy.

Both group religion and nationalism, however, require polity. Without some clearly recognized and adequately organized community, neither a religious group nor a nation can sustain itself. This is obvious as applied to nations, but is only vaguely recognized in connection with religions. For the most part, people are accustomed to view religion as a matter of dogma and theology. They rarely see a church as a sociological structure. Yet the organic connection between religion and polity is demonstrated both in the tight organization of Catholicism and in the weaker association of Protestant churches. The Catholic Church, for all its emphasis on doctrine, is one of the best-knit organizations in modern society. In the ecumenical movement Protestants are struggling to find an effective form of organization to implement the basic elements of Protestant doctrine. To achieve this organizational objective, Protestants will have to legitimize their many doctrinal divergences and to expand the areas of religious concern beyond theological and ritual matters. The realization of this is reflected in the activities of the National Council of the Churches of Christ in the United States and of the World Council of Churches.[15]

We constantly hear it said that "America is a Christian country" and a phrase like "the Christian roots of democracy" is a commonplace. What is usually meant is that Americanism and Protestant Christianity are two sides of the same coin. These sentiments are expressed even by liberal forces. We expect the "100 per cent Americans" and proponents of "America for white Protestant Christians" to make no pretense about rejecting the American democratic creed of pluralism; they do so openly in their appeals for an American *Gleichschaltung*. But there are many sincere and devoted democrats who unthinkingly accept the thesis that the only plausible ideological substructure for American democracy is Christianity, and specifically, Protestant Christianity. Some Protestants in the United States, recognizing the relative weakness of Protestantism in this country, have sought to solidify its foundation by integrating it into the structure of American democracy and government.

This narrow interpretation of the American creed does shocking violence to the facts of American history. Of course America has been enriched by its heritage from Christianity (and Judaism as well) but it is also heir to many intellectual and spiritual legacies brought to these shores by generations of immigrants. But the American creed is more than the product of these legacies; it is the outgrowth of over three centuries of the exciting adventure of a new people on a new continent. What Americans of all creeds share is not the spiritual baggage that each immigrant brought with him from his birthplace; it is the new life that all—some in spite of themselves—have help to create.

It follows that the American creed, or American nationalism, is an emerging group religion. The ingredients are all there—ideals, heroes, civic festivals, each with deep universal significance, ritual, sacred literature, etc.—but they are still to be consciously formulated and accepted by Americans as of religious significance. At present, they are considered part of the secular experience of the American people. I have sought to show that the classification of such experience as secular is misleading. But it will be a long time before generations trained to see religion only as a creation of the past will be able to grasp the idea that new religions can come into being.

The concept of group religion implies the likelihood (or at least the possibility) that a person will during the course of his life experience more than one group religion. This will be the case where he is able to share in the evolving cultures of more than one group. In the United States today Christians and Jews are actually living two religions, however unconscious of the fact they may be. On the one hand, they experience their historic religion; on the other, they share the American religion. For example, the celebration of Thanksgiving Day, which, incidentally, is an adaptation of the biblical festival of Tabernacles, is deeply religious in intent. The common practice of holding interfaith services on this holiday is just one manifestation of the religious significance with which American civilization has been invested over the years.

But while many Americans live simultaneously as members of two religious groups, they do not always do so with spiritual consistency. Though American democracy grants equal rights to all religious creeds, one cannot be a democrat in theory and at the same time logically accept the exclusivist claims of a traditional religion. The fundamentalist Protestant who finds truth only in his version of Christianity and who would transform the common education of the American public school into a sectarian system does not subscribe to the American principle of religious liberty. The Catholic who believes there is no salvation outside the Church and who would, therefore, if he had the power, impose the limits of a Catholic philosophy of education on all Americans, either does not take the doctrines of the Church seriously or is fooling himself. Were he to acquire power, he would, if he were true to his doctrine, abandon certain pluralistic features of American democracy —for example, the ideal of free inquiry in public education. At the present time he is able to give the appearance of accepting the American creed because that creed permits him complete freedom, which he is unable to use against others for his parochial purpose. However, the storm clouds of a Kulturkampf hover overhead. Exclusivist or missionizing religions cannot long exist side by side in a state of perpetual tension and suspicion any more than can mutually contradictory social systems. The challenge of American group religion to the historic religions is directed to the fundamental question, "Can the historic religions so adjust their theologies and institutions as to enable them to abandon all presumptions to absolute truth and all hopes for soterial imperialism, for the eventual conversion *by means other than persuasion* of all nonbelievers?" Only if the answer is affirmative will a free society be secure from

the ravages of religious tensions. For if religious issues were
to be determined by state apparatus, no matter how democratically fashioned, the freedom of American society would
be well on its way to dissolution. The alternative to religious freedom is a return to the tempestuous struggle for
men's souls which would break forth at the first possible
moment.

Group religion, then, is a natural product of the corporate
existence of peoples. Its character is dependent on the
quality of group life—both material and spiritual. It is
subject to the influence of time and place. Consequently,
when writers speak of religion as reactionary or as obscur-
antist, they must learn to specify what religion, of what
people and during which period in its history.

It is a revealing fact that a discussion of group religion
can get to this point without mention of what is generally
regarded as an essential of all religions, namely, God. Is not
the idea of God basic to all religions, group or doctrinal?
Here it is necessary to see the continuity of experience between ourselves and our ancestors and between ourselves
and our contemporaries. It is undoubtedly true that almost
all sophisticated ancient group religions fashioned God-ideas
and that those God-ideas were based on belief in the supernatural, the belief that a conscious power, beyond human
ken and control, rules the world. Yet, scholars tell us that
ritual preceded the God-idea. Thus there were probably
early stages of religion in which the God-idea played little
or no role. Moreover, when man first conceived of God he
probably associated the concept with the personality of particular objects rather than with a supernatural power. That
is to say, the earliest animistic religions assumed that every
object in nature had a personality of its own, with some
objects more powerful than others. It is possible, therefore,

that group religion came into existence without any conscious association at all with a concept of a supernatural God. Ancient man was undoubtedly keenly aware of the mysterious universe, but it was not until man had achieved a high degree of intellectualization that he was able to formulate the concept of a supernatural deity. When that level of thought had been reached, protoscience, government, art, history, agriculture, social relations, etc., also fell prey to supernaturalism.

I have argued that a group religion, functioning in the twentieth century, need not adhere to this supernatural approach to the universe. If by definition religion is belief in the supernatural, then of course there can be no religion where this factor is absent. But I have shown that such argument by definitions is unwarranted. Hence it is possible for group religion to arise even in a world that is conceived of in naturalist terms. An idea of God may be built up from a *completely naturalist position.* Some group religions currently operating with no apparent recourse to God, or in declared opposition to the application of the word to their ideologies, can be interpreted as actually centering in a concept of God. The issue, however, is not germane at this point in our discussion. Suffice it to say for the time being that the philosophical basis for a group religion need not be avowedly theistic and certainly not otherworldly, or supernatural.

In ancient group religions the God-idea functioned as the intellectual explanation of the mysteries of nature and of society. God was conceived of as the ultimate guarantor of salvation and as the final authority for the group's cultural patterns, political, social, and moral. Intellectual and social needs, however interpreted, are present in every society. It is these needs, rather than the particular theo-

retical structure built to embrace them, which determine the
origin and the character of the group religion. Not all the
answers that religions have given are valid ones. Hence, the
affirmation that religion is an indispensable part of man's
experience is based not on the answers but on the needs
which give rise to them.

It is true that there are other disciplines, like philosophy
and science, which provide their own answers to human
needs. Group religion frequently employs these disciplines
as aids in its own enterprise. The distinctive character of
group religion, however, is that it seeks answers within
the context of a particular historic tradition.

I suggested above that "religion" accurately designates
certain aspects of Soviet Communism. We are now in a
better position to assess the degree to which Soviet Communism approximates group rather than doctrinal religion.*
This question is important because if Communism actualizes
the spirit of Russian polity, it becomes even more dangerous
than it would be if it were merely a doctrine imposed upon
the Russian people.

Russia's avowed espousal of the cause of atheism and its
concerted fight against all religion would seem, on the face
of it, to place Communism outside the realm of religion.
(The war and postwar concessions to the Orthodox Church
are obviously strategic retreats rather than recognition of
the validity of the Church's claims.) But, by theism it is
apparent that the Communists mean belief in a supernatural
God. Simply because the Communists declare they oppose
any recourse to belief in God is not reason for automatically
reading them out of the sphere of religion. When a person
today says, "I don't believe in God," the natural response of

---

*The reader can apply the same criteria to Fascism, Nazism, and the
totally different but nonetheless religious overtones of democratic nationalism.

anyone who wants to understand the assertion is, "What do you mean by God?" Invariably the answer is in terms of an anthropomorphic supernatural power. If, however, God can be conceived of in other than supernaturalist terms, it is possible to span what appears at first to be an unabridgeable chasm between religion and Soviet Communism and to call the latter by its true name, authoritarian religion.

Actually, the theory of dialectical materialism functions for the Communists almost exactly the way a supernatural God serves the purposes of orthodox religions. Dialectical materialism is the explanation of natural evolution and social history, just as God is the answer of formal religionists to the mysteries of nature and man. Science has not—any more than politics and art—been permitted free development in Russia. No discovery is accepted which does not fit into the dialectical scheme. I recall the defense of Stalinist mental gymnastics advanced by one of my college instructors in a course in philosophy of science: If a theory has been validated beyond question, no fact is fact unless it accords with that theory; dialectical-historical materialism has proved to be the best and truest explanation of man's struggle with his environment; *ergo,* the Soviets have a perfect right to shut off investigation in certain fields and to denounce as counterrevolutionary any findings that contradict the theory. Thus do the Soviets meet the need for explaining the meaning of life, for giving some assurance of its fulfillment and for providing an authority for their pattern of society. Shades of the Middle Ages! The Russians may not define their beliefs in theological terms, but surely a false god has been enthroned in modern dress. Even recent efforts by the Communists at revising the Soviet line can be interpreted as an orthodox answer to challenge. The changes are easily absorbed into the all-embracing framework of Marxism, as they are held to have been inherent in the doctrine from the outset.

Aside from the question of a God-idea, however, every other element of group religion is found in the Communist cult. There are saints galore in a hierarchy ascending to Marx and Lenin, with the latter occupying an even more important role in some aspects than Marx. Lenin has lain in Moscow in a state of remarkable preservation for the adoring masses of Russians to see.*

Holy days, too, are plentiful. On May Day, on the anniversary of the Bolshevik Revolution, on the birthdays of heroes, the people, in mass, emotion-rousing demonstrations, are reminded of the purpose for which they exist. Sacred books abound (*Das Kapital,* the works of Lenin, and the writings of other theorists currently in favor), and some of the volumes which have not yet been canonized but which are even truer reflections of the Communist mind exhibit all the fervor of religious literature. The Communist Party in these works is always referred to as "the Party." Throughout, it is the Party and its functionaries who are the Savior. Only the Party can provide revolutionary leadership; only the Party is "free from opportunism, irreconcilable towards compromisers and capitulators."[16] The Party owes its strength to Marxist-Leninist theory, for that theory "enables the Party to find the right orientation in any situation, to understand the inner connection of current events, to foresee their course and to perceive not only how and in what

*We should not underestimate the psychological reality of the ups and downs in the deification of Stalin. In a lecture before a Columbia University economics class, a counselor for the Soviet Embassy in Washington, Constantin G. Fedoseev, declared, "The cult of the individual attributed to certain persons supernatural qualities. They were regarded almost like miracle workers and were worshipped as such. Such a conception of men and, specifically, Stalin flourished in our country." (*The New York Times,* April 13, 1956.)

direction they are developing in the present, but how and in what direction they are bound to develop in the future."[17]

Orthodox group religion and Soviet Communism, no matter how far apart they may be in specific details, belong in the same frame of reference—that frame of reference in which man seeks self-fulfillment through the medium of his group.

There is some question about the lasting power of the Communist-planned group religion of contemporary Russia. Whether or not the genius of the Russian people is truly expressed in Marxist philosophy and in the ritual sanctified by the Communist Party can be answered only in the future. As yet, it is impossible to determine whether Communism is the religion of the elite segment of Soviet society, of the Communist Party, or of the majority of the masses. The reports of unrest, the mass deportations, the periodic trials and liquidation of "conspirators," all corroborate the feeling of many Westerners that the Russian people and the people of Russia's satellites accept only through fear the brand of Communism that has been imposed upon them. On the other hand, almost two generations of indoctrination cannot be overlooked. If one may hazard a guess, however, it is highly probable that a religion forced down the throats of the masses will eventually be spewed forth. The Communist Party theology, ritual, and ethic may well be abandoned when the Russia people have a chance to do so. Nevertheless any future religion of the Russian people will doubtless retain the concern for the masses, the devotion to science, technology, and art, and the love of the homeland that have been the core of Communist Party ideology—however twisted these motifs may appear to us today.

4

If there is confusion about the meaning of group religion there is utter chaos as regards its intellectual content. There are so many definitions of religion that it would take a tremendous volume to catalog them. Even the derivation of the word is the subject of controversy. Perhaps the dominant view is that it comes from the Latin *religio,* meaning taboo or restraint, which is akin to the verb *religare,* meaning to bind fast. This derivation would seem to cast light on our previous discussion of religion as a characteristic expression of group solidarity, although some would insist that the "binding" refers rather to man and God. José Ortega y Gassét proposes another derivation: "To live not wantonly, but warily—wary of a transcendental reality—is the strict meaning of the Latin word *religiosus,* and indeed the essential meaning of all religion. What a man believes, and what he therefore regards as unquestionable reality, constitutes his religion. *Religio* does not derive from religare, to bind —that is, man to God. The adjective, as is often the case, has preserved the original meaning of the noun, and *religiosus* stands for scrupulous, not trifling, conscientious."[18]

The derivation of a word is important only in so far as it can provide a clue to proper usage. Unfortunately, the supposed knowns in terms of which religion is usually defined are almost always really unknowns or badly in need of clearer definition themselves. Hence the origin of religion is of no help to us when we search for its meaning. But let us try not to add another definition to the stockpile. We are concerned with describing religions as they are manifested in the life of groups of people (the subject of the preceding section of this chapter) and in the minds of thinking individuals (our present subject). We are studying, in other words, the phenomena to which men have applied the term religion, and seeking to isolate some common elements in all these phenomena. In this way we can hope to make the word religion more understandable.

Group religion is both made and in the making. That part of it which is made is the tradition; this is always a selection out of the total and vaster experience of the group. Tradition is the product of a people's unique genius. It is the final distillation of many years of preparation, and as long as the people lives, it is the starting point of a new process of refinement. But although tradition may represent a people's soul, it relates itself differently to every individual member of that people. The majority of a group at any one time may be completely at one with tradition, yet there are always points of tension, produced by the pull of the inevitable flux of life, which disturb the skeptic and deny rest to the religious genius. Those points of tension are the areas of conflict between the religion of the group and the religion of the individual, or as it is commonly called, personal religion. When the group religion is flexible enough, it absorbs the new insights of those religious virtuosos who arise from time to time to urge the group on to greater spiritual heights. Where it is inflexible, new insights eventuate in schisms, sometimes giving rise to new religons, sometimes sounding the death knell of the old religion. The world has witnessed many such cases of the individual genius in conflict with the tradition of the group—Ikhnaton, who lost; the Jewish champion of ethical monotheism (whether it was Moses or a later prophet), who won without forfeiting his place among his people; Jesus, who lost as a Jew but whose disciples succeeded in creating a new religion; Luther, whose heresy split the church.

These ever-recurring flights of the human spirit lead to *doctrinal religion.** This may be defined as *the approach to self-fulfillment, or salvation, which is dependent on the acceptance, in whole or in part, of a particular system of theology, set of principles, ethical code, and ritual regimen.* Unlike group religion, in which behavior often temporally precedes belief, ideational religion must in its genesis rely completely on prior assent. The communicants of an ideational religion are first united intellectually or by an act of faith; then they sometimes assume a new communal or organizational form or provide a rationale for an old one. Contrastingly, the members of a group religion first interact with one another in the arena of life and create a civilization; then they become conscious of their common purposes and self-conscious about their own relationship to the group. In Chapter 5, I shall examine in greater detail how the doctrinal and group aspects of religion grew within Judaism. Here, however, it is worth while to illustrate the difference between the two aspects by reference to the wide difference between Judaism and Christianity, both as to origin and as to essence.

The best instruments for making this comparison are the Old and New Testaments. The most striking fact about these two Bibles is the historical character of the Old Testament and the homiletical emphasis of the New. The Old Testament, for all its theology and ethics, is first and foremost the early history of the Jewish people. Religion emerges out of the collective experience of the Jews; each stage of their history brings its new understanding of God and its new

---

*The point about doctrinal religion is that it consists of ideas which are to be accepted as essential to salvation. One might also call this type of religion ideational, philosophical, or theological, depending on the emphasis. In all cases, however, it is the idea that is central to ritual, ethics, and polity.

or refined interpretation of His way with men. There are many heroes, but they are all human—even the legendary figures among them. The people learn from their faults as well as their virtues, and none of the heroes is deified. It is significant that in later generations Jews rarely used a name like Mosaism or Abrahamism for their religion. They would not limit it even in name by associating it with any one of their ancestors, however great and revered. Judaism is the group religion par excellence. An exception can be used to prove the point. The German Reform Jews spoke of themselves as "Germans of the Mosaic faith," but these Jews had already decided to renounce Jewish nationalism. Their religion was thus doctrinal or philosophical, and it could well be associated with the name of a particular founder of basic tenets of their faith.

The New Testament presents an entirely different picture. Here the people enters only tangentially as it affects the life and works of the central hero. Jesus was a great preacher, and the New Testament is a biographical study of him, with vivid examples of his parables and teachings.

Jesus propounded a theory of religion usually in harmony with his own Jewish tradition but sometimes with an altered emphasis. That emphasis, in the hands of Paul, became something new, something otherworldly, and captured the hearts of a lost generation. Christianity appealed to peoples of unrelated backgrounds, who found in it an answer to their search for the spiritual harmony that their own traditions could no longer provide. Since the European world ostensibly accepted Christianity, it has with varying degrees of success been trying to integrate the doctrines of Christianity into its pattern of living.

Obviously there is no absolute line of demarcation between group and doctrinal religion. People create doctrines, and doctrines help shape the form and character of human associations. Group religions, when they become fossilized, pass over into doctrine that has little relation to the life of the people who gave birth to them. Doctrinal religions, when they capture the true spirit of a group or when they meet the needs of a people, can enter into the fiber of that people's being. For the purpose of clear communication on the subject of religion, we must make a distinction between religious doctrine and the contemporary religious expression of a people. The two are sometimes identical, but when they are not, a tension inevitably exists between them.

There remains the matter of personal religion. People are constantly heard to declare their emancipation from organized religion. They speak of themselves as being religious, even, sometimes, as believing in God, but as seeing no purpose in belonging to a religious community or participating in group ceremonials. The only religion they profess is their personal outlook on life. Yet most of the people who today stand outside the circle of organized religion owe their philosophy of life either to one of the historic religions or to the intellectual, ethical, and spiritual character of the society in which they live. Usually their personal religion is either a miniature reflection of the dominant ideas of a total culture or a rebellion against it.* Whichever is the case, although they feel no attachment or need to belong to a group religion, they are most certainly the products of one. All this, of course, does not gainsay the fact that those who would favor the dissolution of organized religions or who are unconcerned about their fate owe nothing to those religions

---

*It may be argued that being influenced by a "secular" culture is not the same as being conditioned by a group religion. I refer the reader to Tillich's treatment in *The Protestant Era* of the religious involvements of all so-called secular culture.

simply because they may have learned from them. Nor does it deny that personal religion, even if deriving from social sources, is an individual and private matter. But the individual "emancipated" from organized religious ought to comprehend fully the context of his personal religion.

Take, for example, a typical American of this variety. He believes in acting humanely, but his humane values are derived from those which serve as the ethical basis of American life. Some are native to American experience, others are rooted in Judaism and Christianity. Since he was most likely born into one of these religious groups and received his childhood indoctrination according to its ethical standards, it follows that his personal morality is in large part the distillation of many centuries of ethical experience on the part of his ancestors. And whether or not his early upbringing was influenced by formal religious training, there still remains the profound moral impact of American democracy. Everyone raised in the United States belongs, in effect, to a community with a distinctive ethical viewpoint, or, in view of sectional differences, to a community with a characteristic moral tradition.

Thus the thinking and the behavior of the "free" religionist are the products, in great measure, of the intellectual and cultural scene of which he is part. That scene—a specific geographical, temporal and ethnic setting—is social in character. Here too, personal religion is personal only in the sense that it is experienced by an individual. In a larger sense it is public, because without the presence of the group, it could never have come about. What has happened is that participation in a religious community based upon adherence to a more or less flexible system of ethical, theological, and ritual doctrines has largely given way to interaction with a social environment in which these ethical, theological, and ritual doctrines have often not yet been crystallized, formalized, or systematized. Such doctrines nevertheless subsist in the American environment. What Myrdal calls "The American Creed" is a spiritual influence on American citizens. That creed, as I have said, is embodied in such sacred writings of our country as the Declaration of Independence, the Constitution, the Gettysburg Address, in many of the decisions of the Supreme Court, in the utterances of our national heroes, in the ideals of our civic festivals. In short, although no one would designate the American society as a formal religious group, it inevitably serves to fashion the personal religions of Americans not affiliated with a church.

Personal religion, then, is the pattern of thinking in which an individual reacts to the fundamental questions of human existence. But, contrary to prevailing opinion, personal religion is not exclusively a private creation; nor is it solely a private concern. Its source is the immediate social group, which serves as the main educative force in the life of an individual, and its outlet is his daily actions and expressions of thought, all of which affect the character of his group.

No progress in organized religion can ever be made without the cultivation of philosophies of religion by spiritually creative men and women. Until now, the dogmatic mold in which religion has been cast has discouraged such individual thinking. Those whose intelligence, aesthetic sensibility, and ethical sensitivity have been outraged by the tradition of their father have found it necessary to break with their religious community and either find a new one or lose themselves in some other community which grants them freedom of expression. A democratic group religion, having absorbed the lesson of human freedom, would cherish such free and soaring minds and encourage them in their search for truth, beauty, and goodness. It would seek continually to arrive at an ever more satisfactory synthesis between the inherited tradition of the group and the religion of the noblest minds of the present. If such an attitude could be generally achieved, those men and women who now call for the dissolution of the historic religions in favor of "personal" religions would finally come to realize that they are practicing isolationism rather than universalism.

I have not meant to imply by anything I have said that all individuals can be expected to participate in equal measure in group religion. Nor do I argue that the only valid type of group religion is that which culminates in one of the present forms of church or synagogue worship. Group religion is today at a crossroads, and there is no signpost to point in the proper direction. I have tried merely to indicate that just as social progress requires the active participation, in groups, of interested citizens, so religious progress depends upon the spiritual contributions of those men and women who are able to give of themselves in organized groups without surrendering their critical faculties. A philosophy of ethics requires constant cultivation; worship must be made relevant to the real spiritual needs of each generation; and rituals, if they are not to be ends in themselves but are to point to ideals of great human significance, must likewise keep pace with the intellectual, moral, and aesthetic demands which they symbolize. All this requires organization and cooperation. Those who want their personal religion to function at its best will try to locate it in the community that most adequately appreciates and fructifies it.

3

WHAT IS A GOD-IDEA?

Most discourses by men about god tell
us more about men than about God. (I do not, of course,
exclude the present volume.) Nevertheless, the compulsion
to search for the divine is one of the glorious attributes of
the human species. Whether it take the form of a Prome-
thean storming of the heavens, an Abrahamic insistence upon
absolute justice, a reasoned Aristotelian analysis of the ultimate source of motion, or any other of the manifold ways
in which men have sought to explain the mysteries of
existence, the very striving testifies to man's refusal to accept
life as it is. Somehow the ignorance and evil that weigh so

heavily on human existence can and must be swept away. The unknown, man feels, contains much that can justify his optimism as he struggles to understand and achieve his destiny.

Whether we adopt a naturalistic or a supernaturalistic view of the universe, we must all come to terms with the crucial question posed by all religions: What is to be said about God? I have put the question in this nonspecific form because although this chapter is devoted to ideas about God I want to show that there are certain issues, such as whether God exists and how a good God can countenance evil, which can never be resolved and hence can only be misleading. Modern religion must learn to be more reserved in its assertions about God.

1

It will be useful to begin by making a distinction between a philosophical and a religious conception of God—between the God of the thinker and the Holy One Blessed Be He of the pietist. I have already commented that Aristotle's idea of God played no role in Greek religion yet exercised a profound effect on Maimonides and Aquinas in their reformulations of Jewish and Christian theology. This single fact points to the complexity of our task. It is often hard to determine where philosophy ends and religion begins. The separation between them was, as we know, a late development in cultural history, and it will probably never be final and complete.

The fundamental difference between philosophical and religious ideas of God is not one of content but rather of the degree of their own involvement in the life patterns of the group or the individual entertaining them. Religious God-ideas color the entire way of life, God being conceived of sometimes as the legislator of that way of life and sometimes as the guarantor of the achievement of its goals. On the other hand, philosophical God-ideas are not translated into terms of group culture; they serve a universal, disinterested, and intellectual function.

But although religious and philosophical God-ideas serve different functions, they invariably act upon each other. Religious thinkers frequently appropriate philosophical God-ideas to bolster the position that God holds in their group or personal religion. In the process, of course, the original theology is transformed; sometimes the religious thinker, in adjusting his own or his group's traditional theology to a philosophical idea of God, formulates a revolutionary concept but camouflages it by the employment of traditional terminology and symbolism. Sometimes, as in the case of Maimonides, the camouflage is effective enough to prevent its penetration by any except the most perceptive minds. For this reason, Maimonides' *Guide* has been accepted even by ultra-traditional Jews, who fail to recognize its radical reformulation of the biblical and Rabbinical conceptions of God. The interaction also operates the other way round. Many independent philosophical minds have acknowledged their indebtedness to a traditional religion, while refusing to acknowledge any affiliation with that religion.

The problem of trying to establish a boundary between theology* and philosophy is further complicated by the fact that a man may hold to a naturalist idea of God and yet belong to and feel genuinely a part of a religious group

---

*I use "theology" here as synonymous with that aspect of religion which deals with the idea of God. In other contexts, as I try to show in this chapter, both theology and philosophy can and do serve to establish religious views on the nature of the universe and on the nature and destiny of man, on which the idea of God hinges.

whose formal worship and ritual are founded upon belief in a supernatural God. Is such a man a religious thinker or is he a philosopher? He is probably both. In this instance his philosophy is, I believe, in advance of the conventional religious thinking of his group. We must acknowledge that in the sphere of God-ideas, as in other concerns of life, there has been and is a tremendous lag between the ideas held by the many and those propounded by the more thoughtful few.

Since the objective of philosophy is to understand the general principles underlying things as they are, the true philosopher—a scientist in ideas—follows the logic of his thinking. Consequently, philosophical speculation about God, when it commends itself to those within the religious fold, often leads into paths which require subsequent readjustment of religious God-concepts. This was certainly the experience of medieval theology, when neo-Platonism and Aristotelianism revolutionized ideas about God. Philosophy is as influential today in its effect on theology, but something new has been added. Science now sometimes exercises a direct influence on theology without the benefit of mediation by the philosophers. One need only cite the immediate reaction of religious thinkers to the Heisenberg principle of indeterminacy. Some theologians were quick to seize upon the principle as "proof" of free will.

In the main, religious God-ideas develop more slowly than do their philosophical counterparts. Thus when we speak of the contemporary attempts to revise the concept of God, it would be more accurate if we were to designate the thinking of our advanced theologians as philosophical. It is only when their God-ideas seep into the popular consciousness and color the religious experience of the man in the street that these ideas can be said to have become religious concepts in the technical sense. As of now, neo-Orthodox, existentialist, liberal, and naturalist theologians—all of them in all their variations—are developing philosophical conceptions which may function religiously for themselves and for small groups of followers. But for the large congregation of believers these are still abstract notions that will take time to be digested and absorbed into the religion organism.

There is no question that religious God-ideas held by twentieth-century men and women differ vastly from those which inspired their forebears. The present generation is probably less well-equipped than its ancestors were to describe its God-concept: in losing its ability to believe in the God of revealed religion the present generation seems also to have lost its power of articulation. In many cases, there is no concept at all, but merely a vague feeling of a Power who requires good behavior of men. Thus for large masses of people there is no real religious conception of God. The more educated may find some philosophical idea appealing; the others are satisfied with the vague feeling just mentioned. This may account for the current crisis of worship. The few do not pray to an intellectual construct; the many are impelled to worship only in moments of great emotional stress —their weak spirit is aroused only during such moments.

For better or for worse, we are today living in an era when only a concerted philosophical effort to orient man anew to the universe can bring about the restoration of religious faith. A modern religious revival cannot be based on preaching "that old-time religion" or on arousing guilt feelings about rebellion against the faith of the fathers. It cannot be called into lasting existence by the oratory of evangelists. It can only come about if men and women are helped to formulate a satisfying conception of God that will infuse their vague feelings about life's meaning and purpose with substance and vitality. This will not be accomplished overnight, and it certainly will necessitate very radical changes in the structure of religious belief and practice. There are still many people who view philosophy as an enemy of faith and who therefore consider philosophical speculation about God to be a threat to the historic religions. I, on the contrary, believe that only such a philosophical endeavor can save organized religion from becoming completely irrelevant. But we have a long road to travel. For the most part, even those of the world's intellectuals who are religiously oriented and function with philosophical ideas of God have not yet succeeded in converting these ideas into emotionally compelling religious influences.

The distinction drawn above between philosophical and religious types of God-ideas, while it illumines our contemporary religious problem, will not be strictly held to in the analysis of God-ideas that follow. Religious concepts, when they become the subject of analysis, are apt to assume a philosophic coloring. Moreover, the most effective philosophical God-ideas of the past have been absorbed in one way or another into religious thinking.

In the previous chapter, I dealt with the possibility of developing a religious society without recourse to belief in a supernatural God. Such a society will become possible only when it is realized that the popular conception of God as an all-powerful, all-good, and supernatural Power is only one of the many ways in which men throughout the ages have tried to picture the deity. Some of these ways have followed a naturalistic path. My concern in the present chapter is to analyze a representative group of God-ideas, and to develop the suggestion that all of them can be helpful in the development of religious understanding. If we take them as final conclusions, however, they can only obstruct the search for the divine.

2

It has been said by many religious thinkers that human nature thirsts for the Absolute. In philosophy, Dewey has given currency to the phrase "the quest for certainty." But Dewey, of course, spent his entire life trying to indicate how men can live happily and creatively without the kind of certainty that so many of them seek. He believed that "human nature" requires no absolutes. This is a lesson that religionists must learn if they are to lead their fellow men into a new age of faith and spirituality. For the search for the Absolute cannot possibly be a successful human venture. I think it important to indicate briefly why this is so.

What is this Absolute which, it is said, men seek? It is difficult even to put one's finger on what is meant by the term. For some it is simply another word for a mysterious God who has nevertheless revealed His will to man. For others the Absolute is the indescribable Being who appears in mystical visions. For still others the Absolute is the Undifferentiated Oneness, the ground of all being. For most seekers of the Absolute, God is infinite, not subject to description by human standards of right and wrong or by human understanding of cause and effect. This prompts us to ask why so many absolutists try to describe the indescribable. The Absolute is sometimes conceived of as a kind of metaphysical catchall, the ultimate but mysterious explanation of natural and moral law. In other words, when people speak of their yearning for the Absolute, they already have a picture of what it is they seek. The search is really not a search for an unknown; it is a great effort to prove the existence of some sort of ineffable Being whose ineffability they have already violated with their metaphysical assertions.

What the absolutists proclaim is not a hypothesis about the motive force within and/or beyond the universe, but a leap of faith, an acceptance of some picture of the Absolute as an objective fact. To say that God is all-good or all-powerful, or that He is neither all-good nor all-powerful, or that He is responsible for everything is to make the Absolute subject to rational thought and discourse. Thereby, the absolutists contradict their own definition of the Absolute as the infinite and indescribable ground or creator of being.

The truth is that mortal man can never hope to grasp all of "space, time and deity." That obviously could be within the power only of a mind coexistent and coeternal with the entire universe. Joseph Albo, in paraphrasing Saadia Gaon, a ninth-century Jewish philosopher, put this thought simply: "If I knew Him, I would be He."[1] Indeed this very fact about God's knowledge has misled some thinkers into positing it as a proof of God's existence. Since only an infinite Mind could encompass all of reality, it must exist. But why? A circular argument proves nothing. In this case all that can legitimately be asserted is that it is possible to imagine an infinite Mind in which all eternity is encompassed. The bare assertion in no way testifies to the truth of the statement.

The Absolute is an outstanding example of the confusion which has persistently surrounded the God-idea. For some reason or other it has been thought that declaring God to be absolute can silence all doubts or solve all mysteries or cultivate spirituality, particularly humility, among men. Yet the history of religion reveals at least as much doubt, uncertainty, and lack of spirituality among absolutists as among other men. No idea of God can do more than tell us what conclusions men, at a particular stage in their intellectual development, are able to extract from their knowledge about the universe. It merely obscures the issue to assume that an idea of God can ever exhaust His nature.

3

The biblical concept of God is that of a Deity both totally beyond the world and yet involved in it. I do not pretend to understand the full implications of this paradox, upon which so much ink has been spilled. Some make a virtue of paradox and proclaim it to be one of God's virtues. There is, it is true, a sense in which no paradox is involved in the same entity's being both immanent and transcendent. The human personality, for example, is involved in the activities, physical and mental, of the individual but is also more than the sum of those activities. But this is not the paradox of the biblical Deity. For He is conceived of as all-powerful and all-good, creator and immanent law of the world, giver of the moral law and determiner of history, wholly other than man, yet concealed and revealed in man's conscience. In other words, God's transcendence does not grow out of his immanence, as does the transcendence of human personality out of the nature of man. For God, in His transcendence, is said to be the creator of that universe in which He is immanent. In biblical religion God's transcendence is, at the same time, a complete mystery, not to be fathomed by even the most profound understanding of the physical nature of the universe or the moral nature of man. If the personality of man is not exhausted by its involvement in his physical nature, it can at least be seen as necessarily connected to it and conditioned by it. No such relation of connection and conditioning can be established between such a transcendent God and the world. In truth the term transcendent does not properly belong to the biblical God. "Supernatural" is a more accurate designation.

The total mystery of God can be gleaned from the Book of Job. There we are presented with a deity whose workings in nature can in no way be inferred from a knowledge of nature's order. For how did that order come into existence? That is God's secret. Nor can man's moral intuitions be trusted. Job *knows* he is innocent, yet in the end he is satisfied to accept the dictate that the conventional-minded friends with whom he has carried on a courageous, honest debate are in a sense correct. Who is he, a mere mortal, to challenge God's justice? There is infinitely more to it than even his clear conscience can hope to fathom. Indeed he cannot any longer allow himself to think of God as just or unjust, at least as these terms are understood by man. These categories have no meaning when applied to God.

There is much in this conception of the author of Job and of other biblical passages to appeal to even the most stubborn unbeliever. In the first place, this conception takes account of the contradiction between fundamental beliefs of men about right and wrong and the behavior of an all-powerful God who is at the same time all-good. It faces the problem squarely. And if the answer is given in the authoritative and overpowering rumble of a whirlwind rather than in the still small voice of reasoned analysis, there is at least no presumption that man's positive convictions about what is right are erroneous. The biblical conception of God limits the extent of man's ethical insights; it does not deny that within those limits he can suggest valid principles of conduct. Surely the most ardent modernist must reckon with man's inability to grasp completely the complexity of ethical behavior. We are still a long way from formulating a pattern of conduct which can harmonize all human values, however much we may be satisfied with the validity of many of them.

Secondly, the biblical view has the merit of admitting when it has reached the outer limits of understanding. God is described in anthropomorphic terms, but there is little question that at least the sophisticated portions of the Bible had abandoned anthropomorphic assumptions. The biblical God, in general, is a Power known only through His manifestations.

Had this biblical concept been posed as a theory, the course of religious history would, of course, have been vastly different. But the God-concept of the Bible was not mere theory. The Bible insisted that a single supernatural deity existed. The conception of unity was a great contribution to human progress, for implicit in the monotheistic assumption is the positing of a world possessing an intelligible order. Only such a view of the universe could have made scientific investigation a fruitful enterprise. No comparable gain followed from the assertion of God's existence. The Bible begins with the creation, but before creation there was the God who was responsible for it. "God exists" is the implied introduction to the Bible. Now what is to be criticized in the assertion that God exists? My point can best be clarified by making explicit the schematization implicit in the biblical view. It would run something like this:

[1. God exists.]

2. Man can know nothing about God, whose mystery is infinite.

3. Man knows about creation and about God's conduct of the world through the revealed Law. He knows, for example, that God created the world *ex nihilo*. (This, it should be pointed out, is the prevailing traditional interpretation of the biblical account,

although it is equally possible to read the epic of
creation as involving a preexistent substance from
which the world was fashioned.)

4. Man knows that his own conduct and the behavior
   of the physical world testify to God's existence.

5. Therefore, God exists.

The first statement in the schema, "God exists," is
bracketed to indicate that it appears to me to be the premise
of the biblical argument rather than its conclusion. It
is not true that the essential argument of the Bible for
the existence of God is inductively reasoned.

At first glance, the Bible appears to say the following: Man
is unable to achieve any positive knowledge about God. However, there are in human experience certain manifestations
which can at least point to His existence. Without a completely unconditioned Creator and Planner we could not
account, on the one hand, for the orderliness of nature, the
changing seasons, and the supremacy of man, and, on the
other, for the miracles which demonstrate the contingent
quality of nature. Then, too, man, benighted mortal that he
is, has to be instructed toward the good life. Without a
revealed doctrine, the Torah, mankind would have an eternal
career of ignorance, error, and sin. We must conclude,
therefore, that God exists.

The foregoing argument is no proof, as Maimonides long
ago clearly saw. For all the premises—and the conclusion as
well, that God exists—are unprovable assumptions. How can
we possibly prove creation *ex nihilo?* Aside from the questionable procedure of inferring an event which antedated
human experience and which could not have left any traces
that might supply some grounds for the inference, there is
the whole logical difficulty of a God who creates something
outside Himself. If God is omnipresent, how can there be

anything outside Him? And if, indeed, the world is in God, how shall we account for all the evil that pervades it? This very problem has occupied many a believer in creation, with none of the answers, it must be admitted, proving very satisfactory.

Nor does the Torah—or any of the other supposedly revealed traditions—provide a sound basis for inferring God's *existence*. I think it unnecessary here to review all the difficulties that confront believers in revealed religion. It should be sufficient to indicate that no one has ever proved the authenticity of revelation. All the modern reinterpretations of revelation as inspiration, intuition, or genius serve only as further testimony to the human origin of the revealed texts. A clear statement as to the real nature of belief in revelation is given by George La Piana, who writes the following in regard to the Christian theological system:

> Divine revelation is assumed to be a fact of history. The claim of possessing a divine revelation is not unique with Christianity. Most great historical religions have advanced the same claims and have also had their sacred Scriptures. From the point of view of Christian theology all these other revelations are merely figments of human imagination or the work of evil powers. Only the Christian revelation is a true and real historical fact. Since, however, the historical reality of revelation is by its nature undemonstrable by the method of historical evidence and since it is not demonstrable by logic which cannot go beyond asserting its possibility, the belief in the objective reality of revelation is a matter of faith in the authority of the Church.[2]

Such faith is scarcely a reliable tool to prove the existence of God.

Finally, the existence of God cannot be derived even from a scientific analysis of the physical and moral world. Each new disclosure of order tells us no more than that the order exists. It makes an interesting theory to declare that every effect has a cause and to reproduce the Aristotelian argument of a Prime Mover (which, incidentally, was unknown to the Bible's authors). But is it not curious that those who today purport to accept the biblical God and his mysterious nature are prepared to attribute to Him the causal scheme about which they know (or assume they know) only through their empirical experience? If God is as mysterious as any supernatural theory asserts, how can we be so sure He is the Power responsible for the phenomena of our experience? Perhaps all experience is a mirage. Perhaps God did not cause the world to exist at all. Perhaps the world is merely God's body and He its consciousness, as some sophisticated theists hold. In that case, the doctrine of creation proves faulty, and the existence of God, as Creator, becomes doubtful.

The above arguments are far from exhaustive. In a more detailed study, attention would have to be given to subtle variations on the theme which are characteristic of other revealed religions, including the many philosophical arguments that have been arrayed in their support. I have tried here merely to indicate some of the many weaknesses in the proof of God's existence which inhere in biblical religion. I believe that they hold for all God-ideas based on revelation.

Atheism was no option to the men of the Bible. It was for this reason that the honest doubts expressed by so many of the biblical personalities are never carried to their logical conclusion. Lacking as they did a clear insight into the workings of nature, if they had rejected a supernatural God they would have been left with nothing to guide them through the labyrinth of life. It was not humanly possible for them to abandon their belief. It is only after centuries of investigation and heart-rending spiritual struggle that human beings are beginning to gain the courage and the intellectual capacity to realize that it is not given to them to know with certainty that God exists, even a naturalistic God. Until now, religious rationalism has hesitated to take this final step away from certainty. In the face of the limitations of reason, Jewish and non-Jewish theologians alike have called upon revelation as proof of God's existence. Now, modern man must learn to recognize revelation itself as at least uncertain—if not impossible. Man's knowledge of God is necessarily inferential and tentative.

4

The type of God-idea represented in the Bible is only one of a number found even among ancient religions. The one that stands in sharpest contrast to the Judaeo-Christian God who is so concerned with the individual is the naturalistic concept of Taoism. Despite its mysticism, primitive Taoism illustrates the thinking of men who did not expect too much of God in the way of personal salvation. They were content, like the Stoics, to take life as it is, secure in the faith that the universal order is law for man as well as for nature. "The Great (universe) gives me this form, this toil in manhood, this repose in old age, this rest in death. Surely that which is such a kind arbiter of my life is the best arbiter of my death."[3] The ideal man is unconcerned about his personal well-being; he finds his welfare in the conduct of the whole universe. For "Your self is a body lent to you by the universe. Your life is not possessed by you; it is a harmony lent to you by the universe. Your nature is not possessed by you; it is a natural evolution lent to you by the universe."[4]

The universe is an ordered one, even though man's experience often leads him to a false and pluralistic picture of it. If man would only adopt an attitude of resignation toward

life, he would be able to see its oneness more clearly. "Therefore what he (the pure man) cared for was One, and what
he did not care for was also parts, manifestations of) One.
What he saw as One was One, and what he saw as not One
was also One. In that he saw the unity, he was of God; in
that he saw the distinction, he was of man. Not to allow the
human and the divine to be confused, therein was what
distinguished the pure man."[5] In other words, behind the
world of appearances there is an overarching unity which
persists despite man's proneness to cut it into pieces.

What about this unified universe? How does it relate to
man, and how should man relate to it? It is not the universe
created by a good God for the benefit of man. "Nature is
unkind: It treats the creation like sacrificial straw dogs."[6]
Man is treated no better than the rest of creation. But this
impartiality can be turned to man's benefit.

> How the universe is like a bellows!
> Empty, yet it gives a supply that never fails;
> The more it is worked, the more it brings forth. . . .[7]
> And again:
> Continuously, continuously,
> It seems to remain,
> Draw upon it
> And it serves you with ease.[8]

Nature is more or less a passive source from which man can
draw the power to conduct his affairs. But he can succeed
only when he abides by nature's laws.

The source of nature's laws is a great mystery, as is life
itself. But we must resign ourselves to this limitation rather
than strive against it. For Taoism, we might say that the beginning of wisdom is recognition of our ignorance of the
Lord. "Life springs into existence without a visible source
and disappears into infinity. It stands in the middle of a vast
expanse, without visible exit, entrance or shelter. He who

follows Tao . . . does not clutter up his mind with worries, and is flexible in his adjustment to external conditions . . . Fathomless, it [life] is like the sea. Awe-inspiring, the cycle begins again when it ends. It sustains all creation and is never exhausted. . . . What gives life to all creation and is itself inexhaustible—that is Tao."[9]

Other religions foster the feverish activity of exploration and manipulation that man is prompted to by the austere mystery of life. Taoism discourages such a response as foolishness. As Moore puts it, "When man, with his conceit of wisdom and his selfish will, ceases to interfere with the order of the world and impede it, he will find that it goes on perfectly without him."[10] A religion of resignation, Taoism is thus predicated on the assumption that man's blessedness is dependent on his being in accord with nature, rather than in bending it to his desires. It is for this reason, says Moore, that early Taoism viewed petitionary worship as "vain and impertinent."[11]

By today's popular standards, Taoism is no religion. Yet in view of its intention to read the ultimate meaning of life and to point out the road to human salvation, there is no classification other than religion into which we can place it. We should not be misled by the impersonal, natural kind of God that the Taoists postulate. For their God-idea is as emotion laden an interpretation of the nature of ultimate reality as is the most personal, supernatural conception of God. Indeed, there are passages, such as the following, whose piety and sublimity would grace any religion:

> There is great beauty in the silent universe. There are manifest laws governing the four seasons without words. There is an intrinsic principle in the created things which is not expressed. The Sage looks back to the

beauty of the universe and penetrates into the intrinsic principle of created things. Therefore the perfect man does nothing, the great Sage takes no action. In doing this, he follows the pattern of the universe. The spirit of the universe is subtle and informs all life. Things live and die and change their forms, without knowing the root from which they come. Abundantly it multiplies; eternally it stands by itself. The greatest reaches of space do not leave its confines, and the smallest down of a bird in autumn awaits its power to assume form. The things emerge and submerge, but it remains forever without change. . . . Darkly and without visible form it seems not to exist and yet exists. The things of the creation are nourished by it, without knowing it. This is the root, from which one may survey the universe.[12]

It is not so much the naturalism of Taoism that jars our Western sensitivities as the role it assigns to man as an object of nature incapable of initiating change or affecting the course of his destiny. Taoist naturalism, in this case, seems to us not to be naturalistic enough; it fails to take account of the potentialities of human activity. It ignores man's ability to transform the physical world and to create beauty and value that have not existed before. It ignores, too, the dimensions of vision and freedom which enable man to transcend the limitations of his life span and project himself in time and space far beyond the world of his immediate experience. We are more inclined to accept the role assigned to man by the biblical concept of partnership with God. Nevertheless, Taoism's naturalistic emphasis contributes to our understanding by indicating that even an ancient religion could conceive of God largely as a nonpersonal, immanent principle of the universe.

5

In Spinoza's system, God is the formal cause of a natural, mechanistically ordered world. He is not its creator; nor is He a Power who stands over against it as a supernatural entity. He is the essence of all things—an idea poles removed from the "living God" of Judaeo-Christianity. Spinoza's God is the classic example of a philosophical construct to "explain" the necessity that prevails in the ordered universe. Completely imbued with the seventeenth-century vision of a mathematical explanation of cosmic law, Spinoza conceived of a universe in which it would be an illusion for man to assume that he could effect changes in the world which were not the will of God. The world is constructed in accordance with absolutely rigid and mechanistic laws whose rule man and God alike must obey.

Such a God-idea has been criticized as leaving no room logically either for science or for ethical growth. These are points which have been raised many times, and there is no need to detail them here. Let it suffice to note, first, that although modern science draws its conclusions from empirical data and not from logically necessary principles,[13] Spinoza's insistence on a mechanistic universe found ample support in the science of his day. It seems fair to suggest that Spinoza would not have held to his closed and rigid system had he lived in our age of empirical science. The second charge against Spinoza is that a world in which behavior is absolutely determined rules out ethical choice; in short, the logic of Spinozism is said to reduce man's moral awareness to a mockery. Actually, however, as has been pointed out by Bertrand Russell and others, a determinism such as was proposed by Spinoza negates only indeterminism. Free will or choice is possible only in a rational, ordered scheme of things.

We see then that, given the kind of universe that was knowable in the seventeenth century, Spinozism is not so implausible as some of its critics, from the vantage point of three hundred years of intensive scientific activity, try to make it out to be. And it is precisely because Spinoza used so cogently the intellectual materials available to him that we can see why the construction of a permanently adequate God-idea is so hazardous an enterprise. Man's increasing knowledge of the universe continually suggests to him new hypotheses about its structure and mode of operation.

Although Spinoza's formulation may be difficult for some latter-day religionists to accept as the creation of a "God-intoxicated" man, it did serve as a bridge between concepts that place God beyond the universe and concepts that find Him within it. Spinoza's philosophy was undoubtedly an emotional as well as intellectual reaction to the sublimity of the universe. If Spinoza was mistaken, or at least is unsatisfying to us, in identifying God as the essence of all that exists, evil as well as good, he did find the world that man experiences to be the proper locale for man's fulfillment and to be, therefore, suffused with divinity. Spinozism has the merit of placing man in his natural setting. The human mind, as Spinoza described it, is an understandable consequence of natural process. We need not look to a special act of creation by a non-natural cause in order to explain the phenomenon of mind. Both God and man are natural phenomena, God because He is that which nature expresses in its orderly process, and man because he is one of the products emerging in that process.

6

To the modern mind, the idea that God is a person or at least a kind of being who hears and answers prayer is not a compelling one, despite the continued functioning of prayer as a major human activity. This has not prevented some theologians from conceiving of God as the Mind of the universe or as possessing consciousness—a consciousness, however, which is supposedly *sui generis*. This was the culminating idea, for example, in the theology of the late Milton Steinberg, who wrote:

> When I describe God as Spirit, I mean that He is not only a Power but a "Mind." His nature, in other words, is akin to our own. He is rational, which is why the universe is law-abiding. He is conscious with a consciousness like, though infinitely greater, than ours. Indeed, He is the source of human consciousness, our private minds being individualizations of Him, sparks as it were of His fire. . . . I mean further that He is purposive. Whatever the case elsewhere in space, on our planet He has worked through inorganic nature to the plant, thence to the animal, thence to man, through whom He is now driving toward ever increasing freedom, justice and mercy. . . .[14]

What, exactly, was Steinberg trying to say? God's infinite Mind does not think thoughts, nor does it will action in the same sense that the human mind does.* The divine Mind requires no motivation for its activity; it requires no sense impulses in order to function. Its thinking is identical with the operations of the physical universe, for the latter are the very content of divine thought. The Mind of God is both subject and object.

What is the purpose of setting up the analogy? One reason is undoubtedly the limitations of language, which are—or should be—felt most keenly by theologians. It is exceedingly

---

*For the purpose of meeting Steinberg on his own ground, I have here oversimplified. My own view of "mind" leads me to conceive of it as the complex of behavior, externally directed and internally operative, of the human being, and not a separate entity or faculty.

difficult to express the idea of purposiveness without arousing the associations of consciousness and will that are involved in human planning. One is forced to rely on inadequate instruments of expression. The alibi has a long and beguiling tradition behind it. "The Torah spoke in the language of men" was an ancient formulation of the same idea, but it too was a rationalization. For language is certainly incapable of expressing what the human mind has not grasped. Hence the language of analogy is a cover-up to gloss over the dissatisfaction of some thinkers with the limited insights about reality which their reason can disclose to them. They want to believe in something more personal than their own mental construct of the world, and yet they cannot ever know what that something is. So they rely on analogy in the hope that it will be emotionally rewarding in addition to being intellectually acceptable by dint of not straining the bonds of credulity.

Thus Steinberg was actually positing a Power beyond the universe directing its affairs—if not arbitrarily, as in the traditional supernaturalist version, at least in a way that raises serious logical questions about the validity of the concepts of natural and moral law that Steinberg himself held. What Steinberg was saying, in essence, is that the world is not a congeries of chance events; it is a cosmos, but a cosmos that has an eternal Guide. He was not emotionally content with positing the existence of a natural order subject to rational manipulation by man. But that actually was all his reason would permit him to posit. He was too much of a modernist to conceive of a supernatural God capable of arbitrarily playing havoc with natural order, yet he wanted the surety of a universe that was not only responsive to human needs but contained the certainty of their fulfillment. He was, by his own admission, "tender-minded." Hence the analogy of

God with mind. Through this analogy he was able to reify the rational order which he saw around him and raise it above the level of blind force.

The method of analogy fails for a reason that should be obvious. If God as Mind is anything more than a name for the order which is revealed in the universe, then He is the same supernatural God whom we saw in biblical religion. He "wills" things to be as they are and as they must become. What happens to the role of man in engineering plans for the future? However sophisticated the usual resort to paradox may be, a God who rules omnisciently leaves no freedom for man. If He is nothing more than the sum of the constructive forces in the universe, is not the analogy of Mind misleading? The analogists appear to stand on the threshold between naturalism and supernaturalism. For the most part, they are emotionally in the latter camp, intellectually in the former.

7

Another influential type of God-idea might be called the process concept. We find an outstanding presentation of God as process in the thinking of Samuel Alexander, who, among modern secular philosophers, has probably come closest to formulating a systematic philosophy of religion. Alexander's system is particularly worthy of our attention because he was sensitive to the emotional drive behind the rational processes of men.

Like Spinoza, Alexander was a God-intoxicated man. It was his opinion that all men are endowed with a thirst for deity. But for this native passion, worship would be impossible, no matter how much intellectual certainty about God's existence and His nature could be achieved. Alexander did not develop the implications of this view, but it is as significant a contribution to the philosophy of religion as any-thing else in his writings. For Alexander pointed here to the fact that all God-ideas are intellectual rationalizations of a preexisting psychological reaction to life's mysteries. The question is always begged when people try to convey what they mean by "God," because their emotional belief has already conditioned everything they have to say intellectu-ally. A good case can be made for the hypothesis that there is a demonstrable correspondence between certain tempera-ments and certain types of God-ideas. I shall have more to say in the next chapter about the relation between belief in God and ideas about God.

But our primary concern is with Alexander's God-concept and not with his theory about its genesis. Alexander is in the naturalist tradition, holding that nature functions without the control of any force outside itself. But nature is an orderly process and must, therefore, have some principle of operation. That principle Alexander finds in what he calls *nisus,* the creative urge in the cosmos. There is a tendency in the universe for all existents to move to a higher level. Each level, in turn, exerts a pull on the one below it. In this way there is a constant process of emergence, ultimately to cul-minate in a superior form, whose quality we cannot antici-pate.

The objective of *nisus* is deity, "the next higher empirical quality to mind, which the universe is engaged in bringing to birth. That the universe is pregnant with such a quality we are speculatively assured. What that quality is we cannot know; for we can neither enjoy nor still less contemplate it. . . . Deity in its turn is a quality which attends upon, or more strictly is equivalent to, previous or lower existences of the order of mind which itself rests on a still lower basis of qualities, and emerges when certain complexities and refinements of arrangements have been reached."[15] Deity is thus constantly emerging and being transcended as *nisus* pushes and pulls the universe relentlessly on its way to God.

God, in turn, might be described as the ultimate deity, never achieved, but always in the process of approximation. Alexander explains that "God as actually possessing deity does not exist but is an ideal, is always becoming; but God as the whole Universe tending toward deity does exist."[16]

Alexander's striking distinction between deity and God is one of the hallmarks of his philosophy. He was faced with the same problem that later confronted Whitehead, namely whether to identify God with the creative process in the universe. If he established such identity he could affirm nothing about God beyond what man's reading of nature could tell him. Whitehead, as we shall see, was prepared to make such an identification, at least in part, but he reserved for God an ultimate harmonizing function, toward which the process as a whole was striving. Alexander chose the device of identifying God with the goal of the universe, while confining the process of nature to its empirical character. Deity is merely another word for the continual emergence of ever higher forms which seems to characterize the universe of space-time. Yet deity, which is infinite in scope, is part of the nature of God. For it is by means of his deity that God realizes himself.

Alexander seems to be torn between his feeling that the world of natural events cannot be explained in terms of transcendent categories and his emotional drive to go beyond the world of experience to a more speculative construct of the natural process. His concept of deity would have been enough of a foundation for an idea of God, because it is a reading of nature in the light of an immanent, but hypothetical, causal principle. By adding God Alexander was able to satisfy his craving for surety that deity is not blind and that the universe is necessarily responsive to the needs of man.

Alexander's God-concept is a highly optimistic view of the universe. It acceptableness is largely dependent on whether or not one chooses to see nature as constantly improving, as ever giving rise to superior forms. However, a sympathetic expositor of his philosophy has stated that Alexander's position could not be substantiated if the scientific hypothesis of entropy, that the world is running down, were to be confirmed.[17]

In addition, Alexander failed to make a really clear distinction between God and deity, although this distinction is important in his system. Here is an example of a man struggling with a false issue and ignoring the issue which should have been of concern. Alexander thought, rightly, that he had to avoid confusing God with God's manifestations, his transcendence with his immanence. Therefore, God could not be defined in terms of any verifiable experience. Experience could give man only a faint insight into God's working. Nevertheless, the world of experience does possess attributes of deity in the emergent process. But the issue, I say, is a false one, for in so far as the distinction is clear it is insignificant. For the most part, however, it is not even clear. Deity, like God, is a process, a principle, an outcome, and a goal, all at the same time. Deity, like God, is infinite, although it is found only in a part of the universe. (I shall ignore the difficulty of a limited infinite.) But God, in Alexander's words is "the whole Universe tending toward deity." In this characterization, deity appears to be God. This turnabout appears to be inevitable whenever God is conceived of as synonymous with natural process or as the goal of that process. Collingwood points out that Alexander reverses the traditional conception that God created the world. In his system, "in the end the heavens and earth will create God."[18]

The real issue, however, is the validity of the cosmic urge postulate. To what extent is Alexander's assertion borne out that every level of existence strives to a higher level, or that the universe as a whole is creative? Certainly evolution has produced some marvelous results. But if we accepted Alexander's thesis, we should have to assert that the ape strives (not consciously, of course) to become a man, while lower animals strive to reach the level of the ape. Man, in turn, instead of devising superior techniques for blowing his brains out, should be perfecting his mind in order to become "little lower than the angels." Perhaps, in the light of eternity, he is, but no proof can possibly be deduced from the facts before us. The search for divinity cannot be completed by postulating the existence of a force that relentlessly works itself out toward an ideal outcome for man. No basis for such a hypothesis exists.

In wrestling with the problem of evil, Alexander is as optimistic as he is in his cosmology. Evil is natural; it is, again, the result of causes which man can perceive and understand. Evil need not be viewed as divine retribution. Indeed, until the natural process culminates in God, evil is a necessary part of existence, for only by conquering evil do more perfect types acquire their value. Particular evils, however, are temporary. Alexander sums up his doctrine in this way:

> For goodness, whether we are considering the human values of the sub-human values, is the character of the permanent as opposed to the impermanent contrasted evil. The universe works in experience so as to secure the survival of good, or rather that which survives in the long run in the contest establishes its value thereby

and is good. To repeat a saying already quoted, "morality is the nature of things." The history by which new types of finites come into existence is the natural history of values.[19]

Is it valid to locate the good in that which survives? Are the victims of tyranny bad and their oppressors good? What is the judgment to be leveled against an eternity that strides to fulfillment over the corpse of even a single innocent being, that causes even one human life to meet an unjust and untimely end? Good cannot be defined as that which survives, for that which is life-giving is generally held to be good—even Alexander accepts this—and yet life itself culminates in death. Now Alexander would probably maintain that man's role in bringing the good about is crucial. If this is so, why speak abstractly of the universe's working in human experience? Why not, rather, speak of man's working in the universe of experience, seeking to achieve ends that he deems good? The latter approach, of course, lacks certainty, and Alexander, like most theists, seems unable to conceive of a world without certainty.

8

In line with the philosopher of *Space, Time and Deity* comes Alfred North Whitehead. Both Alexander and Whitehead represent a compelling interest in the structure of the universe.

There is, however, another point of departure among philosophers of process from which to approach the problem of God. That point of departure is the moral nature of man. In this second approach the study of man is pursued in order to determine whether and how ethical values can be validated and concretized in human institutions. In the major historical religions, God is variously viewed as the legislator and guarantor of ethical values and as the rewarding and punishing judge of human behavior. In the naturalist tradition represented by philosophers of process God is a principle of harmonization among conflicting ideals, in a sense the ideal goal toward which human beings strive when they try to read meaning and direction into their lives. It is such a naturalist analysis that John Dewey makes and which I shall consider in the next section.

Whitehead's way of conceiving of God is the way of the metaphysician who tries to understand the flux of nature. I might call it the way of Aristotle rather than of Plato, although in suggesting such a comparison I am fully aware that neither Plato nor Aristotle can be pigeonholed in any one category. Nor, as we shall see, can Whitehead be accused of ignoring the problems of good and evil and of man's moral nature. I want simply to point to the striking difference between the type of conceptions of God in the highly abstract analysis of Whitehead and in the more ethically-centered formulations of other philosophers.

But whatever the approach, naturalists, it would seem, are disposed to consider God as immanent in the universe. Transcendence, in so far as it has any meaning, is conceived of as being a quality of the universe itself rather than a property of some Power controlling the cosmos from beyond it. Thus God is an explanation of the world as it really is—always, however, with the understanding that such reality embraces discontinuity, mystery, surprise, and creativity, which man often cannot predict but which nonetheless are part of an orderly natural process.

For Whitehead, the universe is process. Understand the nature of that process and you understand reality. Process and reality the flux of events—is all that the universe discloses to man. Therefore, if one would apprehend God, one must know the nature of the universal process. Science and theology are partners.

Whitehead's philosophy, as I have suggested, has a kinship with that of Samuel Alexander. This is true particularly in the major points that Whitehead makes about God, namely that He is both a goal and an immanent formative principle of the universe, both the integrative objective of the cosmic process and the integrating force that renders this objective achievable. Like Alexander, therefore, Whitehead has as his main problem the task of explaining God's "primordial" and "consequent" natures, God's vision of things to come and their ultimate realization in Him.

Whitehead's organismic, or (as I prefer to call it) integrationist, approach is firmly planted in this world and is unsympathetic to supernaturalist flights.

We know nothing beyond this temporal world and the formative elements which jointly constitute its character. The temporal world and its formative elements constitute for us the all-inclusive universe.

These formative elements are:

1. The creativity whereby the actual world has its character of temporal passage to novelty.
2. The realm of ideal entities, or forms, which are in themselves not actual, but are such that they are exemplified in everything that is actual, according to some proportion of relevance.
3. The actual but non-temporal entity whereby the in-determination of mere creativity is transmuted into a determinate freedom. This non-temporal actual entity is what men call God—the supreme God of rationalized religion.[20]

I find most difficulty in understanding Whitehead's second point, "the realm of ideal entities" or "eternal forms," as he calls them in *Process and Reality*. These are not the Ideas of Plato, although the Platonic influence is manifest. They exist conceptually realized "in the primordial nature of God,"[21] But God does not create them. Rather does God's nature itself imply the existence of ideal entities; the latter, in turn, require Him for their reality. By this antithesis, I presume, Whitehead means that nothing is actualized in the temporal world without, in some way, implying an eternal form. But this eternal form, even though rooted in the nature of God, possesses no reality unless concretized in some actual event. Plato would seem to have been more consistent in establishing the reality of his Ideas as logical forms whose existence need not depend on their concrescence, however much any temporal object would, in so far as it became actualized, necessarily partake of some Idea.

These reflections cause me to conclude that Whitehead's basic theory would have been better served had he not complicated it with the confusing doctrine of forms. For notions of logical and ontological entities are actually derived through generalization or imaginative construction from a study of existents. While it is possible to read these notions back into the natural process as residing in its very primordial state, it is much more difficult to see what proof could be advanced whereby such entities could be conceived of as *causal elements* in the process. And since Whitehead employs these entities as a bridge between God and the world, between eternity and temporality, between anticipation and actualization, one wonder what their status really is. Are they merely logical entities or do they act as forces? In what sense does a temporal object *partake* of them? In attempting to avoid the idealist position of placing the whole cosmos as an idea in the mind of God, Whitehead suggests that every event bears some logical relation to the primordial nature of God. In this case, however, why speak of God's "primordial nature"? Is it not logical to assume, for example, that the idea of a table actually came into being after men's experiences with flat surfaces, measurement and raised supports? What is gained by locating such an idea in some primordial realm, whether ontological, logical, or temporal?

Nor is it clear what Whitehead has in mind when he speaks of God as "a principle of concretion." By this phrase Whitehead tries to identify God as "that actual entity from which each temporal concrescence receives that initial aim from which its self-causation starts."[22] If Whitehead means by this that advance into novelty is limited by the conditions within which a particular event is set, we can all agree with him. If he means that creativity does not spring from a vacuum but is inspired by future possibilities that grow out of the past, again we can agree. Certainly the entity Whitehead calls God cannot be a power wholly apart from events themselves. That, at least, would necessarily follow from Whitehead's commitment to naturalism. However, what meaning, aside from its metaphorical bearing, can we attribute to self-causation? Whitehead uses terms like subject, aim, feeling, and self-causation in a technical sense that has little to do with consciousness. Consequently, he confuses mechanical and human processes. It is perhaps for this reason that he fails to distinguish clearly between God as a term applied to the creative process of nature and God as participating in and causing that process. Is God the final cause of the universe, the goal toward which nature is unconsciously but purposively heading? Or is He the process itself, determining the course of events only in the sense that events are caused in an orderly, intelligible fashion?

Whitehead's world is an incomplete one; it is constantly emerging as the result of a creative process which is held together by the integrative power called God. Every event in this evolution, while standing in isolation from all other events, bears an organic relation to them in so far as they all come together in one or more real unities. These unities are, as Whitehead declares, a product of a determinate creativity. Were it not for God, the freedom (or better, anarchy) of creativity and novelty would make for a chaos of unrelated concretions. "Apart from God, the remaining formative elements would fail in their functions."[23] As it is, God's presence in every concretion, event, or epochal occasion links it to its antecedents and its consequents.

Whitehead realizes that his answer to the problem of indeterminate creativity raises the question of evil—in highly abstract form, to be sure. If determinateness is the result of God's activity, "then the evil in the world is in conformity with the nature of God."[24] On the other hand, "if God be an actual entity which enters into every creative phase and yet is above change, He must be exempt from internal inconsistency which is the note of evil."[25] Whitehead settles the question by limiting God. Here again the distinction is made between God as goal and God as motive force. On the one hand, the world demonstrates "that its creative passage is subject to the immanence of an unchanging actual entity. On the other side its incompletion, and its evil, show that the temporal world is to be construed in terms of additional formative elements which are not definable in the terms which are applicable to God."[26] In other words, Whitehead ignores the problem posed by conceiving of God as Creator: that the evil manifested in the world would then have to have come into being through His agency, or at least to have been permitted by Him to emerge. This is a problem, like that of immortality, for the solution of which no evidence is available. Whitehead simply takes the world as it is and identifies God with the good. Evil exists, but it disappears in the over-all "esthetic consistency" of the world, the more so as God, the determinate goal of creativity, is achieved.

Put into more familiar philosophic terms, God is an immanent Power in a universe about whose source or origin we must be neutral. We have no basis for assuming either that the universe is eternal or that it is the product of a special act of creation. Given what we experience, however, we find that the world testifies to a Power that fashions it, or at least to an order that characterizes it. That Power is both a creative force and a goal toward which the process of creativity is heading. Since God must possess an inner consistency,* the destructive, but unstable, power of evil cannot be attributed to him. It must be assigned to the incompleteness of the physical universe.

Whitehead thus summarizes his own doctrine:

> The order of the world is no accident. There is nothing actual which could be actual without some measure of order. The religious insight is the grasp of this truth: That the order of the world, the depth of reality of the world, the value of the world in its whole and in its parts, the beauty of the world, the zest of life, the peace of life, and the mastery of evil, are all bound together—not accidentally, but by reason of this truth: that the universe exhibits a creativity with infinite freedom, and a realm of forms with infinite possibilities; but that this creativity and these forms are together impotent to achieve actuality apart from the completed ideal harmony, which is God.[27]

There is an aura of vagueness in Whitehead's conception

---

*Whitehead's explanation of why such consistency is necessary is not convincing. His argument is that God is the "esthetic consistency" of the world. By definition, evil possesses internal inconsistency and hence can have nothing to do with God.

that vitiates his argument. As an integrative principle within
the universe, God can be understood in completely naturalistic terms. In this sense, "God" is the word by which we
designate the causal factors or the principle of intelligibility
in physical events. But what is the "completed ideal harmony"? Does Whitehead mean to assert that the end of the
evolutionary process is already determined? This would
hardly seem to follow from his insistence that creativity pervades the universe. On the other hand, that creativity is declared to be determinate. Does determinacy imply a pre-
ordained end? Whitehead again answers "No." Why, then
speak of a *completed* harmony, which would seem to render
meaningless and blind the strivings of the present to create
values? Ultimately, Whitehead's brand of naturalism means
to rely upon some supermundane but indescribably metaphysical principle, however much Whitehead apparently
sought to avoid writing of the natural order of things as a
metaphysical construct.[28] Any system which attempts to conceive of God as both a force and a goal exposes itself inevitably to the charge of inner contradiction.

Nor does Whitehead's solution of the problem of evil succeed. If evils exists as a positive but destructive force, some
kind of dualism necessarily follows. Whitehead accepts the
dualism but places evil on a lower level than good, since evil
is unstable. Good, since it accords with the aesthetic consistency of the world, must triumph. This, stripped of its
philosophic trappings, is the traditional argument that God
is all-good and all-powerful and must win out. As an act of
faith, this reasoning has had, and continues to have, considerable potency. It should, however, be recognized that it
ignores the moral weakness of man and his undeniable
capacity to create moral chaos. Moreover, to inject a pragmatic note, it is rather difficult to arouse men to moral in-

vestigation and responsibility if they are convinced that they
are mere pawns in the hands of a Power that has already
determined the ultimate nature and the final triumph of a
"good" humanity.

Whitehead's concept of God is too suggestive to be dismissed even in the face of the above criticisms. Particularly
fruitful, in my opinion, is his acknowledgment—unfortunately sometimes ignored in his own works—that we know
nothing beyond the temporal world. All God-ideas have some
roots in the world of human experience. But when men try
to get behind the world, to fathom its mysteries, to explain
its inconsistencies and evils, they often wander off into an
intellectual desert in which they get lost. Whitehead's premise that we do not get beyond the world available to human
experience is in sharp contrast to that supernaturalist view
which holds that man's knowledge of nature is as nothing
compared to the reality of God, of which glimpses are
caught in mystic experiences and in revelation. Yet Whitehead falls prey to this very proneness to read more out of
nature than can legitimately be done. To see the future
fashioned out of the present by a "completed ideal harmony" is to attribute ontologically to the universe a character which cannot logically be inferred from human experience. The existence of Whitehead's God is simply another attractive hypothesis, whose validity no evidence can
ever prove or disprove. Even as hypothesis, however, it has
internal difficulties that Whitehead either ignored or failed
to resolve.

Still, to conceive of nature profoundly it is necessary to
employ methods that advance beyond narrow positivism.
Science, advised Whitehead, requires imaginative speculation, and man must therefore seek to construct cosmologies
and conceptions of ultimate reality which can provide a

meaningful context for research in all branches of human knowledge. It is to Whitehead's credit that he avoided dogmatizing his own particular vision of reality.

Finally, Whitehead's theory commends itself for its willingness to accept evil as a real force in the universe, with which God Himself must reckon. The ultimate origin of evil, like the origin of the world, must forever be a secret from man. Nevertheless, there is nothing in the nature of evil that proves its omnipotence. This leaves man an area of operation in which he can overcome much, if not all, of the evil he faces in the course of his brief life span. Whitehead's position removes evil from the realm of supernaturally imposed punishment and transfers it to the category of a natural reality with which man can deal. Unfortunately he resorts to the too facile solution of restoring evil to a metaphysical plane in which it is dissolved automatically by its own essential inner stability. Such a resolution of the problem of evil in this temporal world is pious but futile wishful thinking.

9

It is probably not an exaggeration to declare that John Dewey is viewed by most conventional, supernatural-minded theologians as an enemy of religion. But if religion is placed in the context of man's search for a saner, more beautiful, and ethically more advanced life, then Dewey's philosophical contributions must be welcomed for their numerous insights into the nature of religion. It is not my intention, however, to discuss Dewey's philosophy of religion, about which there is much to criticize as well as praise. I shall confine myself to his idea of God.

Dewey devoted his long, fruitful career to opposing dualism, whatever its form—body and mind, spirit and matter, nature and supernature. He was a firm believer in the organic character of the universe. Psychologically, he was a monist, if we understand by monism belief in a universe operating according to principles having a rational relationship to one another; intellectually, of course, he was a pluralist, for he held that it is not given to man to embrace the oneness of the universe. Our knowledge of the world cannot be reduced to single causes; natural laws are human constructs, useful as means of advancing our knowledge but constantly being refined with each addition of empirical data; human nature, apart from the common basic needs such as those for food, shelter, companionship, and the releasing of energy, varies from person to person and culture to culture. Dewey's recognition of the manifold character of experience did not prevent his giving expression to his "natural piety" and to his understanding that men must have some means of overcoming the sense of cosmic solitariness. Dewey was not the cold, unemotional thinker we might presume him to be from a reading of his weighty prose. He had great compassion for his fellow men, and his discussion of God testifies to this characteristic.

Dewey has been called to task for applying "God" to his idea that the divine in life constitutes the "ideal possibilities unified through imaginative realization and projecton,"[29] for this idea is miles apart from the supernatural connotation popularly given to the term. Dewey said, in fact, that he did not insist on the terminology, but he felt that the world, through its universal usage, had the power of helping to protect men from despair. He was completely aware of the emotional power of words, and he saw no reason why the supernaturalists should have a monopoly on "God."

Dewey's naturalism, unlike that of Alexander and Whitehead, sought not to go beyond *verifiable* experience. For

visions of the future, ideals, and scientific constructs of
nature all have their origins in natural conditions, in "the
possibilities offered to thought and action."[30] These products of the imagination, however, must ultimately be subject
to verification. The simplest idea is not a mental picture of
some objective existent, it is a plan of action; so is the
loftiest ideal. An ideal can have no separate ontological
status; its roots are in present existence and its flower is dependent on human endeavor. Consequently, for Dewey, God
could only be a name applied to a highly important process
subject to empirical analysis.

What is it that Dewey calls God? It is the "*active* relation
between ideal and actual."[31] Dewey finds that human experience gives rise to many ideals and values—art, education,
fellowship, love, justice, and the like—which are neither
completely actualized nor "rootless." They stem naturally
from the interaction between men and nature. Both
society and nature contain "forces . . . that generate
and support the ideals."[32] This is his point, in a nut-
shell. *God is the name we give to the total process whereby
man's most important ideals arise and are brought to fulfillment.* It is a natural process, one that relies both on human
resources and on those of an orderly nature. There is nothing inevitable about the achievement of ideal ends. Dewey,
despite his avowed optimism, does not assume, as do Alexander and Whitehead, that the good *must* triumph. All he
asserts is that there is no reason for assuming it cannot.

The point need not be labored that traditional religionists
will find little in Dewey's God-idea with which they can
agree. They will deny that ideals, particularly ethical ideals,
are "natural." Moral values are God-given and absolute;
those rising in history can have no more than contingent
value. On this point Dewey and the traditionalists cannot

even join issue. The traditionists will, however, ask Dewey why he chooses certain ideals and not others, and they will not accept the reply that the ideals worthy of being chosen as "good" are those that serve to unify man and his experience. This, at least, is a debatable matter. For the critic of Dewey might well ask: Since the unification of ideals, by Dewey's own statement, is in the process of fulfillment rather than actually embodied in current existence, what criteria other than Dewey's own ethical preferences are to determine which ideals are divine and which are not? Surely, they might say, Dewey would hold freedom of thought dearer than life itself no matter what the current climate of opinion —even if totalitarianism had closed the minds of all other men. Orwell's world of 1984 is a possibility that Dewey would not deny. If it is experience and actual conditions that generate ideals, by what standards do we chose democratic ideals rather than totalitarian ones? Both, after all, are "natural"; the mere fact of their actuality or possibility does not entitle us to proclaim that one or the other *ought* to be.

Dewey's reply, in detail, would take us far afield because it involves his whole logic of inquiry, his rejection of attempts to establish a dichotomy between scientific judgments and ethical judgments, a dichotomy based on the supposition that the former are hypothetical and the latter are categorical. To summarize his treatment of value is to say that values cannot be separated from the process of valuation. As in science, when we are faced with facts that require explanation, we set up a hypothesis to explain them and then proceed to test the hypothesis, so in an ethical situation we have to select the hypothetical end that can best serve to unify our experience for us in accordance with what we consider to be the inherent logic of the events under consideration.

Ethical goals for Dewey are outcomes of ethical inquiry rather than categorical imperatives which antedate their application to particular problems. The peremptoriness of some ethical values derives from man's previous experience with them. Dewey's critics are left only with the possibility of asking whether man's proneness to formulate hypotheses and to establish unifying goals is not in itself a demonstration of some divine force at work. Here there is no further room for debate, for we enter the sphere of unverifiable speculation. Why man is as he is cannot be answered by man.

It is precisely here, however, that Dewey's critics might well take their stand. True, man cannot "explain" whence he derives his peculiar powers of mind. What makes Dewey so certain, then, that the application of the scientific method of logical inquiry to the field of ethics will result in a humane society? Although Dewey was not as naive about the inevitableness of social progress as some of his critics would have us believe—he well understood that such progress would be inevitable only if human behavior were governed by compulsion in the direction of utopia (a compulsion which, in itself, is a contradition in terms) —yet his entire philosophy pre-supposed some objective ordering of things, some correspondence between social ideals and the actual dynamics of social development, which would make the conception of God as ideal possibility more than a pious wish.

Just as the correspondence between a verified hypothesis and the facts it explains depends on an inherent order in nature, so does the workability of ethical ideals have something to do with the inherent unity of mankind. On the other hand, just as hypotheses need not *necessarily* accord with nature (indeed, in the history of science many false assumptions have proved practically fruitful), so is it true that the values that men choose need not necessarily reflect the actual nature of man. In both scientific and ethical judgments, we are dealing, as Dewey rightly asserts, with hypothetical ends. But the hypotheses point beyond themselves to a reality they propose to explain. Dewey's God-idea, therefore, would seem to conceal a premise about the moral structure of man which alone would render plausible the conception of God as ideal possibility.

10

Even so brief and inadequate a sampling of the many God-ideas that men have formulated through the ages suggests a number of propositions that ought to be borne in mind in discussions about God.

The right to conceive of God in terms that do not extend beyond verifiable human experience—and to judge this conception by the same rigorous standards of empirical proof as are used in science—is unchallengeable. By "right" I mean that the charge of semantic confusion should not be leveled against those who demand that hypotheses about God be subject to validation in experience. This is not to say that a God-idea formulated in accordance with contemporary scientific method is necessarily more valid than a theory that runs counter to it. I am aware of the fact that scientific method or knowledge cannot rule out hypotheses that have not been disproved. All I am affirming is that a God-idea may be considered religious even if it denies supernatural transcendence to God.

An example of the kind of thinking I am arguing against is this statement by A. J. Ayer:

> It is sometimes claimed, indeed, that the existence of a certain sort of regularity in nature constitutes sufficient evidence for the existence of a god. But if the sentence "God exists" entails no more than that certain

types of phenomena occur in certain sequences, then to assert the existence of a god will be simply equivalent to asserting that there is the requisite regularity in nature; and *no religious man* would admit that this was all he intended to assert in asserting the existence of a god.[33] (*Italics added.*)

Ayer is correct in stating that a religious man wants to assert more than that there is regularity in nature. He wants to feel and to assert that this regularity is such that men can count upon it when they plan for their future. This inference involves him in no greater logical difficulty than it does the scientist whose experimental method depends upon it. This is not to say that a specific scientific law as formulated at a particular point in scientific development exists objectively in the world. It is merely assumed and tested in the course of an experiment; even when validated it serves as an explanation for a limited number of phenomena. Scientific laws are man-made, serving as tools for the understanding of nature. But scientific laws presuppose the orderliness, if not necessarily the uniformity, of nature.

In other words, the logical positivist position expressed by Ayer is weak at two points. In the first place, it is wrong in overlooking the singleness of the faith that underlies both religion and science. Secondly, Ayer makes the mistake of identifying God with a "transcendent being" and with no other postulate.

As should be apparent from even this brief survey, the conventions of language need not restrict and have not restricted "God" to the usage characteristic of any religious tradition. For the term God, as I asserted earlier, is highly ambiguous. Two men at prayer, reciting the same words, may be addressing themselves to altogether different deities. One God may be an inner conscience; the other may be

Being-in-itself. In the former case, God may answer in the form of a renewed determination by the worshiper to act ethically; in the latter instance, the result of prayer for the worshiper may be an intense awareness of his own insignificance.

Thus God-ideas, being functions of the human intellect, must necessarily be products of the reasoning powers of individual men and women. And inasmuch as reasoning power is affected by heredity, environment, formal education, and experience, it is inevitable that there be many conceptions of God current among men.

The fact that pluralism in God-ideas is a necessary outcome of man's search for the divine does not, however, confer equal worth on all formulations. Concepts of God are subject to the same canons of logic and validation as are all products of human thinking. Contrary to popular opinion, God is a subject for rational debate, and there is a value in disputing the merits of the various God-concepts. Like all rational discourse, discussions of God keep men aware of their changing knowledge and of the consequent need for rethinking their most cherished assumptions about the divine.

But while theological debate is desirable, we must not expect from it final conclusions or proofs. In the long run, "God" is a name that philosophers or theologians apply to certain suppositions about the nature of reality. "God" becomes a subject of *religious* discourse when the reality which it supposedly designates is felt to support and give meaning to the purposes of men. "God" is not a designation for some objective existent to which men can point either directly, as to a table, or indirectly, as to an electron or a virus.

From the religious standpoint, the faith that underlies all

ideas of God is more important than the ideas themselves. For pervading all conceptions of God is their psychological substructure. Men react to the universe as a cosmos. They may differ in their cosmic vision, as widely as Job and John Dewey. But all alike see order in the universe. Furthermore, they see their own mortal lives as having value. For this faith, needless to say, there is no ultimate validation. There can be only an attempt at justifying the faith and at reinforcing it by developing a humane society and a satisfying conception of the universe. The faith is maintained by the average person throughout life; but in the course of his lifetime he probably changes his views several times in order to sustain or give new meaning to his faith. World-faith engenders world-views, but no one view has ever been able to satisfy the demands of faith.

A "pious skepticism" is essential for rational and spiritual religion. This skepticism should be directed toward the many varieties of ways in which man has tried to hold infinity in the palm of his hand. No mortal creature can ever hope to do that, even poetically. In exercising such skepticism, however, man need not lose his faith in the order and value of life. The universe is filled with myriads of experiences that confirm his belief. But in so far as the skepticism helps man to recognize the limitations of his own understanding and the inexhaustibility of the fount of knowledge from which his own rationalized experience draws a mere drop, it will enhance his own piety. He will then be more likely to accept the hypothetical character of his idea of God. Such a state of mind is most likely to stimulate man's continued search for a more satisfactory, as well as more satisfying, conception of God. Perhaps the search itself, the effort to substantiate the native endowment of faith, will be a higher stage of religious development than the acceptance of the ready-made but inadequate conceptions upon which man has been wont to rest.

4

AN APPROACH TO RELIGION
FOR OUR DAY

THE ANSWER WE GET TO ANY QUESTION
of a religious character will naturally depend upon how the
question is framed. As long as man continues to ask "Why
do the wicked prosper and the righteous suffer?," he is
bound to get inconclusive and repetitive answers. No matter how profound may be the insight into the meaning of
suffering which it evokes—and, from Job to Niebuhr, there
have been some profound utterances on the subject—this
question appears to me to be far less fruitful than the one
that asks "How can suffering be alleviated?" Nor do I see

any reason for saying that the second question is less religious in character than the first. The effort to alleviate suffering must be sustained by a faith that nature and man are so constituted as to be capable of control and improvement in behalf of human needs, since there can be no scientific proof that the world is so constituted. Most men live by the faith that it is, and consequently they are reinforced in their efforts to plan and experiment their way out of the difficulties that constantly confront them.

The time has come to transpose religion into a new key, to borrow the phrase popularized in philosophy by Susanne K. Langer. That transposition requires, first and foremost, the raising of new questions. Old problems, of course, persist and call for fresh solutions. Traditional problems cannot be completely ignored. But if we are not to be pulled down into the quagmire of sophistry and casuistry, we must direct our attention to those issues with which our present state of knowledge equips us to deal.

The position which I propose to uphold will doubtless be unpopular with those naturalists whose distate for certain elements in organized religion has led them to resist any move to institutionalize what they consider to be religiously worthwhile. It will be even more unpopular with theological and institutional traditionalists. Neither those who insist that any theology, to be worthwhile, must posit belief in the supernatural nor those whose traditionalism is an emotional attachment to ritual will find any comfort in the position that religion ought now adopt a naturalist theology and a freer, more flexible approach to ritual and worship.

1

Why limit ourselves to such questions as our present knowledge equips us to answer? Man's imagination has solved many a mystery; why, then, adopt so prosaic a view?

I do not, by any means, advocate shutting off imaginative speculation: to do so would be to make intellectual growth almost an impossibility. I do argue that we must learn to distinguish between two types of questions. There are those questions which, even when replied to, remain unanswered. A question of this type is "Who created the world?" Such a question is not a "meaningless" one, as the positivists assert, but it leads to answers like "God created the world" and "The world was not created; it is eternal." These are pseudo-answers; they block further investigation and fail to advance our knowledge. In contrast, such a question as "Does nature operate by chance or according to a rational order?", even if it can never be answered in absolute terms, involves investigation into the workings of nature, including observation and the formulation and verification of hypotheses.

It is the thesis of this book that man must begin to realize the impossibility of finding satisfying answers to the first type of question. No human mind can encompass the whole universe of time and space. In man's stirrings to unlock the secrets of nature, he must learn to satisfy his curiosity by concentrating on those areas which the instruments at his command can probe. The fact is that we simply do not know how the universe came into being or what its destiny will be. All that man can do is to spin cosmological theories; those theories cannot be considered actual descriptions of the ultimate nature of the universe.*

What is rarely realized is that answers to the second type of question, despite their pragmatic value, are founded on

---

*The foregoing should not be taken to imply that metaphysical questions are altogether fruitless. To the extent that they reveal the endless mystery of the universe they serve a cautionary function. My remarks are directed toward those who confuse metaphysical assertions with religious truth.

faith—a profound faith in the orderly processes of the universe and in the power of human reason to read reality aright and to learn to use it for the enhancement of life. It is this faith that underlies all God-ideas, from the most primitive to the most sophisticated. There is no question of proof or disproof, since it is a *psychological reaction* to the impact of life. The great errors in religious thinking occur when human reaction to reality is treated as fact, when belief in God, instead of being accepted as an attitude or approach to life, is considered a theorem requiring demonstration. What causes human beings to take this step from assertion of faith to assumption of fact is that in their craving for the stability and security that faith in life's meaningfulness and orderliness can provide, they inevitably try to picture that meaning and order; in the act of depiction, they ascribe existence to their own creation. But the God-idea can never be God. That would be idolatry.

In Jewish religion numerous thinkers saw this danger and sought to avoid it by asserting that God's nature is unknown and unknowable. Positively, we can know only what He is not. Maimonides put it this way: "Know that the description of God in negative terms is the true description . . . while positive attributes imply polytheism. . . ."[1] (In Kabbalism, God is conceived of as "a sphere, a whole realm of divinity, which underlies the world of our sense-data and which is present and active in all that exists."[2] Man can grasp God only as He manifests Himself in human experience, but God Himself in His essence is beyond that experience.) God, says the tradition (both philosophical and mystical), is unlike anything we humans can grasp; He is wholly other, not only in His transcendence, but in His immanence as well. He defies human understanding.

2

I believe that in the search for an acceptable idea of God, the metaphysics of ultimates with which many religionists have been obsessed are obstructive. They want an explanation of the universe—of the *why* of its existence. They want to know that the world was created so that it has an ultimate destiny favorable to man. They have insisted that ethical values must be grounded in some ultimate reality; unless these values are by nature absolute, man can have no measuring rod by which to judge right from wrong. But to achieve absolute answers, it is necessary to go beyond nature into the stratosphere of the supernatural. This wild flight beyond the gravitational hold of methods of verification makes it impossible for anyone to prove or disprove the speculation of these metaphysicians. There is no denying the attraction which such speculation holds for the human mind. Who has not sought to probe the mystery of creation? Nor, as I pointed out above, is this type of thinking necessarily fruitless. After all, the assumption that the operations of nature are subject to rational study is a metaphysical postulate. However, there is an essential difference between the use of imagination in scientific thought and its use in metaphysical speculation on the Absolute. The hypothesis of the scientist stands or falls on its experimental verification; there is no such check on the speculations of the absolutist metaphysician.

Religion in the new key, while granting everyone the right of poetic construction, refrains from dogmatizing metaphysical theories. The element of mystery and faith cannot and should not be completely rooted out of religious doctrine; it is nonsense to think that man can live completely by the dictum "Seeing is believing." Man ought never and can never lose the sense of the ineffable, of the unplumbed (and most likely unplumbable) depths of the universe. And man's experience has taught him that he cannot automatically rule out as irrational an imaginative construction of reality simply because it is not subject to immediate scientific proof. Flights of imagination have often been preludes to scientific discovery. Einstein's cosmic religion, while it is not necessarily presupposed in his more scientific constructions of the universe, is nevertheless a plausible, stimulating interpretation, which gave impetus to his own search for a unified theory of the physical universe. Most important, a cosmology like Einstein's requires no extension of our reason into unreason and implies no contradiction of verifiable fact.

Proofs of God's existence and metaphysical definitions of God and man are, in the last analysis, unnecessary for religious faith. As Eugene Kohn has said,

> "We cannot afford to rest our faith in God on the validation of any metaphysical dialectic. Attempts to give a definite description of the nature of God afford a very shaky foundation for faith in Him. It is much better to assume from the outset that man's mind cannot grasp the nature of God. We cannot define God; we can, at best, define what we mean by the term 'God,' what experiences we identify with the Divine."[3]

A modicum of humility on the part of religionists would press home to them the truth of Kohn's assertion that all definitions of God are definitions of what we mean by God and not accurate descriptions of a knowable entity. It is a fact that the God-concept which appears in the speech and writings of men is a product of the imagination.[4] There is no other way for man to know God than through his own experience, and, since man's experience is limited, his knowledge of God is limited. No amount of question-begging references to revelation can hide the truth of that statement. Does this mean a denial of God's existence? If God is conceived of as a supernatural being, then we can answer only, "We do not know." If, however, God can legitimately be conceived of in terms of natural processes, then we are called upon to explain what aspects of man's experience as part of nature lead him to form a God-idea.

3

This is a good example of the new key of religion: Instead of asking whether God exists and assuming that everyone understands the word to denote the same reality, we ask ourselves what we mean by God and what significance there is to belief in Him. Before addressing ourselves to this question, we shall first have to recall the common and unique factor in all the myriads of God-ideas past and present.

Religion, as we have seen, arises from two sources, from the experience of the group and from that of the individual. It would be a mistake to suppose that because the group has no consciousness comparable to that of the individual, because it cannot think, it has no cognitive function. Actually, the thinking of the individual is largely influenced by the character of the group. We note the distinct emphasis on history in Jewish conceptions of God. Not that physical nature was ignored; the Psalms testify to an acute awareness of nature. But it was the Jewish sense of history, which largely resulted from the constant struggle of the Jews to exist and the necessity to explain to themselves the vicissitudes of their existence, that provided the frame of reference in which Jewish ideas of God were formulated. If we are to understand an idea of God accurately, we must be able to trace the path of its evolution in our social environment.

It is also true that we must look for the source of God-ideas in the fundamental needs of the human individual. This type of sociological and psychological investigation assumes that the God-idea can, indeed must, be studied naturalistically. We cannot hope to refute belief in revelation or in the assumption by God of human form; we do not deny the "possibility" of their truth, but we do assert, along with Overstreet, that they are immature conceptions, which lower the dignity of man because they render him, by definition, incapable of discovering truth or righteousness for himself. A being who inherently lacks the ability to know right from wrong and who has to depend on an "authority" in order to know how to act is a weak and ineffective personality. I do not use this *ad hominem* argument as proof of the correctness of the naturalistic position but to emphasize that man is morally and intellectually responsible for his assertions about the nature of the universe because all his assertions, even those about revelation, are products of his own thinking. Being responsible and being aware of his limited powers, he ought to seek truth and goodness and hope, rather than know, he has attained them.

However, all God-ideas, whether naturalist or supernaturalist, have sought to answer one universal need of man, the need to find meaning and order. For the universe to have meaning for man, it must, in some way, respond to his wants. This is not the same as saying that when a man wants something the universe must respond positively. Many of man's wants are absurd. They may, on the one hand, be contrary to the actual needs of his nature. A person may want liquor when his health would be better served by abstention. On the other hand, man's wants may be absurd because they are not in keeping with the nature of the universe. There is no point so far as we can determine, to the search for eternal life. Nor does it make much sense to pray for rain or for the birth of a son. That people do these things proves only that they believe the world is so constituted as to satisfy their most egotistical desires. The assumption of meaning or of order, therefore, does not imply that the intelligible order is accurately conceived. But the assumption does bespeak a *belief* that a meaningful order exists. The attempt to disclose and to understand this order has been man's greatest undertaking.

By order I do not mean a prefabricated teleological pattern, but a rational system which man can learn to manipulate for his own legitimate purposes. The assumption implicit both in the biblical story of creation and in the sophisticated account by Aristotle of the Prime Mover is that the universe is a cosmos and not a chaos. Actually, all God-ideas are rationalizations of this premise. Belief in the orderliness of life always precedes the specific estimation of the quality and the significance of that order.

The universality of this need makes it plausible to assume that it is an invariable prerequisite for the God-idea. But since the need is universal, how are we to account for the conflicting interpretations of life's significance and nature's order represented by the various God-ideas? How can some men conceive God to be impatient and some think of Him as forbearing? How can He be thought of by some as the creator of good and by others of evil? The answer is that the meaning of life is always mediated by the group in which one is educated. Modern anthropology and psychology have collaborated to show how the group character affects the psychic make-up of its individual members. Kardiner has even endeavored to prove the existence of a basic personality type for each society. Whether or not his theory can be substantiated, there is no question of the profound influence of environment on the individual. His wants are largely those aroused by the environment, and the way in which they are fulfilled is largely conditioned by the environmental possibilities. This is not the place to argue the point of whether or not the individual is completely culture-bound by his surroundings. Suffice it to say in opposition to deterministic theories of culture that since the individual is an active agent of the environment as well as a product of it, any theory asserting a one-directional impact of environment on the individual cannot be true.

Now, if it is true that God-ideas are conceived in response to the need to interpret the significance of and the order in life which are assumed prior to any reasoning about their nature, then it follows that any power which is identified as fulfilling this need can legitimately be called God. Aristotle's first cause was God; the religious stamp of approval was placed upon this philosophical concept by Maimonides and Aquinas. Spinoza's pantheistic deity is no less a God than the biblical God who sat between the cherubim on the cover of the holy ark. These concepts differ from one another as night from day; yet hardly any studies have been made as to what they have in common. Let me reiterate that *the common factor in all God-ideas is the underlying assumption that human existence is meaningful because of some divine Power that is thought to give direction to human life.* Let it be added immediately, however, that God-ideas are *human* reactions to the universe. *Whether or not the universe is actually as meaningful and as orderly as these beliefs assume is not demonstrable in any final sense.**

---

*Critics of this thesis might point to the notion of Buddhism that earthly existence misleads man and that the ideal state for man is a falling away of consciousness into "nirvana." Actually, the conception of nirvana was employed in Buddhist tradition as an answer to the question of evil that pervaded all conscious existence. Thus while Buddhism lacked the positive emphasis of the Western religions on conscious salvation, it did recognize the need for transcending the present condition of man in the direction of another, presumably superior, state.

I can now state my own idea of God. God is that quality of the universe, expressed in its order and its openness to purpose, which man is constantly discovering and upon which he relies to give meaning to his life. God, I believe, can be no less. He may conceivably be a lot more—a Creator of the universe, a Law-giver, a Judge. He may possess other qualities ascribed to Him by supernaturalists. I see no need for attributing such qualities to God, because human experience, my own and that of the race, makes available to me enough evidence of a divine immanence. But the immanence of God does not imply the absence of transcendence. There is always the mystery of the unknown present and the unpredictable future, there are the infinite qualities of experience that no human being can ever exhaust, there are the creative surprises, and beyond all there is the process of existence itself, of which any one generation of man is but an insignificant part. Surely in all this, there is enough transcendence to evoke the feeling of awe and sublimity in any man.

Because science has discovered order in nature—and indeed has turned that order to man's advantage—some modern minds conclude that science has eliminated man's need for an acceptable hypothesis about God. It seems to me that what science has accomplished vis-à-vis God is only to rule out the possibility of God's conscious interference with an orderly nature. For all its wonderful discoveries and the progressive perfection of its methodology, science has not established as facts that life has meaning and that nature has an order capable of enabling man to fulfill himself. Refusing to bow to doubts about the possibility of his achieving salvation, man assumes the meaning and the order; this is an act of faith. He realizes there is no certainty that he will be able to fulfill his purposes in life, but he knows too that only in a world so constituted as to provide potentially for his success can he make any headway at all toward salvation. His belief that the world is so constituted is his faith in God.

Some naturalist philosophers assert that no meaningful proposition about the orderliness of the universe as a whole can legitimately be made. They contend, for example, that there is no reason for assuming that the world is friendly to the human race. Floods, earthquakes, volcanic eruptions, and other natural catastrophies are proof enough that there is evil in nature. How can we be certain that the earth will will not be demolished by a solar explosion at some future date, as indeed some scientists tell us it will be? The answer to this admittedly strong argument is the pragmatic attitude suggested above. No one lives as if he believed in such an eventuality. Call it animal faith or the will to live; man insists, in so far as he plans his future, on assuming a brighter outlook. Even if the world will be destroyed by a solar explosion, millions of years hence, the naturalist position here taken would still be upheld by the knowledge that there is nothing in the present constitution of men and nature which precludes man's achieving this—wordly salvation, as long as this world lasts.

The view that the universe is amenable to human salvation is validated, if not proved, by every successful scientific experiment and prediction by a scientist. Does this prove that God, even this naturalistically interpreted God, exists? Of course not. But remember that in formulating a religious doctrine in a new key I have the limited objective of explaining what a rational God-idea can be. Certainly, what I have proposed makes sense in the light of our present knowledge. And those who cannot imagine religion without an act of faith, are reminded that my interpretation calls for the same religious spirit and faith that evokes other, supernaturalist conceptions of God. I am not saying that my God-idea is God. All I can hope to do is explain what I mean when I use the word God.

The formulating of God-ideas not only points to a human need for feeling that the natural world does not stand irrevocably opposed to man but also helps man to fulfill his potentialities as a rational, responsible being. If man is a social animal, then it is only in society that he can be fully human. Every man yearns, at times, for solitude, but it is chiefly in his relationships to other men that his human qualities are called into play. These relationships, as I have suggested, both are conditioned by and are conditioners of, the character of every group. Relationships can be either casual or purposeful. When they are imbued with purpose, man must necessarily select from among many possible relations. This entails formulating objectives or ideals that serve both as goals and as criteria for evaluating behavior in the group. Is a particular action good or bad, just or unjust, public-spirited or selfish? The need for valuational judgments is with us every day of our lives.

4

Traditional religion has ready answers for many of life's questions. Rabbinic or canon law seeks to detail every possible eventuality, dictating the correct mode of behavior in a unified body of enactments attributed directly to the Word of God. These enactments are subject to change only by ecclesiastical authorities, and the ethical presuppositions on which they are based are assumed to be clear and valid for all time. What is there about this system of law and ethics to which the rationalists take exception? They object to it, first, on epistemological grounds, denying the basic premise that revelation as traditionally understood is necessary to man's discovery of moral "truth." They deny that law, whether ritual or ethical, ought to be the province of professionals, no matter how erudite, who are not subject to the will of the people. They believe that ethical principles have clear meaning only in specific contexts. And so they prefer a system of ethics and law which, while reckoning with the valuable experience of the past, makes each generation of men responsible for their own moral decisions and which, accordingly, grants them the prerogative of selecting those ethical values and laws which would enhance human life under their particular circumstances.

Clearly, this admittedly relativistic approach has certain problematic areas, and these are seized upon by every scholastic philosopher and orthodox religionist. If man is free to choose his own standards, it is held, his egocentricity will mislead him. Relativism would also seem to play into the hands of human differences in outlook stemming from educational and class distinctions. Thus many are led to think we must seek a firmer anchor than free intelligence for ethical values. But man, as a moral being, must of necessity take risks. Even the acceptance of a traditional morality is a moral risk, for it often involves accepting the authority of the past on faith alone. Who knows how many crimes against God and humanity have been perpetrated by men who have accepted the "revealed" ethics of their fathers? However, even from the standpoint of the relativist, there is a danger, and that is the ease with which the passage from suspended judgment to dogmatism is made. A man, after carefully weighing in the balance all the available ethical alternatives and making his choice among them, might act as if he were absolutely right. It is this proneness of man to dogmatize that makes the idea of God so important.

When a religionist invokes God as the source of his ethical

systems, he is seeking an answer to his yearnings for inner harmony and certainty. Whether the religionist is seeking to prove the correctness of his own stand or is trying to do the will of God, it is the groping for inner conviction that is the psychological basis for his conception of God as Lawmaker. Particularly does the individual want to feel that the mores and moral judgments of his people, upon whom he depends for so much of his self-fulfillment, are valid. All of us want to feel that it is the morality of believers in democracy, rather than that of a Hitler or a Stalin, that is truly human and humane.

In traditional religions, God was invoked to sanction the ethical views of both the individual and the group. A mature religion would invoke the God-idea not to justify its own ethical position but to check any pretensions to ethical certainty. If there were no God, then each man would have a right to press his own urge to power, knowing that authority came from him alone; the survival of the fittest would be as valid as an ethical principle as it was once conceived to be as a law of nature. But if there is a God, then, although standards have to be assumed, no man's judgment can, with certainty, be taken as correct. For God is always more than man can understand. Actions that seem right at the time they are taken often produce unforeseen, disastrous results, not because man's intentions are wrong but because he cannot see the whole of things—because, in short, he is not God. The loving parent often errs on the side of overprotection; he can just as easily, and does just as often, overdo the generally desirable practice of letting his child become self-reliant. In both cases good intentions are difficult to implement. The problem is more complex than it appears on the surface, because conscious intentions are frequently bound up with subconscious motivations that are as decisive in actual behavior as the consciously worked-out acts. No man, therefore, who believes in God, can legitimately absolutize any of his practices or beliefs, not even his ethical values.

In many contemporary discussions of ethical values, questions like the following come up: Are values rooted in existence? Must democracy be grounded in a religious metaphysics? How can man be motivated to ethical living if all values are relative? These are three of the many ways in which the fundemental issue is raised: Are values man-made or are they absolute imperatives which man discovers rather than creates?

In few of the discussions on this issue is the trouble taken to analyze what enters into the idea that values are man-made. Let me now attempt such an analysis.

I take it that most human beings subscribe to the injunction in Leviticus "Thou shalt love thy neighbor as thyself." The question is, why? Is it because the biblical authority sets it forth as an imperative? Undoubtedly some men acknowledge such authority and base their ethical views on it. But even to these men love of one's neighbor commends itself as an attitude worth cultivating for its idealism, regardless of the authority behind it. These same men experience great difficulty in justifying, even in its historical perspective, the divine imperative that required the ancient Israelites to commit genocide against their idolatrous neighbors. Evidently the supposed authority of the Bible is incapable of producing the kind of ethical certainty which human reason sometimes achieves. Human reason seems to insist on applying its own procedure of evaluation even to ethical values found in presumably authoritative sources. The fact that every generation draws its own distinctions between ethically valid and ethically invalid sentiments in biblical literature should satisfy all but extreme fundamentalists that we are dealing with man-made values, or at least human interpretations of divine commands.

Suppose we assume, for the moment, that the command to love one's neighbor is God-given. Is it not also true that it is a significant command only because it commends itself to man's power to hear, interpret, and obey? And how does man hear? Through his power of thinking about his situation, his relationships with his fellow men, and his realization of the consequences of one type of relationship as opposed to another. Even if the Golden Rule had not made its appearance in Leviticus, is it conceivable that the desirability of the attitude it represents would not have suggested itself to man? As a matter of fact, the existence of a version of the Rule in almost every culture provides the answer. Are we to assume that God spoke directly to all the various societies who conceived of neighborly love? Or is the sentiment man-made?

The truth is that ethical values are both universal and relative, subjective and objective, depending on the context. No value would mean anything, even to the most ardent member of the relativist-subjectivist-humanist school, unless it was somehow related objectively to human behavior. If one saw no relationship between the ideals one held and the possibility of achieving them in practice, there would be a psychological, if not a logical, block to pursuing them. This might not affect the type of person who acts solely from the zest for living, but even a person of this temperament must acknowledge that values seem to have certain effects that can be measured by rational standards. There are obvious differences between a society in which love prevails between neighbors and one in which hate prevails. In this sense values have the same kind of objective reference as natural law.

But values are not natural laws. They do not take effect until man creates—or discovers—them. Even these terms, create and discover, should be understood in their context. Man cannot create from nothing. His imagination can run wild by establishing relationships between things and experiences, but the products of his imagination will, like the mermaid or the pink elephant, exist only in idea. He may likewise, in his search for happiness, call into being a set of values which, when practiced, have no chance of success. In such an instance, he may have created values to no avail. Only when the validity of these values are established through rational experience can we speak of them as discovered. For they then have some application to the nature of man in this universe. Since values do refer to man's nature and seem to operate in accord with it we are justified in positing the hypothesis that values—not this or that value, but values as a category of human experience—are not only man-made, but refer to universal, objective aspects of reality. In this sense we speak of them as divine, as inherent in a natural order not created by man himself.

Man experiences his values as universal. That is to say, he believes that they ought to be held by all his fellow men. According to the view just outlined, however, man must not absolutize even those values which commend themselves to him as universally valid. Far from making all moral judgments equally valid, a naturalistic and relativistic ethic would ask only that no judgment be considered absolutely true—certainly not antecedent to its application to ethical problems.

If belief in God serves as a restraining force on ethical absolutism, a mature conception of God can lead man to test his ethical views in concrete situations in the light of their practical effect. Moreover, a conception of God that insists upon the ethical meaning of life can serve to encourage man to search for ethical standards and relieves him of the feeling that his striving is all in vain. Again, does this prove the existence of God? The answer is still in the negative. But the belief in God and the conception of God as the moral force operating in man and in society give purpose to man's striving and induce in him an awareness of his limitations and a sense of humility.

It is not enough, however, to believe that human existence has purpose, nature has an order, and man has a moral duty to seek out and perform. One must be able to fill in the details of this outline. This can be accomplished only within the framework of a society. The meaning of life must emerge from the home, the factory, the school, and the arts. The livelihood which man wrests from the soil and the use to which he puts his knowledge of nature must help nature to recreate rather than destroy itself. The relations among men must make for the maximum fulfillment of all. Why? On what grounds are these values to be preferred to others, perhaps of a destructive character? The traditionalist would say, "Because that is God's will," but such a reply clarifies nothing. The naturalist would understand the traditionalist's contention better if the latter were to say that, of all the common values of men, there are only certain ones that can exist side by side in harmony under given conditions. If we want peace, we may have to rule out absolute justice in favor of intelligent compromise. A naturalistic ethic does not need to have recourse to an Absolute, indeed denies that any such Absolute can ever be known to man. All human problems in which values are at stake can be resolved only by the choice between values. That man sometimes errs in his choice seems to point, as significantly as do his successful decisions, to the existence of a human ethical potential.

That potential, which is expressed in the demands of conscience, is approached but never fully realized—much as the disclosures of science point to an orderly universe whose full meaning has never been captured from the standpoint of ethics. Believing in God, from the standpoint of ethics, is believing in man's ability ever more adequately to formulate, correct, and harmonize his values, and to find the means of implementing them.

5

By the time a child enters religious school he usually has a full complement of theological misconceptions, and these make teaching about God one of the most exasperating problems in the whole educational field. God as "bogey man," as punisher and rewarder of individual acts of behavior, as conscience, as spirit, and as a power possessing the many, often conflicting, attributes that are relevant to the particular questions the child may have asked—all these add up to a confusion that only the most skillful teaching can overcome.

It would be the greatest asset to religion if it could be arranged that a child did not come across the word God until he had had the kind of experiences in life to which the word might well be applied, and until he had reached the age when he could make subtle linguistic distinctions. This, of course, is an idle wish. Merely expressing the thought, however, is sufficient to indicate that part of the difficulty in teaching about God is the necessity to overcome half-truths and adult-induced distortions and that things are further complicated by the child's proneness to reify verbal symbols. Unfortunately there are a number of mistakes commonly made by religious school teachers which exacerbate the problem.

Many teachers assume that all children are unsophisticated

in their thinking about God, whereas children are capable of profound abstraction and critical analysis. One ten-year old boy attending a Jewish religious school conceived of God as a "force that tells us the difference between right and wrong," while another rejected God "as a figment of the imagination." In contrast to these advanced "theistic" and "atheistic" opinions, teachers do not credit children with being able to go beyond the primitive idea that God is a bearded old man sitting up in heaven. I am afraid the stereotype prevails because most teachers avoid discussions about God and never get to know their students' full potential as theologians. Teachers lack confidence in their own ability to handle the subject. The first requisite, therefore, is for the teacher to articulate a conception of God that is convincing enough to him to be taught with confidence. This does not mean that he has to formulate a final, dogmatic God-idea. Far from it! Effective teaching about God requires an ability to admit the unknown—a concept which the average child will readily accept. But it also requires a respect for the child's ability to react intelligently to his direct experience with reality and to the interpretations suggested to him by adults.

It is very common for teachers to fail to assess properly what children have learned about God from their parents and friends. They therefore treat the subject *de novo,* expecting the child to accept what he is taught in the classroom without confusion or resistance. No teacher can succeed in helping his students to a more mature conception of God unless he takes into account what the child has already learned, and, more important, unless he concedes to the child the right to form a concept of God different from his own.

By and large, children's God-ideas are of two kinds: one a

primitive anthropormorphism and the other a variety of sophisticated, naturalistic interpretations of reality. Teachers of traditional texts like the Bible and the prayer book run into difficulty with students whose God-ideas are in the second category. If the teachers try to sustain the literal interpretation of the texts, they run the risk of rendering those texts unworthy in the eyes of the students. On the other hand, if they interpret the texts symbolically, they face the equally hard problem of coping with the literalness that seems to be part of the make-up of even the most precocious child. In this case, the student may count the text as of little value—as "mere" poetry.

It follows that if we continue to introduce our children to classical texts in which the word God, in its various forms, plays an important part, we must be prepared to devote time and thought to expounding the meaning of this term. At present we take too much for granted, the result being that we fail to teach the children how to read and use our classical literature as a source of inspiration for themselves.

When I say that children should be stimulated to think about the idea of God, I do not mean that they should be fed on metaphysical and theological terms. But there is no reason to assume that a child cannot follow a discussion on the meaning of God in the context of a Bible story or of a problem of justice. We have so long underestimated our children's ability to think that we have come to attribute their indifference to religion to every reason except the right one, namely that we have simply failed to challenge them to think deeply. The truth probably is that deep down many of our rabbis and educators fear to open the doors to what they consider a premature skepticism. First, we are told, indoctrinate the child with the traditional, simple view of God, then let the child rebel in his own way. If the indoctrination has been successful, the rebellion will be short-lived. Our job is not to encourage really free learning at the outset and to raise the questions about God that bother us adults. Rather, let us seek better methods of indoctrination.

This psychology of religious education has been the working creed of far too many Jewish religious educators. There is, of course, no guarantee that when Jewish religious schools teach about God in a spirit of free inquiry students will develop mature conceptions of God. Free inquiry without inspiring guidance may lead to mediocrity. A religious teacher has to do more than raise questions. He must, to repeat, also strive mightily to acquire a cogent God-concept of his own. Without such a perspective, his teaching must necessarily be shallow. If it is natural for the child to rebel at some point in his intellectual growth, let it at least be a rebellion against a point of view that he can respect. Such respect will be felt by students for a teacher who has been honest and searching both with himself and with them.

Actually, rebellion against *ideas* is not an inevitable part of spiritual growth. A wholesome growth is marked by the substitution of better ideas for inferior ones, a process that should not be interpreted as rebellion. The child whose imagination renders animate a chair against which he has stubbed a toe understands the error in the course of time and sees the chair as it really is. There is no reason, however, for a teacher to encourage the child to believe in animism. Similarly, the many potential elements of God-ideas can be woven into a pattern of progressive complexity and adequacy if the child is encouraged to accept such development as a healthy manifestation of his maturation. It is only when the idea of God is marked with a label of "absolute truth" that there is need for rebellion.

Therefore, the way for a religious educator to cultivate an appreciation among children of the need for seeking a God-idea is to focus the attention of the children on the questions involved in such a search rather than on the concept itself. The latter is bound to change, but the concern of the child with the quest for God will remain.

Given, then, a situation in which teachers can freely explore the problem of God with students on the students' level, there are several steps in the teaching process which must be borne in mind. These steps are recorded here in a particular order, but the reader will readily understand that in practice the circumstances of the classroom must determine whether to follow the order here suggested. Experience must also dictate whether any of the steps should be omitted in a given situation.*

In the first place, children should be made aware of the pitfalls of language. They can readily grasp how words can arise arbitrarily and how they can change meaning. They can understand also that while some words denote objects apparent to the senses, other words apply to experiences and qualities which are not tangible. They can easily see the difference in concreteness between chair, teacher, my teacher, Smith, John Smith, state and God. Finally, they will come to realize that "God" is the most abstract term possible. (This should be admitted even by the more traditional-minded religionists who acknowledge that man's grasp of God's attributes can never be expressed in other than negative terms.)

Secondly, it must be made clear that the abstraction called

---

*I have purposely refrained from specifying the age at which these procedures should be introduced. There are too many differences in intellectual grasp to make any arbitrary curricular suggestions. What I am setting forth here is a general theory of teaching about God, which can then be adapted according to the requirements of different ages.

God is an attempt to solve many different types of problems. Thus God is an answer to some men's need for ethical conviction, to the desire of others to find the universe harmonious, to the hope of others for immortality, and to the craving of others for psychological assurance of their own personal or group survival. Children should be spared the frustration of most discussions about God, a frustration that stems from the failure to define terms. The word God is a complex notion, covering a great many questions about life's meaning and goodness; in the process of learning this, students absorb the idea that "God" is a word for a theory that men weave about the universe to explain the part of it that they can experience and that it is also a term applied by some men to their surmises about the mysterious universe beyond human ken but not beyond human imagination.

It follows from the foregoing that children must be guided toward mature application of "God" to experiences worthy of the designation. Indiscriminate use of the word by the teacher debases it and confuses the student. Even more important, it is essential for the teacher to consider with the student the unplumbed depths of experience and the infinite possibilities for novelty and growth in the seen and unseen world. Making our children aware of the richness of their world is an indispensable step toward enabling them to arrive at their own God-concepts.

An example comes to mind. A teacher asked her class of eight-year-olds, "What do Jews do on Rosh Hashanah?" The ready response of most of the children was, "They go to synagogue and pray." One boy broke in critically, "It doesn't do any good to pray for anything. If you need something, you have to buy it." The teacher, sensing an opportunity, agreed with the critic: "Reuben is correct, isn't he? If you want chicken, mother need only go to the butcher and buy it. But is there anything that one cannot buy?" Immediately, hands shot up all over the room, and the answers followed freely: "Health," "Love," "Friendship," "Freedom." There was no need to press the issue. But something had been accomplished. The children had realized that there are desirable things in life that cannot be purchased. At some future session the teacher would recall this discussion and go on to consider methods of achieving these ends. In the course of such analysis there would be ample opportunity to consider the divine aspects of health, love, freedom, etc. "God" would then become more than a name. It would be a living symbol of the depths of reality, pointing always to the wonder of life beyond human grasp.

If we approach Jewish classical texts as the literary expression of our ancestors' search for profound truths about reality, we shall be in a position to make these texts live for our children, for we shall have a criterion for determining whether or not to present a particular text to a child. If the question behind the text is one to which his understanding and interest are equal, then it is worthwhile for him to study the answer suggested. If not, the teacher is best advised to postpone discussion of the text, at least from the standpoint of the question it seeks to answer. This educational principle applies particularly to discussions about God.

The approach to the teaching of God that I have outlined leaves untouched many areas of investigation. There are problems of human relations connected with conflicting opinions of parents and teachers, psychological stumbling blocks set up by the differences in emotional stability among students, and intellectual complexities of all sorts that have troubled the greatest thinkers of every generation. My concern here has not been to formulate a fool-proof method of making theists out of our children. Rather, I have tried to clear away some of the obfuscation in current practice and to catalogue some of the obstacles that must be hurdled in our progress toward intelligent presentation of the God-idea to our children. The fact that teachers are generally so ill-prepared to perform the task testifies to the failure of their own religious teachers.

6

Many modern intellectuals go along with religionists as far as accepting a philosophically respectable God-concept but raise objections to the institutionalization of religion and to the performance of ritual. They forget, when it comes to religion, that life does not consist of intellect alone but is an arena in which all the human faculties come into play. Logically there is no reason for man to paint, to compose music, or to write poetry. Nevertheless, life has evolved in such a way as to stimulate man to utilize more and more of his faculties. We have seen that ideas, even philosophies, are conceived as a result of the seminal influence of a people's way of life. Group life has always included folkways that bear on almost every aspect of experience, physical and spiritual, from eating habits to memorializing a great hero.

Sometimes these folkways come to represent important values of the group, that is, they become rituals. Early food taboos among the Hebrews, for example, became ritual laws in which were embodied the important distinction between the clean and the unclean. Susanne Langer believes that ritual is symbolic, "except where it is aimed at concrete results, and then it may be regarded as a communal form of magic."[5] In our own American culture, we have seen the progressively greater significance that has been attached to such days as the Fourth of July and Thanksgiving Day.

Changes in the spiritual climate of a people require corresponding adjustments in ritual. It is because there is a frequent cultural lag between life conditions and ritual that so many sensitive persons find it difficult to subscribe to any formal expression of their personal religion. Yet in most cases their religion actually has been influenced by some cultural tradition in which ritual played an important part.

It may well be asked, why go out of our way to create new rituals or rework old ones? If we can formulate a religious doctrine that seems to answer our needs, why try to wall it in with a pattern of habitual behavior? Some advocates of ritual answer by saying that ritual is inevitable, because it is actually habit. Other advocates agree with Langer that it arises spontaneously but make use of Langer's analysis of its origin and development to justify its practice, which she does not do. "Ritual is a symbolic transformation of experiences that no other medium can adequately express. Because it springs from a primary human need, it is a spontaneous activity—that is to say, it arises without intention, without adaptation to a conscious purpose; its growth is undesigned, its pattern purely natural, however intricate it may be."[6] The origin of ritual should not govern our judgment of its present function. Langer is guilty of the genetic fallacy, which she of course condemns.

No one lives without forming some "natural" habits whether they be walking with poor posture or talking too rapidly. These are not rituals; rituals contain an element of conscious symbolism that is not to be found in ordinary habits. In primitive, and in some sophisticated traditional religions, rituals are expected to influence the Deity. While this connecting link with the supernatural is no longer accepted by liberal religionists, for them rituals convey definite meaning. They are counted on to produce an emotional reaction in the person who performs them. Moreover, it is not true of all ritual that it "arises without intention." The salute to the flag, the celebration of American civic festivals, the various independence celebrations of modern nations are only a few of the many examples of communal ritual consciously created to embody and foster group ideals. This, then, is the real purpose of ritual: the enhancement of life through the dramatization of great ideals. Just as the artist requires no rationale for painting other than the act itself, so the religious man needs no justification for seeking an appropriate mode of expression. Furthermore he can, like the artist who wants to influence others by his art, create ritual for the sake of enriching his own personality and that of his family or group with the emotional force generated by observance. In this way he can give added weight to his conception of justice or to his gratitude for the bounties of nature.

It is true that ritual speaks to man. The heritage of the past operates most effectively in the rituals through which each successive generation is educated. Naturally, rituals that have been sanctified through centuries of usages have an aura of religiosity about them that blinds us to their complex involvement in the social structure and history of the group. To treat traditional ritual in analytic fashion is invariably irritating to more orthodox and mystic minds. According to them, "sociological" attempts to understand ritual miss the point about its true nature: ritual is poetic, it is suggestive, it is prismatic. Not for a moment would I deny these characteristics of ritual; what I am trying to show is that ritual cannot be defended on emotional grounds alone. Resort to emotion is a device to cut off criticism and argument; but in a world in which rituals of one kind must compete against rituals of another kind for the human mind and heart, it seems obvious that the serious religionist will respond only to rituals that do satisfy his faculties of mind and heart.

What applies to the individual applies equally to the group. As individuals are unique, so are groups. They are bound to express themselves in original ways, and in a free society they should be encouraged to do so. Creative ritual implies a pluralistic approach to culture, even though all cultures and hence all rituals may be embodying the same universal ideal. The world needs many colors and many forms of expression.

Such an approach to ritual demands a degree of spontaneity and freedom that no orthodoxy will grant. Orthodoxy, having lost sight of the central purpose of ritual, has fallen into the tragic error of assuming that ritual is an end in itself and therefore requires man to suppress his creative urge and give himself over to the educative influence of the traditional rites. This is not a mode of behavior which commends itself to the free spirit of man.

Yet there is an element of validity in the traditional conception of ritual. For the traditionalist, rituals which have met the religious needs of countless generations of ancestors must have some inherent value. While a modernist would not paint in exactly the same way as Tintoretto or Rembrandt, he can appreciate their styles and learn from them. Similarly, traditional rituals can often be the starting point for our own gropings toward religious expression. Old rituals can frequently be revitalized by being infused with a new rationale.

It is no longer feasible to urge a return to "that old-time religion." Modern man is not a sinner in his abandonment of the old ways, and it is the height of immaturity to accuse him of sinning and turning away from the right path.

We had better stop asking men and women why they fail to come to synagogue or church; we must seek instead to understand their spiritual needs and devise new or revised forms of worship to meet them. It may be painful to those who have a vested interest in particular religious institutions or who are deeply attached to a certain hallowed tradition, but it must be said that unless an institution or a tradition is meeting real needs in an adequate fashion it is doomed to extinction.

There is no question that the materialism of our age has played havoc with our appreciation of the finer things in life. The rise in the general standard of living which has been an outcome of the technological revolution has not been an unmixed blessing. Children grow up with a blasé attitude toward everything. A new toy, a special treat—things that would have delighted youngsters a few generations ago are today taken for granted. Grownups have become so accustomed to dynamic change that they scarcely notice novelty. In truth, our generation is one that is being revolutionized every day, yet many of us think "there is nothing new under the sun." No wonder ritual today is neither appreciated nor practiced. For ritual flourishes in an atmosphere of childlike awe before the sublimity of life. The sophistication of many so-called moderns prevent them from expressing their deepest and loftiest emotions. Most noticeably lacking is the capacity of modern industrialized man to experience and to express gratitude and to enjoy the simple pleasures. There is a hard crust of hedonism encasing the dominant middle class of American society.

There are, of course, many roles that ritual plays, and a more extensive study of the subject would analyze particularly the nature of these roles among various classes. For some poorer groups, for example, ritual affords an escape from the sordidness of everyday life. Thus instead of releasing emotions of protest, it sometimes acts as a deterrent to or a substitute for the expression of bitterness and longing for a better life that consume the poor of all societies. In such a circumstance, ritual will become, justifiably, an object of attack on the part of those who would seek to bring about social change.

Ritual is clearly involved in the total life patterns of human beings. Its role cannot be understood or perfected in isolation, as a result of ecclesiastical decisions or suggestions. Like other institutions in the social life of man, it can be vitalized only through skillful engineering, involving the cooperative efforts of laymen, clergymen, and experts in many fields of knowledge. We can expect that ritual will arise spontaneously as the spiritual dimensions of our social life expand, and we must learn to recognize and enhance it consciously when it does arise. But we ought also to put our finest talents to work, trying to transform existing rituals and to create new ones that, in time, will inspire masses of men. Certainly we ought not to be satisfied to have ritual play the role of an opiate or be a diseducative influence on our children.

7

The knottiest question that can be posed to one who holds a naturalist God-idea has to do with the function of worship. If God is not a person or a conscious power, what is the purpose of prayer? To whom shall we pray? And to what end?

Let us first distinguish clearly between prayer and worship. Worship is the broader category, prayer being only one of its various forms. By worship we mean the way in which men try to establish a connection betwen themselves and the reality they conceive to be God. In prayer, whether silent or spoken, this connection is established verbally. We must remember, however, that in the course of religious history worship has taken such forms as human and animal sacrifice, asceticism, masochism and altruistic behavior. When we discuss worship in our time we must therefore maintain an open mind about the currently accepted form, prayer. It has not been coextensive with worship, and there is no reason to believe that it must be maintained in exactly the way it has been presented to us by our fathers.

Prayer is misunderstood by the average worshiper. He conceives it to be a series of verbal petitions, in which God is asked to satisfy certain human needs. Consequently the most prayerful moods are those which occur at crucial moments, when human resources are of no avail. "Foxhole religion" is the outstanding example. But the proportion of petition in traditional prayer is small compared to the praises, thanksgivings, meditations, testaments of faith, and appeals to ethical sensitivity. The literature of prayer is filled with poetic affirmations of a fundamentally philosophical character. And, to take the Psalms as a prime example, prayer has also been an outlet for deep-felt emotions. Man addresses himself to God, and while there is an implicit expectation that the prayer will be answered, the self-expression itself has a valuable cathartic effect.

When the nonpetitionary functions of prayer are recognized, it can be seen that the problem of the naturalist arises basically from the petitionary function. In the other areas he is no less capable than the supernaturalist of meaningful and sincere prayer.

For the naturalist the real problem concerns the practice of regular and formalized prayer. Where prayer is the spontaneous bubbling over of emotion, it scarcely needs to be justified or philosophized into being. We may question the wisdom of a prayer for divine help in the face of a severe crisis, but no one seriously doubts that human beings require a mode of emotional release in moments of sorrow, joy, or fear. This seems to be an inborn need of man. Nor do those who are disappointed in formal worship fail to recognize that personal inadequacies of expression can often be overcome by recourse to the aesthetic creations of others —to a poetic passage, a paragraph of beautiful prose, or a musical composition. All of us have experienced moments of gratitude to artistic and spiritual geniuses whose inspired works have made it possible for us to express adequately a particular emotion that we have wanted to articulate.

It goes without saying that some emotional expressions are not prayer. The spontaneous uproar following a home run and the applause at the conclusion of a concert are not prayer. An expression of emotion becomes prayer when it serves to unify us with the source of life itself, confers spiritual significance on the felt emotion, or evokes within us a more adequate understanding of that which makes life valuable. When traditional religionists speak of "communion with God," "subjecting oneself to the Infinite or the Absolute," "sensing the presence of God," or use any of the other expressions bearing upon the experience of prayer, they are stating theologically that prayer is a groping for emotional reinforcement to deeply held convictions about the ultimate nature of the universe. Some thinkers believe that the highest form of prayer is an act of complete resignation, throwing onself on the tender mercies of divine grace. But even if fulfillment in prayer be conceived as an act of grace—as a coming down of God, rather than a going up of man—its ultimate intent is to raise man to godlike behavior. All prayer, then, has as its final goal a human effect.

We can now address ourselves to the questions: How can worshipers once more find in formal public prayer a rich spiritual experience? Is such prayer capable of achieving the lofty purpose for which it was established? When prayer is accepted as a divine command, so that traditional liturgy becomes a sacred, inviolable formula, the fault lies with the worshiper if worship fails of its purpose; he is said to rebel against God, to have fallen prey to secularism, or to possess no understanding of religion. These are the charges leveled against the majority of people who fail to pray, or who pray perfunctorily and without conviction or feeling. This is too facile a dismissal of the fact that something is lacking in the modern synagogue and church that drives or keeps away some of the most ethically sensitive and spiritual men and women in our society. No amount of beautification of the traditional liturgy is likely, in my opinion, to stem the tide which is undermining the type of worship to which we are heir. Mankind is groping for some more satisfactory method of worship.

Why is this so? What is there about church and synagogue services that has caused them to fail in their function despite the desperate need of mankind for spiritual inspiration and sustenance? I do not wish to oversimplify the problem. Patently, the materialism of the clergy, their lack of imagination, and their general failure to come to grips with the problems that stare them in the face have something to do with the situation. Likewise, the middle-class, comfortable, and comforting character of public worship has contributed its share to the spiritual enervation of our churches and synagogues. But essentially, modern men and women are either so spiritually disoriented that no form of worship can satisfy them or they are so naturalistically inclined that no traditional pattern can draw them back to houses of public worship. The former are still to be found in the churches and synagogues, and I should hazard the guess that they constitute a majority of the worshipers. They are the men and women whose convictions about the efficacy of prayer were long ago shaken but who attend out of a fear of social disapproval or a sense of duty or nostalgia. The latter, consisting of intellectuals and nonintellectuals alike, have been trained to regard prayer as a dialogue with a God who hears the human voice and responds to it; having renounced this naive notion, they regard public prayer as an anachronism.

If this analysis is correct, then the solution of the problem of worship in our generation calls for some far-reaching efforts by our religious leaders. In the first place, serious thought and study will have to be devoted to theology in the pulpit and in the religious classrooms. Those in and close to the naturalist camp need to be fortified in their faith. They (or is it their religious leaders?) must learn that a vigorous expression of faith in God is not "old-fashioned" but is rather a *sine qua non* of intelligent living. Expressing a faith in God is not a mark of obscurantism, provided that faith is buttressed with a tenable conception of God.

Secondly, prayer should become a subject of disciplined study. For naturalists the starting point of this study is the fact that personal prayer is a dialogue within the self, an attempt through introspection to achieve a larger perspective. In a moment of grief, for example, there is need to relate oneself to a context of life within which one can continue to function effectively, without in any way underestimating the tragedy of one's loss. That context need not include belief in immortality or afterlife. Prayer for the courage to bear grief may well prove effective if the bereaved individual can be led to discern the love which still surrounds him or to accept the responsibilities toward his fellow men which still devolve upon him. Prayer of this type may be more difficult to achieve than the traditional appeal for supernatural help. But naturalistic prayer, no less than supernatural supplication, requires a receptivity to the wonders and depths of reality that render the internal dialogue more than "talking to oneself." There is still in naturalistic prayer a reference to "something other," but a something other that falls within the experience of man in his natural setting. How to cultivate the ability to pray in this fashion should become the concern of Jewish educators.

I recently had the opportunity to consider the question of prayer with a group of fifteen men and women in their twenties and thirties. In a seminar of eight sessions lasting about two hours each, this group of young people who found it spiritually impossible to attend synagogue services admitted the need for some type of worship experience. It was the dominant feeling of the group that prayer is an essential form of expression for the human personality—not only for the achievement of "peace of mind," but more significantly, for the development of that which is most distinctly human: the ability to transcend the self.[7] The problem of these young people is more than a theoretical one. They want to pray but find they cannot. They find the synagogue services irrelevant even when they understand the meaning and the historical overtones of the traditional prayers. For them even so-called modern services are cast in a form that fails to inspire. Good conversation inspires them more than responsive readings; listening to a symphonic recording arouses more introspection than the finest choir or cantor; a study hour on the Pentateuch provides far more spiritual enrichment than the chanting of the Hebrew text in the synagogue. In brief, it is the *whole form* of worship that they cannot accept.

This experience has convinced me that public prayer as a device for harnessing the force of communal fellowship (in order to strengthen certain ideals and feelings that a group experience can best accomplish) requires reexamination and recreation through considerable experimenting with the formal liturgies. Prayers of petition, except those of self-exhortation, should be discarded, and excessive doxologies eliminated; new prayers or readings will have to be introduced that can serve to tap deep-rooted feelings, and completely new forms of worship will have to be attempted. Variety, not necessarily novelty, will have to be introduced into every service. We should, of course, try to discern those elements of the traditional service that have lasting significance, but we must also be prepared for revolutionary steps.

It is important to stress the difference between public worship as a means of group identification and public worship as a means of spiritual growth and communion with God. The contemporary synagogue, as Heschel has well stated, highlights the former function of prayer but fails to fulfil the latter. The object of any study and experimentation in prayer should be to fill that need.

It is too little realized that opportunities for personal and group worship abound outside the confines of church and synagogue. We constantly experience occasions of happiness and sorrow in family life and participate in civic events involving the spiritual and ethical strivings of the group—a veritable flow of everyday activities that should arouse us, individually and collectively, to count our blessings, and to check our pretensions to omniscience and to power. If we can learn to bring the spirit of worship into the mundane affairs of life, perhaps we can regain some of our lost sensitivity. Then perhaps we shall be able to come to our houses of worship with a depth of feeling that will make group prayer a real outpouring of emotion rather than a search for elusive inspiration from on high. Expression of such inner emotion is bound to be self-enriching.

Finally, we must try to recapture for our children the wonder of the world, which is all but lost to them. The mysteries of nature, of birth, love and death, the beauty of a blade of grass, a poetic or musical masterpiece, and an ethical personality must all become occasions for cultivating that sense of awe before the majesty of life which is a necessary prelude to prayer. But we shall fail to accomplish this end until we have the kind of religious education in which the teaching of prayer is more than the transmission to the children of the sterile form of worship now current in our religious institutions.

Surely the spiritual plight of modern man is desperate enough to impel genuine seekers after a more satisfactory pattern of worship to invest their cooperative efforts to solve this most crucial problem facing organized religion. There is no ready-made answer. Yet those of us who find the traditional form neither compelling as an act of duty nor inspiring, except in an occasional moment, cannot conclude that worship is unessential. There seems to be no other way out than to think and plan. At the very least, we can open up areas of thought that may suggest other lines of investigation and behavior.

8

I see no basic difference between the religious spirit that searches humbly for truth and justice and the scientific mind that gropes with equal humility for the same objectives. A search for truth whether conducted intuitively by a religious genius or experimentally by a master scientist ought never to be governed by a determination to preserve the status quo of institutions or knowledge. The insistence that religion must give *de jure* recognition to scientific method should be viewed as a continuation of the age-old demand for the freeing of the human spirit, which now, as always, requires the courage to abandon the old—or at least to try the new.

Organized religion can no longer avoid a revolution in method that has been long in coming but that must take place if the historic religions are not to wither away. Liberal religionists today recognize that religion cannot afford to be dogmatic and that many of the sacred concepts and practices require abrogation or adjustment. Religion can no longer operate on a basis of interpretation and reinterpretation alone. Theories that have long been accepted by traditional religion as facts—revelation, immortality, original sin—must be reclassified as theories; the power of the organized group must (indeed, can) no longer be used to enforce belief in them as facts. The crying needs of today in organized religion are for new departures on a trial and error basis—in ritual and in worship—and for a thorough overhauling of its theoretical structure to incorporate all those elements of the modern spirit which make for greater freedom and the maximum spiritual fulfillment of man.

This is not to be simply a surrender to science. There are two sides to the relationship between science and religion, theoretical and practical. Science in our time sorely needs a reexamination of some of its inherited assumptions. The element of faith inherent in science has long been under-estimated. Substitution of the concept of probability for faith in the uniformity of nature appears to me to be no retreat from question-begging. To say that it is probable that a ball thrown from a window will land on the street below is to make an assumption about the future based upon the experience of the past. But that assumption depends upon the further supposition that the events of the future will follow the same orderly pattern as those of the past. Clearly, this calls for an act of faith. Both mature religion and science admit the absence of certainty; they must both, therefore, if they want to be logical, admit that plans and experiments are, psychologically at least, dependent upon an act of faith in the order of nature. Whether that order be called God or a theoretical construction of the human mind is an intriguing question of semantics and epistemology but actually has little bearing on the psychological reality.

Practically, scientists must be called to account for their ethical irresponsibility. There was a time when scientists could legitimately have opposed any check on areas of experimentation. Today it is a matter of grave doubt whether or not scientists can be white-washed for their part in the production of atomic weapons. Those scientists who claim that if they did not participate, others would have done so, or that if the United States had not manufactured the atom bomb, Germany would have, are merely demonstrating that science, as an institution, is not free of practical (and often diabolical) considerations. A religionist could accept this argument with better grace if thinkers who are ready to rationalize any moral defect of science or of scientists would allow the same latitude in reasoning about religion. If there is German science, Russian science, and American science, if there is free science and prostituted science, it may as truthfully be said that there is true religion and false religion, prophetic ethics and pagan ethics.

All this theorizing does not alter the basic fact that the religious experience is not confined to those who have a well-formulated philosophy of religion. After one has finished analyzing a poem or a piece of music, there is still the direct enjoyment that makes up the aesthetic experience. The religious experience is similar. It is of such theorizing that Max Otto remarked:

> Something seems to me left out which is more profoundly characteristic of the religious mood than any kind of special knowledge, devotion, or service. This is a response to the awesome and mysterious in life and the world. A positive response to the awesome and mysterious has had a central place in the most various religions throughout religious history. Without it religion seems to me to lose its differentiating quality and to become identical with morality, differing from it, if at all, in emotional tone. In theistic religions and in religious mysticism the response is not so much to the awesome mystery itself as to the Being behind the mystery, even though what this Being is may only be stable in symbols or not at all. In the nontheistic religion with which we are concerned the response is to the mystery as mystery. The difference between these two attitudes is deeply significant, but there is at the same time a relationship between them which justifies the application of the term religious to both.[8]

I have shown above why I feel it legitimate to apply the term God to a naturalist approach to reality. We need not make apology for the assertion that the religious experience can be as direct for a naturalistic religionist as it is for the

man whose intellectual position is not well formulated or
who is a supernaturalist. Two men at prayer in church or
synagogue may, as I have said, have entirely different conceptions of God, yet both be undergoing a profoundly stir-
ring spiritual transformation.

To summarize, then, I have been trying to show that
religion may and does arise naturally. This applies to the
theological, ritual, and worship elements in religion. As
regards the meaning of God, I have shown that God is
actually believed in before He is conceived of, that all God-
ideas are rationalizations based upon the unprovable assumption that God, as the answer to man's quest for self-
fulfillment, exists. I would call for a more creative attitude
toward the role of ritual than it now plays, with due regard
for the possibilities of traditional ritual. As a naturalist, I
take my stand for an ethic tempered by an attitude of
humility and suspended judgment, though not always of
suspended action. Finally, I have tried throughout to show
that religion is a phenomenon both of group life and of
individual experience. Some of these ideas will be further
elaborated in the coming chapters.

5

THE NATURE OF JEWISH
RELIGION

IT HAS BEEN POINTED OUT MANY TIMES
that the Hebrew language knows no word corresponding to
"religion."* The absence of the word from Hebrew terminology should shed some light on religion in general and on
Jewish religion in particular.

The word religion, in modern culture, is generally conceived of as pertaining to a single aspect of the life of any

---

*The word that is commonly used now as the Hebrew equivalent is *dat*
(law), which is the closest approximation in biblical and Rabbinic literature; *emnuah* (faith, or belief) is also used. In Israel a religious person is
called *haredi* (God-fearing, or Orthodox).

group. In our own American situation religion is considered to be so partial an element of culture as to be relegable to the realm of private conscience. But in the culture of ancient peoples religion was not a separable element among many others. There were times when religion required no special terminology, since the name of a people also constituted the name of a religion. "Greece" meant not only a social and political entity; the term covered a cult, as well. "Egypt" referred not only to the land of the pharaohs but also to the land of the Egyptian gods. And the Land of Israel was the territory of the Jews and of the God of Israel.

Among most modern peoples, religion has come to be differentiated from secular aspects of life, and the once all-embracing nature of religion and its organic relationship with the rest of culture have been forgotten or, in order to harmonize the interests of a multi-cultured state, rejected. The Jewish people, however, have retained much of the earlier conception of ethnic religion, and Jewish religion, therefore, cannot easily be pigeon-holed in the category in which other religions seem to fit so well. The absence of a term for "religion" in premodern Jewish writings is symptomatic of the sociological uniqueness of Jewish religion.

Traditional Jewish scholars have never had any difficulty in explaining this uniqueness. They have attributed it to the election of Israel and to Israel's possession of the instrument of salvation, the Torah. It was the intimate, organic relationship between God, Israel, and Torah that accounted for the peculiar characteristics of Jewish life. "The Holy One, blessed be He, Israel and Torah are one." Religion, peoplehood, and culture were inextricably interwoven in Jewish life. What was secular in other groups was religious among Jews. What was nationalistic in other groups was religious

among Jews. Jewish religion was the core of their nationalism and culture.

All this has been elaborated on interminably from synagogue pulpits. But today a new condition exists. Nationalism,
religion, and culture in Jewish life are now recognizable entities, each in its own right. And so the question arises as
to whether or not their original organic unity can be recap-
tured. Is it possible to put Humpty-Dumpty together again?

1

It will be profitable to indicate the scope of the problem
by comparing the past and the present character of Jewish
life. No student of Jewish history will deny the centrality of
traditional Jewish religion in Judaism up until the period of
the Emancipation. Unless this is understood, not all the
critical apparatus of the modern historian can help to make
sense of the Jewish odyssey. Economic, political, geographic
factors—all are important for an intelligent reading of the
Jewish past, but it is religion in the Jewish idiom that is the
key to the riddle of Jewish existence. No matter what period
in premodern Jewish history is considered, and no matter
what the event in question may be, religion is involved. The
origin of the Jewish people became, in the mind of later
generations, an act of God and an acceptance of a divine covenant by the founding fathers. The entire biblical narrative
was interpreted as the record of Israel's alternately abiding
by and rejecting the terms of its covenant with God. Israel's
politics were more than a matter of power, taxes, public
works, and international relations. Everything was related to
the central, revealed purpose of Israel's existence. The Exile
was first understood as Israel's punishment for renouncing

the covenant; later it was conceived of as an opportunity for spreading God's word to the nations.

Organizationally, the Jewish people underwent many changes from the early tribal structure in Canaan to the community councils of the East European era. But throughout, it was the revealed tradition that provided both the rationale for the communal structure and the detailed legislation by which the community was ruled. Art, literature, dress, folkways—all were religious concerns.

It can readily be seen that Jewish religion up until the advent of the voluntary Jewish community was "totalitarian," in the sense that there was no area of life into which it did not enter. Its totalitarianism, however, was by no means a tyranny. The Jew accepted the "burden of Torah" joyfully and with eager assent. It was only at the threshold of the Enlightenment and the Emancipation that definite signs of revolt appeared. Spinoza had been one of the rare exceptions to the rule of conformity. Jews were committed by acceptance to the total religious civilization into which they were born.

Much misunderstanding of the nature of Jewish religion has arisen from the failure to grasp a second important factor in Jewish life of the past: its roots were in the Jewish group. Despite all its universal features, Jewish religion has been identified with a single ethnic group. At the dawn of civilization in the Near East this was not a unique feature; every people had its own religion, and every religion, despite an overlapping of pantheons and a borrowing of gods, was identified with a particular ethnic group. But after the rise of Christianity and other universal doctrinal religions, the folk character of Jewish religion became an unusual phenomenon, and the people who adhered to the religion and who in turn were sustained and kept alive by it became a complete

mystery to the nations. They were, in the words of Leo
Pinsker, a "ghost people," and according to all the laws in-
vented by those who speculate on the history of nations
they should have ceased to exist when they were driven from
their land.

Even while the Jews possessed their state structure in
Palestine, full citizenship was accorded only to religiously
committed Jews. There was no such thing as the secular
power of the state; the king, who had to be a Jew, derived
his power, as did the Temple officials, from the Torah. Thus,
while the Jewish state exhibited great hospitality to the
various categories of *gerim* (aliens) and even granted them
numerous privileges, only the full-fledged convert was considered a first-class citizen. The circle was complete. In no
area of Jewish life was religion missing. Quite the contrary,
religion was the sum and substance of Judaism.

2

The triple strand appears now to be broken. Nationalism,
religion, and culture seem to be separate and distinct within
Jewish group life. Along with the opportunities for individual self-fulfillment presented by the Enlightenment and
the Emancipation went certain other conditions that have
produced this result.

In the first place, the Emancipation required both Jews
and non-Jews to establish a new status for the Jewish group.
Previously, so far as non-Jews were concerned, the Jews had
been a nation apart, without a land it is true, but with a
corporate status conferred upon them as much by the non-
Jewish world as by their own inner desire to retain their
identity. In the religion-centered world prior to the nationalist movements of the eighteenth and nineteenth centuries,
the religious character of the Jewish people helped to confer

a definable status upon them, even if it was that of a pariah people doomed to bear witness to the fate of those who denied the Savior. Now, with the conferring of citizenship rights upon the individual Jew, the problem arose of redefining the status of the people. It is not necessary to recount here the process of emancipation and the demands that were made for the obliteration of every vestige of Jewish nationalism. The story is to be found in any history of the Jewish people. It should be emphasized, however, that from the standpoint of many non-Jews the problem has still not been satisfactorily solved. Jews have accepted citizenship in many lands, but the Jewish people somehow persists as an ethnic entity. The peculiar nationalism of the Jew is as much a puzzle as ever.

On their part, the Jews had to react to the Emancipation by defining their status anew in their own eyes. The first such redefinitions were those of the Sanhedrin of Jewish leaders convened by Napoleon in 1806 and of the Reform movement, which, acting in accordance with the logic of events, proclaimed the end of Jewish nationalism and the adoption of a status commensurate with that of other religious denominations. The Jews would be a religious entity possessing no ties other than joint communion in the Mosaic creed. The Reform solution might have succeeded had it not been for the ethnic and racial nationalism that sprang up in Germany and in tsarist Russia and that excluded the Jews once more, this time on biological and cultural grounds. In the Middle Ages it had been the Jewish religion that formed the barrier between the Jewish and the Christian world; now, with Christianity no longer unified, it was still possible for non-Jews to unite on a program that excluded the Jews from taking full advantage of civic freedom. The response of the Jews was to develop a nationalism of their own in the style of nineteenth-century Europe.

The new Jewish nationalism differed from the old. It had to, for many Jews had already come to terms with the new outlook, and the organic relationship that had existed between the other-worldly religion of the Jews and the way of life in which it had been integrated had been destroyed. The new nationalism relegated the traditional religion to the realm of individual choice. What had been a clear-cut group religion became a matter of doctrine, to be accepted or rejected. Membership in the Jewish group no longer automatically conferred religious status on the Jew.

The historic tie between religious leadership and reactionary political forces had alienated many Europeans from religion as such; they were in no frame of mind to differentiate between religion and its misuse by their oppressors. In the same way, Orthodox Jewish leaders had made the mistake, in too many instances, of playing along with the ruling powers in the suppression of revolutionary impulses among the Jewish masses, impulses which the religionists undoubtedly felt were equally as dangerous to traditional Judaism as to the political tyranny against which they were directed. Thereby these leaders, probably motivated by the feeling that Jews had no concern with the affairs of their temporal oppressors, added fuel to the intellectual fire of revolt against supernaturalism that was burning in Jewish hearts, as it was burning in the hearts of the rest of the European intelligentsia.

It was for these reasons that almost all the movements springing from Jewish nationalism, whether Zionist or Diaspora nationalist, were largely unconcerned with religion, and in a great measure hostile to it. The break between

Jewish nationalism and religion apeared to be a clean one.

With this as the initial reaction of the Jews to the modern world, it was inevitable that Jewish culture, as well, should lose its traditional religious anchor. For the first time in Jewish history, Jewish culture that was the product of non-religious or antireligious forces in the Jewish community became a reality.

The change in the character of Jewish culture shows up perhaps even more clearly on the organizational level, particularly in the United States. Whereas in the pre-Emancipation Jewish community all interests of life were served through the medium of religion-centered institutions, in the modern American Jewish community, no such integration can be found. The synagogue represents Jewish religion, but the charity that was once its domain, the culture and education that once emanated from its rabbinical leaders, the discussion of mundane affairs that went on within its walls—none of these is any longer the exclusive concern of the synagogue. In many cases these functions have been pre-empted by organizations which at best are neutral to Jewish religious values and at worst are hostile to them.

This abbreviated comparison between the old and the new Jewish world points to a number of questions that challenge the Jewish mind and soul. Rather than be appalled by their magnitude, Jews ought to be grateful for their creative possibilities and for the opportunity to exercise the age-old Jewish skill for responding to new challenges. The challenges to Jewish life in our times ought to be welcomed as a chance to embark on another great spiritual and intellectual advanture.

The first problem to be faced is the issue of status. Whatever the world may think of the Jews, it is essential for their own future that they adopt for themselves a status that will express the purpose of their corporate existence.

Then there is the never-ending question of how best to adjust Jewish tradition to new conditions and to evaluate and seek to change the environment in terms of what is of superior human value in Jewish tradition. Too often philosophers of Judaism have neglected this second question, thereby revealing either gross ignorance or an inferiority complex about the positive and universally worthwhile values of the Jewish heritage.

The remainder of this chapter, I shall devote to the problem of status; the problem of tradition will largely occupy our attention in the next two chapters.

3

The two questions just put, however interrelated they may be, must be treated separately. For it is difficult to establish a one-to-one relation between people and idea, *Volk* and *Volksgeist,* nation and religion. However central ethical monotheism may be to Jewish tradition, it is not in the Jewish blood stream as some early Reformists suggested. Moreover, there is never a complete rapport between a people's conduct and the high ideals it professes.

An interesting example of indiscriminate amalgamation of ideas is the thesis of Will Herberg that the Jews are "a *supernatural* community, called into being by God to serve His eternal purposes in history."[1] Jewish existence, asserts Herberg, cannot be explained exclusively or even mainly in nontheological terms. "Every attempt to give meaning to the concept of Jewishness in such [naturalistic] terms must necessarily end in failure and lead to the conclusion that the concept is empty of intrinsic content and really refers to a 'nothing' generated out of a persistent and rather malignant delusion on the part of Jew and non-Jew alike."[2] "The covenant of election is what brought Israel into existence and keeps it in being; apart from that covenant, Israel is as nothing and Jewish existence a mere delusion."[3] Lest the reader form an erroneous impression of the author of these statements, let it be said at once that Herberg is a thinker who understands and appreciates the naturalistic forces that shape the destinies of men. His insistence upon the supernatural character of the Jewish people does not connote an abandonment in other areas of the critical instruments of science. It will not do simply to brush off Herberg's viewpoint as supernaturalism and dismiss it with the arguments usually marshaled against that position.

My objection to Herberg's stand, aside from my general rejection of supernaturalism, is based on his scrambling of ideas, his too easy transition from "Jewish existence" to "the concept of Jewishness." Using these phrases interchangeably is logically and existentially unwarranted. Jewish existence is entirely explainable in historical terms. Every stage of Jewish history can be understood in terms of naturalistic canons of thought. That the Jews are a unique people in no way argues that they are supernatural, any more than the peculiar status of the Catholic Church indicates to anyone but a devout Catholic, that it was called into being by a supernatural God. Herberg covers up his illogical inference that Jewish existence as a covenanted people is "an objective supernatural fact" by his identification of Jewish existence with the *concept* of Jewishness. There can be no doubt that the concept of Jewishness so clear in Herberg's mind is to be found among others in biblical and Rabbinic literature. The whole universe of discourse of those ages in Jewish history was supernaturally oriented, and it was inevitable

that the thinkers of those times should have expressed themselves as they did. Covenants of a similar, if not identical,
nature were common in the ancient world. But to speak of
such a world view as "an objective supernatural fact" is
simply to dogmatize a particular interpretation of history.
It constitutes also a misappropriation of language. A *fact,*
in general discourse, bears at least some relation to a process
of validation and proof. Since, by Herberg's definition,
Jewish existence is not subject to any such process, the covenant with God can at best be termed an assumption. Calling
it a supernatural fact is simply idolatry, to follow Herberg's
own logic. For it is reading into the mind of God a human
interpretation of His purpose in history.

Herberg would admit that the covenant has never, at any
period of Jewish history, been operative among all segments
of the Jewish people. This he attributes to the fact that
some Jews have always tried to escape their responsibility.
But they will never completely escape, he continues, because
the covenant is an act of God. Is there no other explanation
of Jewish history? Suppose that we take the ethical purposes
of the covenant as a desirable vocation for Jews rather than
as an imposition upon them from above. We can then
understand Jewish history just as well, nay better, because
defections from that vocation are then seen to be the natural
weaknesses characteristic of men in all ages, rather than a
monstrous sin dooming the individual Jew to perdition and
the Jewish people as a whole to suffer till the end of time.
There are many concepts of Jewishness that can be extracted
from the facts of Jewish existence, and there is no special
virtue to one that posits the Jew as the suffering servant of
humanity.[4] Undoubtedly it is to the credit of the Jewish
people that it has been able to draw valuable ethical insights
from its centuries of martyrdom, but some Jews at least look

forward to the end of Jewish suffering. They do not believe that there is a special merit in accepting suffering as a theological imperative. Nor can they worship a God who would subject men to such an existence.

Jewish status, if it is to be developed so as to help Jews adjust to changing conditions, must be the subject of rational study. The establishment of the State of Israel makes this an indispensable prerequisite for the future creativity of Jewish life. For however *sui generis* the Jewish people may continue to be, it must not be an anomaly either to fair-minded non-Jews or to its own members.

The Jewish people is now in possession of an instrument wherewith it can read itself out of existence, in a manner which will not be cowardly surrender to outside pressure. That instrument, strange as it may seem, is the State of Israel, supposedly the bastion of Jewish survival. Consider how this fateful paradox has come about.

The ancient Jewish state, as we have seen, was Jewish in every sense of the word. Its citizens were Jews, by birth or by adoption, culturally, religiously, and civically; its civilization was monolithic, being integrally bound up with the single people who were the citizens of the land. When the long Exile occurred, that people, spurred by the hostility of the host nations, had to transform itself from a state-nation founded upon the Torah into a spiritual nation, centered around the Torah tradition that had previously been the foundation of the state. The transition was not an easy one, and certain of the civil aspects of Torah had to be suspended; but on the whole, the religious orientation of the Moslem and Christian societies provided fertile ground in which a stateless Jewish religious culture could grow.

The Enlightenment, as we know, weakened the religious foundations of the Jewish and the non-Jewish traditions

alike. For the Jews the Enlightenment was a direct challenge
to their group existence, which had been built upon religion.
Zionism was the answer to this challenge to Jewish group
survival, the assumption being that once Jews reestablished
their national existence in their own land, the problem of
status would be solved. Now that the state has been established, however, it is apparent that insufficient attention has
been paid to the revolutionary change that has come about
in the conception of state held by Jews throughout the democratic world. Israel is no exception to the probability that
the monolithic state will some day be a thing of the past.
The Kulturkämpfe of the nineteenth and twentieth centuries are the dying gasps of an outworn urge for national
cohesiveness based on uniformity. Wherever the democratic
ideal of state is accepted, citizenship can no longer be prof-
fered with strings attached; religious or cultural requirements are no longer recognized as legitimate prerequisites
for full participation in the political, economic, social, and
cultural life of a democratic state-nation. Consequently, non-
Jews are entitled to full-fledged citizenship in Israel.

How then can Israel be called a Jewish state? Only in
the sense that a majority of its citizens are Jews and will
thereby influence the character of the country. But these
Jews are no longer of one mind in matters of religion, while
in political, economic, and social matters the interaction
with non-Jewish citizens will inevitably make of Israel a
new nation in more than a temporal sense. Israel, as time
goes on, will be more than a Jewish state, however much
influence its Jewish citizens may have. It will be the resultant
of all the forces, ethnic and individual, operating within its
borders. In a few generations, then, it will become increasingly hard to equate Israel and the Jewish people. If Jews
now insist upon making that identification, as so many of

them in Israel are prone to do, and if they read out of the
Jewish fold all Jews who remain in the Diaspora, the death
knell of the Jewish people will be sounded. The Jewish
problem will have been solved, but it will have been replaced
by the problem of a new nation, the heir, but not the loyal
offspring, of the Jewish people. That this eventuality is not
far-fetched is realized when we remember what Herzl himself
predicted about the future of the Diaspora: "As for those
[Jews] who remain behind, since prosperity enfeebles and
causes them to diminish, they would soon disappear altogether."[5]

A Jewish people identified solely with the State of Israel
would thus be a short-lived reminder of a people whose
sense of common destiny outlasted the plots of tyrants to
destroy it. Such an identification would be a surrender to an
assortment of social scientists whose failure to pigeonhole
the Jews in neat sociological categories has led them to
underestimate Jewry's power to survive as a collective entity.
It would be a tragic and unnecessary denouement if Jews
were, of their own accord, to accede to the following "description" of them: "Jews are people who practice the Jewish religion. . . . Wherever Jews are persecuted or discrim-
inated against, they cling to their old ways and keep apart
from the rest of the population and develop so-called 'Jewish'
traits. But these are not racial or 'Jewish'; they disappear
under conditions where assimilation is easy."[6] An extended
analysis of this passage, penned by supposedly acute anthro-
pologists, would be of interest in a study of the efforts of
social scientists to understand the Jews. I need only cite, by
way of refutation, the low percentage of synagogue attendance as compared with the number of Jews recorded in any
population statistics or point to the opposite fact that assimilation is often accompanied in a free environment by a

concomitant process of Jewish creativity and communal activity. Many Jews are not religious; many nonreligious Jews are among the most creative forces in Jewish cultural life.

The alternative to the exclusively national status has been clearly formulated by Mordecai M. Kaplan: *"The status most appropriate is that of peoplehood, based on the principle that any group with a 'we-feeling,' consciousness of kind, or homogeneity, has a right to make the most of that consciousness for the salvation of its members."*[7] Kaplan's specific terminology, though it has been the subject of much discussion, is less important than the social reality to which he refers. "People," it so happens, is an inadequate translation of the Hebrew *am,* which is the term most descriptive of what Kaplan has in mind. *Am Yisrael,* the people of Israel, was the traditional designation of the Jews throughout much of their long history and served to describe their collectivity no matter what the particular polity may have been. What is most important in Kaplan's conception is the emphasis on salvation as the purpose of Jewish group existence. Wherever that purpose of self-fulfillment for all Jews motivates the establishment of some kind of polity, Jews owe it to themselves to draw into their fold all who want to find their salvation within the Jewish group. As a transnational people, concretizing in its existence the principles of a new, yet old, conception of spiritual nationalism, the Jews would be accomplishing a number of objectives.

In the first place, they would be abiding by the apparent logic of world history, which renders undesirable a return to the old world of monolithic state-nations.

Secondly, they would be preserving Jewish corporateness as a spiritually dedicated people. Instead of organizing for physical power, as every state is prone to do, they would have to concentrate on the ethical, religious, and cultural values of Jewish life, that is to say, on the spiritual elements of self-fulfillment which would provide the rationale for their organization.

Thirdly, the conscious identification with one another of Jews throughout the world and the resultant interaction among them would fructify Jewish life immeasurably, as does every such exchange of experience and point of view among peoples living in varied environments.

International status for the Jewish people in no way eliminates the need for each local Jewish community to organize its own polity, in keeping with the conditions of life imposed by the environment. This is what Jews have done throughout their history. Thus in Israel, where Judaism has up to now been identified with the state, it may soon be desirable for some internal Jewish organization to be set up, similar perhaps to the *Keneset Yisrael,* the Assembly of Israel, to which almost all Jews in Palestine belonged during the days of the British mandate. It is interesting to note that before the State, both leftist and Orthodox Jews banded together voluntarily to achieve a common political objective. It remains to be seen, now, whether the cause of world-wide Jewish unity is of sufficient concern to the Jews of Israel to enable them to overcome their current political divergencies and to participate as a united Jewish community of Israel in a world-wide plan to make Jewish life worthwhile for all. Here in the United States, Jews will have to begin experimenting with a view to determining which form of community organization will enable the largest number of them voluntarily to associate themselves on the highest possible plane with Jewish life. It stands to reason, that the American environment will be hospitable to some form of religio-cultural development among Jews, which is exactly what is implied in the conception of a people dedicated to helping its members make the most of their lives.

In discussing the status of the Jews we have once again come upon an idea that should by now be familiar, namely that the civilization of the Jews is best characterized as a group religion. If Jews will look upon their membership in the Jewish group as an opportunity for self-enrichment carrying with it a responsibility for enhancing universal culture, they will raise Jewish group religion to a higher level. We cannot predict the exact nature of that development, but one thing is certain. Jewish nationalism, traditional religion, and culture cannot be brought together in their old concatenation, for the traditional religion is now a matter of individual acceptance, rejection, or adaptation. Any plan for artificially restoring it to its original place in the scheme of Jewish life is bound to fail. The new form of Jewish group religion must grow out of the needs of a Jewish collectivity. At the moment, all that can be done is to stimulate a widespread feeling for Jewish unity and a corresponding recognition of the need for polity. When such unity is established and a functioning, democratically organized community has been created (the form must, as I say, be worked out by trial and error), the integration of peoplehood, religion and culture will take place as a matter of course. The unity of Judaism is entirely dependent on the unity of the Jewish people—in so far, at least, as Judaism is conceived to be the evolving civilization of a living people. Doctrinally, Jews can achieve many varieties of religious philosophy, but the people as a whole will not live by doctrine. Doctrinal uniformity, as proved time and again in the history of religion, cannot be achieved among free men. Only a small fraction of Jewry accepts today as normative the thirteen Articles of Faith formulated by Maimonides. The same applies to any tenet of faith whose intellectual content is bound to be interpreted from the vantage point of individual experience. Group unity based on common needs, interests and feeling is another matter, and it is for this that Jews must aim.

The status of the Jews as a *people* has to be achieved. Status is never conferred upon a group by an iron law of history. If Jews so will it, they can read themselves off the map. But they can also will to seize the opportunity which their history has afforded them and to turn it to the mutual advantage of themselves and their fellowmen. The gains accruing to mankind from the new form of polity that would unify world Jewry would justify every effort made by Jews to preserve their age-old identity. The loss that would ensue from the breakup of a united Jewish people would be incalculable. But it is hardly likely that Jews, having struggled through two thousand years of exile, having fought tyrants and sacrificed their lives for the right to freedom and self-fulfillment, and having shed their blood for a homeland, will now declare that the Jewish adventure should be brought to an end. They could conceivably reach such a conclusion only by betraying the very purposes for which they and their ancestors have dared to live.

4

The concept of group religion illumines a question about Jewish religion which continues to bother many Christians and some Jews. "Why," they ask, "if Jews believe their religion is of universal worth, do they not missionize? Why do they not seek to convert the world to their way of thinking, just as Christianity does?" The reasoning behind this question has a certain plausibility, since it is natural for those who feel they have the truth to want to share it with others. In less tolerant times, it was not so much a desire to share that motivated the activity of missionizers as it was a compulsion to force others to adopt their own point of view: however, in discussing missionizing let us deal with it as an altruistic urge to share the secret of salvation.

In the first place, it is pertinent to remark that missionizers would have a stronger case if their activity embraced more of the spirit of inquiry. One initiates a process of converting others only if one is convinced of the truth of one's point of view. But the history of missionary work has demonstrated that the missionizing group is almost always transformed to some extent by contact with those whom it is engaged in missionizing. This should have taught us that religious truth is too complicated to be either discovered or taught through a one-directional method. If missionizers would really act in a spirit of *learning*, as well as of communicating to others whatever part of their own ideology they feel to be of universal value, no one could take exception to their activity.

From this standpoint, the Jews who have absorbed the cultures of the world probably more than any other group, have been far too reticent about sharing with the non-Jewish world the best insights of their experience. It is time for them to enter more vigorously the arena of open exchange of ideas.

Why, then, has Judaism not sought converts?* The answer lies in the Jewish conception of religion as being most effective when it is organically related to the total life of a people. In the Jewish view, the theoretical and dog-

---

*I am restricting myself in this discussion to the factor of ideology. I cannot here go into the interesting psychological problem of Jewish self-ghettoization, compounded of a defense reaction to external oppression, an inner sense of superiority, and a fear of cultural inundation.

matic aspects of religion must be embodied in social institutions, which, by virtue of the necessarily unique experiences of all peoples, are always peculiar to specific groups.
Consequently, conversion in religion would involve the
adoption of a total culture. Since such wholesale upheavals
in the lives of individuals and groups seldom occur as a
matter of intellectual preference, the Jews have always been
content to live and let live. This rule has had only two
exceptions, and those were the biblical campaign against
idolatrous neighbors and the brief flirtation with enforced
conversion during the later Hasmonean period. For the rest
of its history, the Jewish people has been careful to distinguish between the universal values of its tradition, which
it has given to the world without fanfare, and the particular
embodiments of those values, which it has cultivated as-
siduously, to the continued annoyance of those neighbors
who somehow or other have failed to discern the universalism contained therein.

It should be clear that universal values can arise only in
particular contexts. Ethical insights emerge as reactions to
social maladjustments. Artistic creativity, however much it
may be universally appreciated, is stimulated within the
narrow confines of a single cultural and geographical setting. It is hindsight operating unwisely to assume that,
since universal values once manufactured can be shipped
anywhere in the world, it is therefore desirable to eliminate
the particular settings within which these values were fashioned. Many missionary groups have accepted this critique
of their original methods and have tried to help native
converts to adapt Christianity to their local cultures. In
this, at least, they have come closer to recognizing the group
basis of effective religion.

Understanding the group aspect of religion should help

solve the problem of particularism and universalism. Christians often contrast Christian universalism with Jewish particularism, praising the former as a superior brand of religion. Actually, Christianity is as particularistic as Judaism in that it has its own form of polity, the church. In addition, Christian particularism expresses itself in the great stress it places on the acceptance of theological dogma. Whether particularism leads to emphasis on polity, dogma, ritual or ethical conceptions makes no difference. Universalism is as possible in ritual as it is in the transmission of abstract ideas and values, as can be easily gathered from the prevalence of such practices as singing national anthems, saluting the flag, and praying. It is as easy (or as hard) for non-Jews to become Jews as it is for non-Christians to become Christians. The fact that Christianity has won over so many more people is, of course, no "proof" of its superiority. All that is proved is that Christians have succeeded in accomplishing some of their missionizing objectives. Both Christianity and Judaism are particularistic religions, each capable in its own way of expressing universal values.

But the questions which should be posed to all missionaries are these: Is it not possible for so-called inferior groups to be raised to a more universally acceptable standard of belief and behavior in terms of their own traditions? Is it necessary, for example, for the Hindus to adopt Christianity in order to approximate religious truth? Is there not a sufficient basis for such transformation in the age-old Hindu culture? I raise these questions, of course, in terms of the prevailing Western opinion of the inferiority of Hindu and other Eastern religions to those of the West. The assumption, in my opinion, is gratuitous, but let us grant it, for the purpose of our discussion. The naturalist (and Jewish) approach would involve the West's religions meeting that of the Hindus in free cultural interchange, sharing each other's insights and, where it seems desirable, adopting views of the others which can be rewarding.

Jews believe they have much to teach the world. Many of them should and do believe they have much to learn. But neither the teaching nor the learning necessitates converting others or being converted by others. A particularist religion, if its particularism is restricted to the cultural forms within which universal values are set, can be of universal worth. A universal religion, composed of a set of doctrines which its adherents would like the rest of the world to adopt, must inevitably seek embodiment in particular social forms. Both types of religion can live at peace and can be mutually helpful if they will pursue their objectives in a spirit of humility and honest appreciation of each other's worth.

6

JEWISH RELIGION IN THE
STATE OF ISRAEL

THE DEVELOPMENT OF JEWISH RELIGION in the State of Israel is a fascinating study for the theologian, the sociologist, the political scientist, the psychologist—indeed for any student of human behavior. Just as the revival of Hebrew as a spoken language after almost two millenia is a subject for considerable speculation, so the effort to revive many practices of Jewish religion, which for centuries had survived only in the scholastic discussions of Talmudists, is bound to be watched with intense interest. Similar interest attaches to the question as to whether Jewry's

renewed contact with the Land will result in religious creativity comparable to that of the biblical period.

It was to be expected that considerable confusion would
be generated in regard to religion in Israel. The status of
Jews as a majority in a country dedicated to the democratic
ideal of the state creates the problem of the extent to which
traditional Jewish law can become part of the machinery
of government. And if such law is incorporated into national legislation, is it to be applicable to all the citizens of
Israel or only to the Jews? The intense disagreement among
Jews concerning their own attitudes toward the civil laws
in Jewish religious codes adds to the difficulty. These religious problems among Jews are peculiar to the Jewish
community of Israel, by virtue of its majority status. In
other Jewish communities, Jewish civil law remains for the
most part a subject for academic study.

While considerable attention has been paid since the
establishment of Israel to the restored dimension of Jewish
religious law, relatively little has been written about the
problems of tradition that Israel Jews have *in common*
with Diaspora Jewry. In this chapter, I shall be concerned
with exploring the relation between Israel civil law and
Jewish religious law and with the remarking of tradition
that is now taking place in Israel. In the course of this
exploration I shall try to show how an understanding of the
nature of group and doctrinal religion can shed light on
current religious developments in Israel.

1

Democracy is an approach to government as well as a
form of government. The fact that the British government is
a monarchy no more detracts from its democratic character than the republican form of the United States gov-

ernment guarantees that it is pervaded with the democratic spirit. It follows that the particular content that we Americans have given to our conception of democracy may differ from the content of democratic philosophies among other peoples. The history, customs, and peculiar local conditions of a people determine the extent to which the democratic spirit informs its institutions. An interesting instance of this relativism in democracy is the variety of ways in which the role of religion in the state is handled.

The American system calls in theory for the complete separation of church and state. There are clear historic reasons for the adoption of this principle in American government. Of the many religious sects that established themselves in the new world, some were determined to fashion that world in their own image. Religious affiliation was even a prerequisite for citizenship in some of the early colonies. The Puritan theocracy in New England is the outstanding example of what might have been the general pattern on the American continent. Fortunately, power was fairly evenly distributed, and this, together with the common problems of conquering the wilderness and removing the oppressive hand of the English king, made it essential to compromise religious differences. The principle of the separation of church and state was thus born of necessity; it has since grown into an ideal of American democracy.

Actually, the principle has never operated practically in a clearcut way. There have been abridgements of the principle, constant attacks upon it, and, in general, a good deal of confusion about its meaning. One of the still unresolved issues is whether separation of church and state means separation of religion and state. To judge by various practices, the latter is not implied in the former.[1] Sessions of state legislatures and of Congress are opened with invocations delivered by ministers of various faiths; the Army asks each denomination to provide chaplains; the Bible is read at public school assemblies; Christmas is tantamount to a national holiday, and its celebration is a tradition in many a public school. As has been pointed out, by religion many Americans have demonstrated that they mean Christianity.

Although the problem of church and state or religion and state is still unresolved, both theoretically and practically, the burden of American tradition is unalterably clear on one major issue, namely that no state church shall be established on either a sectarian or a nonsectarian basis. Thus a few years ago, when Clarence C. Morrison wrote a series of articles in *The Christian Century* entitled "Can Protestantism Win America?," he in no way favored making Protestantism the state religion of the United States, although he felt that the majority status of Protestants in America conferred upon them the right and duty to foster the spirit of Protestantism in every area of government and daily life.

Many Americans are unaware when they speak of the Christian spirit that they are referring to an ethical outlook generally current in Western (and to some extent in Eastern) civilization; they do not realize that there are elements in this "spirit" which have been unconsciously absorbed from the experience of American society and which, in great measure, have transformed the Christian outlook. The willingness to recognize multiple paths to salvation, the One God worshiped by all in their own way, the disestablishment of churches, the "brotherhood" approach of the National Conference of Christians and Jews—these are only a few of the many elements of the current Christian spirit which are a far cry from the exclusivism of early Christianity. And they are largely a product of democratic thought and experience. They illustrate how American group experience has transformed the doctrinal religion which American Christians inherited from Europe. But the training of most American Christians makes them unable to discern the degree of change that has occurred in the social views of Christianity, particularly as they bear on intergroup relations. As a result, while there is a jealous resistance to the encroachment of any one sect upon the principle of separation, there is a continuous groping after a method of providing some form of Christian doctrine with a significant role in American civilization. The groping will prove of no avail until American religion is recognized as the natural and distinctive outgrowth of the common group life and as not being associated with the doctrines or practices of particular sects. The United States needs a conception of group religion which will find within the American way of life the necessary ingredients for a full religious experience. Only when such a conception becomes generally current among Americans will it be advisable to permit any closer relationship between the government and religion than that which now exists. It should be unnecessary to add that even such organic connection between American polity and American religion should be fostered only if the following conditions can be met: 1) full freedom must be preserved for the continued functioning of the historic religions, and 2) American religion itself must be thoroughly democratic and voluntaristic.

In Israel, an entirely different situation prevails. First and foremost (and this is often forgotten in discussions of the subject), the majority religious group, the Jews, have a long history of self-government. In the Diaspora communities, particularly in Eastern Europe up until the First World War, the Jewish people led a semiautonomous existence, with practically every power of government except self-determination in their own hands. Second, the Jewish governments were always religio-political; that is to say, the law was based on religious traditions and largely interpreted by religious functionaries. Upon their attainment of majority status in a state of their own, it was to be anticipated that significant segments of the people would expect some continuation or revival of the historic precedent. Third, the religio-national character of Judaism, which produced festivals that could be interpreted religiously or nationalistically or both, would naturally have a tremendous influence upon the character of a state in which Jews were a majority, particularly a state created for the express purpose of providing a home for the Jewish people. Fourth, at this stage of its national development, Israel must be in practice, if not in theory, a binational state in many cultural matters. For the Jews of Israel to have forced the Arabs to abandon their right to corporate existence and to their own educational system would have been unthinkable at this point in history.

All these considerations require that we consider the problem of church and state in Israel from a special perspective. I have already touched upon the over-all question as to the degree of identification between the Jewish people and Israel. As a practical matter, Israel will be as Jewish a state as Jewish majority status will make it. The minority groups in Israel, by virtue of their active participation in Israel life, will undoubtedly in the future be able to affect the course of politics and of culture. We cannot now foretell the extent of their influence, for illiteracy and unsettled living conditions make their present impact on the common life of Israel an insignificant one. But while the State of Israel and the Jewish people may continue to be two dis-

tinct entities, there can be no question that the former will
clearly express the influence of the latter. In no other state
in the world in which Jews reside can they expect to exert
a comparable influence.

But to what degree is it proper for Israel Jews to impose
their religious culture on the non-Jewish citizens of Israel?
Let us look again at the situation in our own country. In
the United States the Christian majority has put its imprint
on the law of the land in such matters as recognition of
Sunday as a day of rest and Christmas as a legal holiday. In
some states it is illegal to open certain places of business on
these days, which are definitely part of Christian, rather
than American, tradition. Thus Jews and other non-Christians, to whom neither Sunday nor Christmas is a holy day,
are penalized. If a Jew is a Sabbath observer, he must be
willing to make the economic sacrifice entailed in closing
his shop for two days instead of one. To this extent, it is
accurate to speak of America as a Christian country. However, there is considerable controversy over the wisdom of
this type of legislation, for it involves the tacit assumption
that minority religious groups are welcome only if they abide
by the cultural demands of the majority. No one suggests
that it would be practically possible for the American economy to function full blast on a festive day like Christmas,
which is celebrated by the large majority of American citizens. The question is whether that day is an *American*
occasion, to be shared by all citizens, and if not, whether it
is fair to penalize a minority group economically because
of the majority's religious needs.

The answer in the affirmative, that is, the argument that
Christmas and Sunday are American civic occasions, and
that therefore Jews and other non-Christian citizens have
no right to take exception to the restrictive legislation asso-

ciated with these days is utterly fallacious, as anyone familiar with the evolution of our Constitution knows. But guarantees of religious liberty and equality are not always carried out in law, as is well documented by Chester Inwald. He quotes, among other examples, an early enactment which reads: "For the better observation and keeping holy the Lord's Day commonly called Sunday, be it enacted that all and every person shall on every Lord's Day apply themselves to the observation of the same by exercising themselves thereon in the duties of piety and true religion publiquely and privately and that noe tradesman, artificer, workeman, labourer or other person whatsoever shall doe or exercise any worldly labor. . . ."[2]

Inwald points out that legislation of this kind has been consistently upheld in the higher courts as not violating the constitutional guarantee of freedom of religion. The courts notwithstanding, these laws do discriminate against the Jewish religion, so much so that "a Jewish *religious* organization was denied incorporation because its articles provided that the annual meeting of the corporation be held on the second Sunday in January of each year." None of this legislation alters the fact that American civilization is not identical with Christianity. Most of the laws restricting business activities on Sunday can be interpreted as safeguards enabling the majority to observe their Sabbath without the disturbance of mundane activities by the minority, rather than as legal recognition of Christianity as the official American religion. It is well to bear this in mind as we examine the parallel problem in Israel.

According to current law in Israel, non-Jews are privileged to work and operate their businesses on the Jewish Sabbath and on other Jewish holy days, although these are legal days of rest for the entire country. Thus despite the admittedly Jewish character of national festivals, the non-Jewish population suffers no legal economic discrimination. What is difficult for the non-Jews in Israel is the consciousness of their being guests. The Arab Israeli can share in the celebration of the 5th of Iyar, Israel's Independence Day, but he has no stake in Passover, the High Holy Days, Shavuot, or any other of the traditional Jewish occasions which are legal holidays. This is the plus in the problem of church and state in Israel, the intimate tie-up between the Jewish religio-national heritage and the law of a state in which there are non-Jewish citizens.

Is this phenomenon out of keeping with the democratic spirit? Again the American scene gives us a point of departure. No one disputes the right of the Christian majority in the United States to assure itself of the freedom to observe its sacred days in a fitting manner and to set them aside as legal days of rest for the communicants of the Christian faith. The point of doubt is whether restrictions imposed by Christians upon themselves ought to apply with equal weight to non-Christians. It is ironical that in Israel the nonobservant Jew is forced to observe the Sabbath as a day of rest, while the non-Jew is free to choose whichever Sabbath appeals to him most. And the nonobservant Jew, by virtue of his identification with the Jewish community, has no grounds for complaint; his only recourse is to exercise his democratic right to protest a government policy and fight for its revision.

As Israel grows, there will be many more experiences shared by its Jewish and non-Jewish citizens. Arab as well as Jewish statesmen will achieve recognition as representatives of the national spirit of Israel, and both Arabs and Jews will make contributions to world culture inspired by the common sources of Israel's evolving nationalism. In the

course of time there may be a shift from the original dominance of Jewish tradition to the dominance of a joint culture
sprung from the soil of Israel. Jews and Arabs alike may in
the future relinquish some of their historic ties, just as
many Americans, as the result of a satisfying participation
in a broad American civilization, have loosened their ties to
the historic religions. For these Americans the spiritual content of American democracy has come to replace in their
lives the role formerly played by Protestant, Catholic, or
Jewish religion. Estrangement from the forms of Jewish religion by the Israelis is not a far-fetched possibility, for it is
implicit in the rather shallow, but understandable view of
many Israel Jews that Jewish religion is unnecessary in
Israel because there life as a whole is Jewish. These people
understand that the synagogue is important in the Diaspora,
since it helps keep Jewish consciousness alive, but they see
no need for the institution in Israel. The attitude has led
to some curious aberrations, such as that of a Jew from
Israel, reported by Robert Gordis, who insisted upon eating
kosher food while visiting the United States though he paid
no attention to kashrut when at home in Tel Aviv. An attitude like this one, as we have seen, by implication excludes
non-Jews from participation in an evolving Israel civilization. In the present state of exultation of Israel's Jews at
their recently acquired statehood, this reaction was to be
anticipated, but sooner or later they will have to look
around them and take more careful note of their relations
with minority groups of citizens.

Meanwhile, Israel's Jews are engaged in the task of planning for their own communal needs without violating the
basic democratic rights of other sections of Israel's population. This process is following the logic of Jewish existence
by combining "secular" and "religious" features in a dis-

concerting way. We turn now to a brief examination of
these features.

2

There is, first, the entire issue of the foundation of Israel's
code of law. How, practically, can Talmudic and Rabbinic
law be adapted to the needs of a modern state? Even those
who oppose the theocratic basis of traditional Jewish law are
prepared to accept as many features of the law as are applic-
ble to modern society. The problem is one of bridging the
gap between the extreme left-wingers, who might be willing
to learn from the spirit of the religious codes (as in the
matter of the abolition of capital punishment), and the
Orthodox elements, who have long dreamed of the establishment of a Toraitic state, a state based completely on revealed
law interpreted within the spirit of the religious tradition.

Orthodox Jewry in Israel is united in the belief that "the
state is the framework set up since the six days of Creation,
for the concretization of Torah and its vision."[3] The logic
of the theory of government expressed by authoritative
Orthodox spokesmen leads to the conclusion that the State
of Israel is a *Jewish* state, with minority rights granted to
non-Jewish citizens, but with only the Jew (by birth or by
conversion) legally entitled to citizenship. That many Orthodox spokesmen refuse to draw this implication about
non-Jewish citizens is a credit to their liberalism but not to
their logical coherence.

In a Toraitic state, severe curtailment of the rights of
citizenship would be imposed upon non-Jews. In the case of
the judiciary, for example, since, according to the *Shulhan
Arukh,* non-Jews could not legally adjudicate cases involving a Jew, it would be a problem of considerable *halakhic*
ingenuity to devise a way, within Rabbinic law, of granting

non-Jews their democratic right to serve as judges. A passage in Maimonides illustrates the problem that would arise
in regard to non-Jewish public officials in all branches of
government.

> It is forbidden to place as king (over Israel) one who is
> from an assembly of strangers, even one several genera-
> tions removed in origin . . . as it is said, "You may not
> place over yourself a foreigner who is not your brother."
> And not only as regards the monarch, but as regards
> all positions of authority in Israel, whether it be a
> general in the army, a captain of fifty or a captain of
> ten, even one appointed to take care of the well which
> is used for irrigation. And it goes without saying, that
> a judge or a nasi (presiding officer of the Sanhedrin)
> must be a Jew, as it says, "From the midst of your
> brethren shall you place over you a king?" All appoint-
> ments which you make must be from your own group.[4]

Although the traditional attitude of Jewish law toward
non-Jewish officials is clear, even the Orthodox do not want
to turn the clock back too far, nor can they. Some provision must be made for adequate democratic rights for non-
Jews in the State of Israel. In the case of judges, the problem might be resolved by allowing the Arabs to set up their
own courts and judges. As an exponent of Mizrachi puts it:

> The whole force of the prohibition (in regard to non-
> Jewish judges) is in the appointment, and *that* only
> when the judge is appointed to preside over the trial
> of a Jew. But it is permissible to appoint a non-Jew
> as a judge for non-Jews. Since, therefore, non-Jews
> would be appointed in the Jewish state by virtue of
> minority rights, according to which each group would
> be recognized as a distinct entity entitled to demand
> its share of the governmental positions in order to con-
> duct its own affairs, it follows that non-Jewish judges
> would be officially appointed to service the minorities.[5]

However, the Orthodox if they were to enforce Jewish law in the state could not logically establish a government in which non-Jews could judge cases involving Jews.

Similarly, in a state based on traditional Jewish law, non-Jews could not exercise their democratic right to serve in any legislative body whose decisions affected the Jewish community. For even a non-Jew who was expert in Talmudic law could not be granted the authority to interpret and expand that law. An act of religious conversion would have to take place before the right to legislate could be extended to him, for such authority is by definition the exclusive prerogative of Jews. A Toraitic state would essentially have to be a monolithic state; extending limited rights of autonomy to minorities could scarcely be termed giving them adequate democratic rights.

So far, the Orthodox have not succeeded in selling the majority of the Jews in Israel on their conception of law. But they have succeeded, by virtue of their power, in having enacted a number of measures which correspond to the blue laws so common in early America and still on the statute books in some states. Examples of these measures are the prohibition on the operation of buses on the Sabbath in some sections of the country, the closing down of all movie theaters on the Sabbath, and the ban on government importation of non-kosher meats. In addition, as a carry-over from the mandatory regime, the Orthodox retain possession of a powerful instrument in the religious courts, which have jurisdiction over all matters of personal status within the Jewish community—marriage, divorce, and inheritance. The Moslem and Christian communities are given the right to establish courts of a similar nature, but no provision has as yet been made for civil marriage between members of the various "religious" communities of Israel. Thus, even a

Jew who does not subscribe to a single tenet of Orthodox
Judaism cannot legally marry an Arab girl unless she has
been converted to Judaism by a rabbinical court.

This policy is "justified" by Sh. Z. Shragai, former mayor
of Jerusalem, as follows:

> If in Israel the Government were to allow secular mar-
> riages, it would automatically allow Jews to marry non-
> Jews. As both Jews and non-Jews in the State will have
> equal rights, it is certain that in a very short time the
> 100,000 Arabs in this country whose numbers will cer-
> tainly increase, will in time enjoy a high standard of
> life equal to that of the Jews. Inter-marriage on a big
> scale will naturally follow, and as a result there will
> live in Israel not a "Jewish" people, but a mixed Jewish-
> Arab people, or, better still, a Palestinian people. Not
> for this have we longed and struggled and waited for
> two thousand years.[6]

This area of personal status is one that requires much
more exploration by the Israelis. Admittedly, the upper
hand held by the Orthodox rabbinate is a tribute paid by
Mapai to expediency. Whether or not it is to be a lasting
abridgment of the right to personal happiness is a question
which the Israelis will have to face as soon as other, more
immediate problems are ironed out.

Clearly, planning for the Jews as a people, as an ethnic
group consciously concerned with its unity, survival, and
spiritual growth, is not the same as legislating for a modern
state in which Jews are a majority. To base the law of the
State of Israel entirely on the doctrines of traditional Jewish religion would require restoring the ancient distinctions
between the Jews and the various categories of *gerim*
(strangers). Under a democratic concept of state, all citizens
must be eligible to participate equally in the framing and
execution of the law as well as in the enjoyment of its

privileges; traditional Jewish law can be only one of many sources from which specific laws will be drawn.

Applying the *spirit* of the tradition to the political, social, and economic life of Israel is another matter; this is not only a possibility but a duty, wherever that spirit can help make the society more humane. Not even the antireligious Mapam party takes exception to the incorporation, wherever possible, into Israel's penal code of the Talmudic attitude toward capital punishment. In all of Rabbinic legislation it is evident that the death penalty was looked upon as a measure to be resorted to only in the rare instances when the enormity of the crime called for extreme measures, and it is in this spirit that the State of Israel has outlawed capital punishment, except for treason. Similarly, the biblical legislation designed to alleviate poverty has exercised a profound influence on the architects of the welfare state, and the socialist forces currently in power derive their inspiration for an equalitarian society as much from the Bible as from Marx. Socialism in Israel is largely ethical rather than Marxian, since it arose in a society where private capital was insignificant, and where, therefore, the class struggle would have had to be manufactured. Among the influences in the establishment of the agricultural communes in Israel, according to Buber, was "the half-unconscious after-effects of the Bible's teachings about social justice."[7] Judging by the emphasis placed on the teaching of the Prophets in Israel, I am inclined to believe that Buber underestimates the attention paid by the so-called antireligionist fathers of the *kvutzah* to the Jewish ethical tradition.

3

The unique nature of the church-state problem in Israel

is particularly apparent in education. Here in the United
States, use of the Bible (whether Old or New Testament)
in the schools is one of the key points in the controversy
over religion in public education. American educators agree
that the Bible is a religious document. Those who favor its
use in the schools declare it is nonsectarian, while their opponents argue that since it is a religious text and its trans-
lations are sectarian, its incorporation into public education
is an entering wedge for turning the schools into a battle-
ground for sectarian religions. Contrast this situation with
that which prevailed in Israel even before the unification of
the school systems, where in every Jewish school—labor,
general or religious—the Bible was, as it remains, a basic
text. (The unification put all schools under the supervision
of a Ministry of Education but left more or less intact the
prevailing practice of maintaining separate schools for labor,
general, and religious ideologies.) From Mapam to Agu-
dat Yisrael, from "atheist" to supernaturalist, there was
not one iota of disagreement about the centrality of the
Bible. It is in the interpretation of the book that controversy continues hot and heavy. The labor-oriented educators teach the Bible either as though the word God never
appeared or as though the religious orientation that per-
meates every line could be ignored or viewed as an old, worn-
out container which can now be scrapped. Among the religionists, on the other hand, there are degrees of funda-
mentalism, ranging from the attitude that every letter is
holy to recognition of the merits of some aspects of biblical
criticism.

The Orthodox, in their schools, treat the Bible as the
word of God, not subject to challenge or question. In a
lesson which I observed in a school for girls in Jerusalem a
twelve-year-old child asked the teacher why it was necessary

for Jews in modern times to abide by the rules of *orlah,* the law forbidding eating the fruits of a tree until after the third year. The teacher's reply, which I remember verbatim, was *"En makshim al pekudat hamelekh* (We do not question the command of the king)."

Thus Israel's educators are confronted with the exceedingly difficult task of trying to build a shared Israel Jewish culture in a divided school system. A first step toward unification has taken place with the placing of the various educational *zeramim* (trends) under one governmental department of education, but there is still a long way to go to the achievement of a common school system. Except on the college level, it seems likely that Jews and non-Jews will continue to conduct their own separate schools for a long time to come. But whether or not the present form of highly sectarian education within the Jewish community can contribute to the cultivation of a genuine democratic atmosphere remains to be seen. In a country in which religion and politics are so interwoven, it would seem as if partisan education could only exacerbate a dangerous situation.

4

The return to Eretz Yisrael has also been a return to Judaism for those who had strayed from it, and it has been, for traditionalist and nontraditionalist alike, an opportunity to revitalize it. There is a widespread habit in Israel of speaking of the Jewish population as divided into two sections, the Orthodox and the nonreligious, the former seeking to refashion modernity in the dress of Torah and the latter seeking to find a way of life in which "religion" will play no part. This generalization has a basis in fact in that the only formal religious movements of any consequence are gradations of Orthodoxy, but it is no substitute for a careful analysis of the evolution of a new era in Jewish religion, to which all Jews in Israel, the religious and the avowed secularist, are contributing. Like any other social phenomenon, religion is apt to change as the result of unconscious, unforeseen, or neglected factors. This, of course, does not absolve us from the responsibility of trying to solve problems by planning.

Although the nonreligious elements in Israel are outspoken in their rejection of religion, they are at one with the religionists in their awareness that even a secular Jewish culture must be based in great measure on the tradition. As a matter of fact, many of them speak of themselves as *mesortiim* (traditionalists). It is my conviction that the future of Jewish religion will be greatly affected by the efforts, conscious and unconscious, of these non-Orthodox elements in Israel to remake the tradition in accordance with their own physical, social, intellectual, and spiritual needs. This is not to say that the conservative influence of Orthodox Jewry will cease to operate. If Orthodox Jewry gains control of the government, the activity of the *mesortiyim* will certainly be severely circumscribed, and they will make little progress in effecting radical changes. On the other hand, if the Orthodox remain a militant and vocal opposition, they will still make an important contribution, as every cultural challenge does, to the thinking of the liberal opponents.

If one wants to capture the real spirit of present-day Israel, one does look not to the Yeshivah student, the bearer of the Orthodox tradition, but to the *halutz,** the pioneer; not to the tradition of the past but to the tradition in the "remaking". Ernst Simon has spoken of a new Jewish type

---

*The term refers to all those pioneers who have striven for the development of a cooperative society. In current popular usage, the *halutzim* who are settled in Israel's collectives are referred to as *kibbutzniks*.

that will some day emerge, a combination of the *talmid hakam,* the scholar, and the *halutz,* the pioneer.[8] But that type has not yet made its appearance, and it is the *halutz* who embodies the spiritual outlook that today is representative of the group religion of Israel. But Israel's religion is not static, and profound changes are taking place daily in the social thinking of the Israelis. The influx of Oriental and North African Jews is altering the character of Israel's society and its culture. These comments about *halutziyut,* therefore, may apply only to that element in the population which has been dominant in the building of modern Israel. Simon is correct in forecasting a meeting of the extremes. There are many doctrinal approaches to Jewish religion that are struggling for recognition in Israel, and it is the outcome of the struggle that will determine the next stage in the group's religious development. Orthodoxy, which could once claim to speak for the Jewish group religion as a whole, is today only one of a number of competing philosophies.

That *halutziyut,* the philosophy of the *halutzim,* has most of the ingredients of a group as well as a doctrinal religion should be apparent after a careful study of its scope. The word does not lend itself to ready translation, but its origin suggests the spirit it conveys. *Halutzim,* in Biblical usage, were the armed vanguard who preceded the Israelites on their travels. As more recently understood, *halutzim* have been the pioneers of the Jewish people, those who have blazed the trail in resettling Eretz Yisrael and who have formulated a new social ideology to stir the hearts of all Jews.

Halutziyut has deep roots in Jewish tradition. Its insistence upon fructifying the soil of Israel and protecting its productivity once it has been restored, is more than an answer to a social need. For it bespeaks a sentiment that has been a force for spiritual striving among Jews—the feeling that the right of possession of the Land of Israel is contingent upon the ethical purpose to which it is put. That force has not always evoked a uniformly vigorous response, but it has never ceased to operate.

A favorite saying that has come down in Jewish tradition declares, "The air of Eretz Yisrael makes one wise." In so far as Judaism is concerned, there is no question that the marriage between the Jewish people and its land has been one of the most spiritually fruitful unions in the history of mankind. One need not be a mystic or a poet to note that the intense love of the Jewish people for the soil of Israel has been manifest in the ethical purpose assigned throughout Jewish history to the settlement of the Land. That ethical purpose has not been abandoned in the new return. On the contrary, modern Zionism has stressed the responsibility of the Jewish people for restoring the soil and making it bear fruit again; the loving care of nature is conceived as an ethical imperative. The assumption is that men who know how to cherish God's gifts will know how to treat one another.

The spiritual vocation inherent in the Zionist efforts was first given expression by Aaron David Gordon, in the first two decades of this century. His ideas have since been elaborated in the philosophy of *halutziyut*. Gordon summed up the objectives of Jews in Palestine as follows:

> We who belong to a people that has suffered more than any other, that has been torn up from its soil, alienated from nature, yet continues vigorous; we, a nation which has not been destroyed by two thousand years of misfortune, we consider that in our aim for a complete regeneration there can be no other possibility for attaining the life we seek except to base it wholly upon its natural foundation. We must direct it toward

the development of the human spirit, toward the
search for truth and righteousness in its relation with
other peoples and with all mankind.[9]

Gordon's idealism is characteristic of the venerable Jewish
tradition of expressing universal ideals through the medium
of Jewish group life. That tradition is still the chief justification for the survival of the Jewish people, as it has been
ever since the dawn of prophetic religion. It is worth noting,
is it not, that a people which had never, for two thousand
years, had a chance to live for itself, should, when that opportunity presented itself, immediately shoulder an ethical
responsibility? The Exodus was followed by the acceptance
of Torah; it has happened again. But the carrying out of
ethical responsibility has never, in the history of any people,
been fully achieved. Granted that it is idle to expect any
group of people to become angels overnight, it is still pertinent to inquire how seriously Israel's Jews take the ethical
values they profess. We might inquire, for example, whether
Israel's Jews have been as generous in their attitude toward
the Arab refugees or toward their own Arab citizens as
would be consistent with their ethical profession.

Gordon's vision of what the reconstituted national existence should mean to the Jewish people embraces only one
aspect of the revitalizing of the Jewish religious tradition.
Also involved are ritual and ideology. These three—ideology,
ritual, and ethics—however they may be separated dialectically, are organically related, particularly in Jewish religion.

Gordon looked beyond the task of providing an agricultural basis for Jewish life. The contact with nature was to
cleanse the Jewish soul and purify the character of the group.
To do that, the Jews had to learn how to appreciate the
gifts of nature. It is no accident of history that the Jews,
whom restrictive legislation had kept from the soil for

centuries, should proclaim this ethic of the conservation of nature. Jewish religion had taught that God's work of creation was only partially completed and that it was up to man to carry on that work. Biblical legislation concerning the sabbatical year taught the Jew that he could not abuse nature, that he might even have to plan his social order so as to preserve the soil from the ravages of a greedy and thoughtless population. Men are gradually becoming aware that there is a close relation between their social behavior and the response of nature; in our own country, we have seen that floods and dust bowls are not the irresistible, perverse assaults of an unfriendly earth but the direct result of our misuse of it. And that misuse can be prevented only by a new attitude toward nature and a revised social system that will make the attitude possible.

The social system that has sprung up under the impetus of *halutziyut* is not the working out of the plan of a social engineer. The *halutzim* who founded the *kvutzah* originally looked forward to the kind of prosperity which would enable them to share the profits of their work in typical bourgeois fashion. The idea of a collective life came to them only when it became apparent that profits were not likely to be forthcoming in the near future; it was in the process of trial and error that the theory of a cooperative and collective society was conceived. Israel's is truly a voluntary and evolving group project. One need only compare Israel's cooperatives and collectives with those of Russia to see the difference in spirit. In Russia all cooperative and collective schemes are government planned and controlled. Where introduced, they are considered essential forms of social enterprise, and any who disagree or who fail to follow the government's instructions are penalized. The price that Russia has had to pay for its collectives has been the death, torture, imprisonment, or enslavement of literally millions of human beings. In Israel, whatever producers' and consumers' cooperatives or agricultural collectives have been formed are the creations of free men and women. Without compulsion, *halutzim* have abandoned the psychologically easier road of individualism and pooled their efforts to create a new society founded on political democracy and economic equality. They have refused to impose the collective way of life on anyone; all are free to come or to go. They have refrained from becoming dogmatic about any single form of cooperative or collective. The *kvutzah*, the *kibbutz*, the *meshek shittufi*, and the *moshav* exist side by side. From the complete collectivism of the *kvutzah* to the familial cooperation of the *moshav*, there is universal concern for the psychological needs of the individual.

This freedom has deep spiritual roots in the conception of the sanctity of the individual. It not only implies, it firmly avows that all social systems must be justified by the opportunities they provide for individual self-fulfillment. When this feeling rises to the level of consciousness and purpose among a people, they can be said to have achieved a religious approach to life. It is not merely a matter of ethics; it is a matter of faith in the moral potentialities of man and in the power he possesses to make the most of his life. Nor is it simply humanism, for the faith involves nature as well as man in the pattern of optimism.

The burden of *halutziyut* is the burden of all liberal religious philosophies, namely that life is worthwhile, worth fighting for and living for, and that man and nature are so constituted as to make possible the achievement of the highest human goals. *Halutziyut* emerges as a this-worldly religious philosophy.

Halutziyut is the central philosophy of Israel Jewry, even for those in its midst who have not personally identified themselves with a cooperative or collective. Almost all Jews recognize the practical achievements of Israel's socialists in settling the land, establishing a firm economy, making room for successive waves of immigrants, and creating a new spiritual and cultural atmosphere. It is expected even by the *halutzim,* that individualism, in the form of private farming and small business, will remain—at least for a long time to come. But no Israeli denies the impact of *halutziyut* on the whole character of the community.

There is no question that *halutziyut* is the product of an unusual era in Jewish history, one that called for drastic steps, politically, economically, socially, and ideologically. The true test of its validity and lasting power will come when conditions in Israel are more settled and its citizens can pay more attention to their own personal desires, as they are now beginning to do. It will then be apparent whether or not the spirit of *halutziyut* is so ingrained in the people that they will protect the institutions that direct the natural drive of man for self-aggrandizement into creative, socially beneficial channels. *Halutziyut* has made great demands upon the individual, calling upon him to make many sacrifices in behalf of the group. Thus far those sacrifices have been compensated for by the achievement of national independence and the steady building of a community. Whatever a man does in Israel, from collecting garbage to running a department in government, visibly adds to the community's growth and is appreciated. The future of *halutziyut* will depend on its ability to handle the problem of the individual when conditions are such that the individual is able to live for himself to a much greater extent than is the case now. Israel has already begun to see the operation of the black market, of color and cultural prejudices, and of many petty inequities out of keeping with *halutziyut* or any other ethical philosophy of life. How will this challenge be met?

Ben Gurion summarizes the problem when he says, "It is possible that no such thing as a final goal exists because there is no limit to the constant development of peoples, nations and humanity. After we attain our vision of national redemption, we will not have reached the end of the road. History will confront us with new tasks, and when these will be accomplished, there will be others. . . . A human being is not only an instrument of his people, of humanity or of history. He is an absolute value in his own right. . . . The same is true of human life and of human freedom. We have created many such values that are ends in themselves: labor, mutual assistance, human freedom and equality."[10] Ben Gurion, representing the spirit of Israel's Jews, conceives of the State of Israel as a means to what is essentially a religious end: the formation of a community dedicated to the cause of human decency and to the construction of a society in which the individual can live to the full extent of his own genius. In Ben Gurion's remarks we find a broad understanding of that interaction of group and individual which I have outlined in my analysis of group and doctrinal religion.

5

Jewish group religion once again is at work and is being gradually articulated by the leaders of the community. No matter how Jews differ from one another in fundamental theological and philosophical ways, as a group they rededicate themselves again and again to exploring the spiritual path that their ancestors have beaten out through the ages and that they must themselves extend. The direction in which they extend the path will be the resultant of the ideological forces now in tense interaction.

If we are to judge by the serious way in which the relation of the individual to the group culture is being treated in the *kvutzot,* the Israelis themselves are keenly aware that it is the problem of the individual Jew that Zionism must now solve. For, in the final analysis, why was it necessary to solve the Jewish problem? It was to provide the Jews everywhere with the option of living freely, creatively, and decently in a community where they would constitute the majority of the population and where Judaism, consequently, would be the primary, rather than the secondary, civilization. Therefore, unless the people makes proper use of its independence to provide for the needs of its individual members, Zionism will have been in vain.

It is to be expected that individual Jews will seek their personal fulfillment largely through their reactions to Jewish culture. The happiness of the committed Jew has always been bound up with the spiritual welfare of his people; it has never depended on physical well-being alone. Indeed, this very propensity of the Jew for finding sources of personal happiness in the cultural experiences he shares with his fellow Jews is part of his cultural heritage.

Having abandoned the Orthodox way of life, large segments of Israel Jewry must now create new patterns of thought and behavior which will lift their lives above the level of monotonous routine. Indeed, the process of exploring the pathways of Jewish tradition that is occupying the attention of many sensitive Jews in Israel is a search of these new patterns. The personal happiness of Israel's Jews depends upon their creating for themselves a new *havai,* or atmosphere, as they call it.

Accomplishing this is one of the objectives set by proponents of *halutziyut*. It was not enough for the *halutzim*
to conduct social experiments in the economic field. They
intended to found a Jewish society; necessarily, they had
to relate their way of life to the Jewish tradition. But the
tradition had to be divested of every element of supernaturalism before it could suit the naturalist-minded men
and women who had rebelled against the orthodoxy of their
parents. This was more easily said than done, for the elements of tradition, particularly ritual, minus a satisfying
rationale, are like an empty shell. This is exactly what the
non-Orthodox *halutzim* have discovered to be the case with
such occasions as the Sabbath, the High Holy Days, the
Festivals, and with such rituals as the ceremonial lighting
of candles and the traditional marriage ceremony. They have
found that the Sabbath simply as a day of rest fails to provide the spiritual satisfaction of the traditional Sabbath, and
that the High Holy Days, shorn of the acknowledgment of
sin, lose considerable meaning. How can the old traditions
be given new dimensions?

For they must be given new meaning. Here and there it
may be possible to abrogate tradition altogether and replace
it by something borrowed or something new. But no people
can afford to throw out all it has inherited. The problem is
well stated by N. Benari:

> It is very much a question how we ought to celebrate
> it (Rosh Hashanah, New Year). . . . We cannot evade
> the issue and say, "Let us allow these days to go naked
> without any kind of clothing whatever." For such days
> as the New Year and Day of Atonement cannot be
> abolished; if we cannot find a positive content of our
> own for them, they will revert to their old form. Many
> of us will turn into "repentant sinners" and begin to
> long for the synagogue, for the prayers that used to be

recited a generation ago. And if some of us do begin to go to synagogue, it will not be on account of an inner belief in religion, but solely as a result of yearnings after the past. That is why something has to be done about these days. Days which are such historic occasions cannot be allowed to pass out of existence without our giving them a content of their own.[11]

It is more than a nostalgia for the past that disturbs the non-Orthodox Jews of Israel; even the native-born *sabra* is beginning to grope for a deepening of the cultural life in which he has been educated. For him there is no question of returning to "the synagogue that was." Not having experienced the synagogue he can look at it objectively. In recent years youth journals in Israel have carried articles in which the younger generation has frankly expressed a yearning for some of the traditional forms—not for traditional prayer, to be sure, but for an adequate substitute. Benari has described what occurs on the Festival of Sukkot. "We have seen," he says, "how the children in our settlements delight in putting up the tabernacles on Sukkot. They sense the lack of ceremonial symbolism far more than we do; and so acutely do they feel this void that they seek a means of filling it."[12] Old-time settlers in the agricultural colonies have frequently been astounded by the interest exhibited by the youth born in the communes in the religious life of the grandparents. (Many "nonreligious" collectives have provided special facilities, such as a kosher kitchen and a synagogue, for the Orthodox parents of members.) Yet the astonishment comes from lack of introspection, for these same old-timers have long been searching for an answer to their own yearning for significant forms of observance: "We have passed from a period entirely devoid of festivals and of set forms in our way of life to one of searching for a path."

Inevitably, the *Sturm and Drang* of any generation in

transition evokes experiments in thought and action. This is so in Israel today, with action, as it so often does, preceding theory. The "secularist" Jews have come a long way from their early revolt against tradition. In the first years of some of the *kvutzot,* it was a matter of bitter controversy as to whether white cloths should be placed over the drab tables of the dining hall on Sabbath eve. Many *halutzim* considered such a step a compromise of their absolute rejection of the traditional Sabbath. From that kind of total rejection to the current earnest search for *havai* there is a long road, a road which has already taken more than a generation to traverse.

What kind of action did the *halutzim* take? They tried to abstract from the tradition all those observances which could be rationalized in accordance with their nationalism, their socialist ethic, and their naturalism. In commenting on the observance of Shavuot, the day on which the tradition calls for remembering the revelation on Mt. Sinai, Benari says, "Nazism reminds us that its hatred of us is not only due to the fact that we are Jews living our life in a special way, but chiefly to our having given morality to the world. And we still uphold that morality in its new guise of socialism. That is why fitting expression should be given to the revelation on Mt. Sinai. This theme should be raised to the level of a symbolic concept that should educate us and encourage us in our new life." Benari is far ahead of many of his fellow *halutzim* in regard to the historical association of Shavuot, but what he recommends here has been accomplished remarkably well in the observance of Passover.

The Passover holiday, connected as it is with the dramatic story of the Israelites' liberation from bondage in Egypt, lends itself easily to reinterpretation in a naturalist and nationalist setting. All the nontraditionalist *kvutzot* have invested the holiday with great significance. The *seder* has become the highpoint of the year in many *kvutzot*. Talented members of the *kvutzot* have written new *haggadot*, culling from traditional sources and from many others relevant to the meaning of freedom, the resurgent nationalism of the Jewish people and the Jewish plight in modern times. All this has come about with no undue intellectualism. Only now, after several decades of experience with the new *haggadot*, questions are being asked about the thought that ought to be universally conveyed and about the advisability of finding a more unified pattern for all the new texts.

In contrast, the High Holy Days have proved a stumbling block. Freedom is easily reinterpreted naturalistically; not so the conceptions of God's kingship and man's sense of sin which are among the central ideas of Rosh Hashanah and Yom Kippur. Hence in many communes the observance of these days, despite Benari's assertion of the need for "clothing" them with decent attire, lacks cultural or spiritual depth. Annual meetings and election of officers are scarcely fit substitutes for the soul searching and genuine reflection on man's limitations and possibilities for growth which are among the themes of the traditional synagogue service. Benari's own suggestions for fitting ceremonials are scarcely calculated to fill the need of spiritualizing Rosh Hashanah, although his comments on Yom Kippur are worth careful consideration. About Rosh Hashanah, he says:

> I can see the possibility of our taking over some of the traditional features of the holiday . . . such as the sounding of the ram's horn, in its ancient connotation of the liberation of slaves. There should also be an appropriate ceremonial gathering. In some places the practice has been instituted of starting annual meetings on New Year's Day. Perhaps this practice ought to be improved upon and its form subjected to change.

> In place of the reading of reports there should be a symbolic ceremony accompanied by an exhibition. Social problems should occupy pride of place in the discussions. But that in itself is still not enough. There should be an artistic opening ceremony with a choir and readings of passages from literature, old and new; and we ought to transcend the local framework and consider the nation as a whole.

The whole proposal smacks of artificiality.

Benari's proposals concerning Yom Kippur deserve extended quotation because they reflect accurately the sincerity of those nontraditionalist Jews who are seeking to capture the spirit of Jewish life and to embody it in an appropriate ritual. The difficulty of this whole enterprise is also readily apparent—not only of creating inspiring ritual, but of overcoming the ideological barriers standing in the way of consistent reinterpretation of the tradition.

> The Day of Atonement was once the greatest of public holidays. Naturally, we cannot go back to those far-off times*; but something of that feeling should be instilled in us on that day. It should be the Sabbath of Sabbaths, a day of communion with the great ideals contained in the teachings of social ethics of all generations. There are ideals that we imbibe from the past, and many new ones have been evolved in our day. There are classic passages from literature that ought to be brought before the community on the Day of Atonement. It is no abstraction to demand that a special day be set aside on which the community as a whole should be plunged into a general atmosphere of poetry and the recitation of chosen passages from our own and world literature dealing with the theme

---

*Note how completely Benari ignores the Orthodox observance which is still, after all, the way of life of a good segment of the Jews in Israel. The traditional way, to him, is a thing of the past.

of the betterment of mankind. We ought to revive emotions of this kind, both for the individual and for the community, at least once a year. The most appropriate day would be the Day of Atonement. After all, we embarked on the task of drawing up a Passover *Haggadah,* and were not alarmed by it. Nor should we be frightened to try and compile a *mahzor* (prayer book for Jewish festivals) for public recitation on other festivals. It is something vitally necessary. With us it is not the liturgical poetry of Rabbi Elazar Hakkallir that counts. There is a rich field of Hebrew and world literature, and suitable passages could be selected. At times recitations accompanied by song can rise to very lofty heights which are in essence not inferior to public worship.

Benari writes in the spirit of traditional Judaism in stressing the universal message of Yom Kippur, and he is far closer to the truth than he realizes when he draws a parallel between formal public worship and his own ceremony of readings from great literature. A modernist in religion conceives a prayer entirely in terms of its effect on the worshiper. He does not expect his words to influence the operations of the universe through any magic effect. Nor does he direct his prayers to any conscious Being outside himself. The object of his prayers (of which meditative readings are one form) is his own inner self, the hidden conscience, the source of his ethical will, which requires constant reassurance and stimulation. What Benari suggests is, in this interpretation, actually public worship—and some day it may be recognized as such.

The Sabbath, which has been the crown of Jewish life, the "queen" of the Hebrew poets, has naturally been the subject of much discussion and experimentation. In the journals of the *kvutzot* there is a continuous forum on the problem of creating *havai* on the Sabbath. Articles abound touching the minutest details of ceremonial, such as the arrangement of the dining hall, the type of songs to be sung, and the manner of dividing necessary work so as to enable all to share the joy of communal ceremonies. And there are ideological discussions of the meaning of the Sabbath and its reinterpretation from a naturalistic standpoint. They all lead to the same questions: How can the Sabbath be observed so that it becomes more than a day of rest? What can be done to recapture for the present generation some of the spiritual joy of the traditional Sabbath? How can the modern Jew acquire the "oversoul" that suffused the Jew of old on the Sabbath?

In assessing the results of the process of adjusting the tradition to a new universe of discourse, the student of religion in Israel must acknowledge the uniqueness of the Jewish religious situation there. In Israel group religion is more fully developed than it is in any other Jewish community. One need not accept the ideology of the Marxist Mapam to agree with this appraisal by Zeev Bloch:

> For what were the holidays in the Diaspora? They were the negation of daily existence there. On Sabbaths and festivals the Jew was a king. He forgot the bonds of actual existence and felt a free man; for the festivals were associated in his mind with the period when he really was free. There was a desire to make the holidays shed some of their lustre upon everyday life. We, on the other hand, are shedding the lustre of everyday life upon the holidays. Our holidays are a summing up; of the six weekly days of labor and of our epoch. They are the culmination of a reality into which we are plunging ourselves wholeheartedly.[12]

Bloch is correct in seeing Jewish holidays as intimately connected with the daily life of Israel's Jews. There is an

organic connection between the holidays and the total economic, social, and national existence of the Jews in Israel
that is not to be found in any other Jewish community.

But Bloch ignores the reality which has now overtaken
Israel Jews. That reality is the necessity for a society to
reckon with the response of its members to the group culture.
If the culture fails to meet individual needs, members of
the group will make every effort to adjust it to their own
philosophies of life. Israel Jews have not yet succeeded in
formulating a rationale on the basis of which they can
adapt the Jewish tradition to their deepest spiritual needs.
But they are engaged in the search.

It is because of the organic relationship between Jewish
religion and Israel's total institutional setup that the doctrinal basis of religion in Israel departs from the academic
and involves practical, political considerations. Orthodoxy,
even in a liberal form, would drastically alter the present
democratic cast of the State in the direction of theocracy.
Law would be subject to emendation by interpretation; only
in extreme cases would abrogation be resorted to.

Illustrative of the ramifications of the Orthodox conception of law is the thinking of two Orthodox leaders, one
regarded as a liberal and one representative of a more traditional Orthodoxy, as expressed in their writings, widely
published in Israel. One of the arguments of Yeshaya Leibowitz, the "liberal," is that modern technology can be a
valuable ally of the Sabbath.

> The religious community need not regard science and
> technology as the enemies of the Sabbath. Rather they
> must be regarded as the most efficient means to facilitate
> its observance. At no time in history was the Sabbath

completely in harmony with current processes of production; and precisely in ancient days its introduction was something of a heroic revolt against the social and technological regime then obtaining. As long as the physical powers of man and beast were the only means by which men could satisfy their needs, and their entire existence was one unceasing, desperate endeavor to achieve this object, renunciation of a seventh part of productive capacity required an immense effort and constituted an incalculable sacrifice. . . . The penetration of applied science into society in recent generations has been responsible for a vast diminution of the importance of human labor in production. . . . Not the slightest doubt exists that all problems of Sabbath observance with which the mechanic and technician are faced can be solved by modern technology, provided a sincere attempt is made to achieve such a solution.[13]

Probably all the non-Orthodox sections of the population would go along with Leibowitz in trying to make the cessation of work on the Sabbath as nearly complete as possible. There might be some dispute over which activities were indispensable, but a plan that would enable as many Jews as possible to enjoy the Sabbath with their families would be supported even by the non-Orthodox.

Leibowitz has developed the theory that the constitution of *halakhah* is such as to embrace all eventualities in some detail. He has extended his theory to include activities which, he claims, could not have been foretold in traditional *halakhah*. He urges that these activities—such as the feeding of furnaces for industries which require perpetual firing, sailoring, the sending of urgent diplomatic messages by wireless, etc.—be decreed as permissible for observant Jews on the Sabbath. He denounces the rabbinate for having failed to take this step forthrightly and courageously, charging that

its reluctance to do so makes hypocrites of all Orthodox
Jews, since they benefit from the performance of essential
functions, which they consider forbidden acts. Leibowitz declares that "organized religious Judaism consciously abandoned the Sabbath for the State and the people in favor
of a Sabbath for a sect of Sabbath-observers amidst a people
of Sabbath violators, through whose work on the Sabbath
the former's needs are met."[14]

Although regarded as a liberal Leibowitz is among those
who still think it is possible to preserve traditional *halakhah*
within the framework of a democratic state. His liberalism
emerges from his recognition that *halakhah* for the most part
could not have anticipated future conditions and was therefore not intended "to order the realistic conditions of Jewish political independence in an historical present."[15] Rather
did it "view this reality as merely a phase and an expression
of an ideal world—of a distant past hidden in the clouds of
imagination or of an undefined future. The possibility of this
reality in the framework of a realistic world of the present
did not occur to it."[16] *Halakhah* must measure up to the
demands of the present if it is to prove its worth. Leibowitz
is impatient with the procrastination of those who are reluctant to make any change unless some precedent can be
found for it in tradition. He understands that such an attitude toward law cannot but fail to meet the challenge of a
fast-changing world.

Yet even Leibowitz places a definite limitation on the
extent to which *halakhah* can prove malleable. The Torah,
for him, is "given, primarily and eternally, for which all
Jewish history serves as a changing framework."[17] In contrast to this view of Torah is the standpoint of the "secularists," for whom the primary fact is historical and national
reality, of which Torah is only one manifestation. It is hard

to understand how Leibowitz can on the one hand make the Torah and its *halakhic* traditions central, and on the other hand call for legislation which would take its point of departure from the needs of the present rather than the principles of Rabbinic law.

As a matter of fact, it is chiefly on this straddling of the issue that Leibowitz has been most severely taken to task. He has been branded as a "reformer," as not really devoted to *halakhah*. In a spirited defense of the rabbinate and of *halakhah* itself, Moshe Zvi Neriah, head of the B'nai Akivah Academy in Kfar Haroeh, accuses Leibowitz of having departed from "the divinely revealed basis of the Written Law and the divine inspiration of the Oral Law."[18] Consequently, writes Neriah, there is really no need at all, in Leibowitz's system, for *halakhah*. Neriah goes on to point out that it is not the rabbinate who are at fault but the secularists, who not only refuse to accept the principles of strict *halakhah* but who have no intention of confining their activities to the bounds set by even a liberal program of interpretation. He draws an illustration from the running of the Foreign Office. Neriah admits the necessity of maintaining full-time services; no one, after all, can predict international emergencies. But if a religious foreign minister were in charge, he would, for example, establish a policy that no message should be sent on the Sabbath unless a matter of life and death for the State was involved. Since present policy sets no such limitation, religious Jews are automatically prohibited from working on the Sabbath in the Foreign Office in any capacity.

The theoretical issue between Leibowitz and Neriah is not hard to define. They are not really quarreling over the elasticity of the *halakhah,* for both think it is adequate to meet the needs of the day. Neriah wants a prior commitment to *halakhah* by the overwhelming majority of citizens before the rabbinate decrees the necessary changes, while Leibowitz believes that religious leaders should take the initiative.

Neither these men nor the thousands of Orthodox Jews of all varieties who stand on the concept of Torah-true Judaism have seriously raised the question as to whether or not the *halakhic* system can be applied to a modern state which accepts democracy. We have seen above that there may be various approaches to democracy. It is questionable whether any political democracy can persist in which the people lack final authority. Under *halakhah*, such authority would be vested in experts in traditional law, and changes in law by amendment or abrogation would be precluded by the assumption that the law is perfect and requires only reinterpretation in order to be adapted to changing conditions. According to Neriah, "Religion does not depend on the opinions of the society or the feelings of youth. . . . Rather is its function to direct communal opinion and to educate the young. Woe to that religion which is directed by the community or which develops according to the views of the young."[19] In other words, "religion," in which Neriah includes *halakhah*, is in a realm apart from democratic considerations. It is intrinsically authoritarian. Neriah's viewpoint is clear and consistent, which is more than can be said for Leibowitz's suggestions, which give an unmistakable impression of emanating from a democratic personality who finds it hard to break away from the bonds of tradition. One can sympathize with the plight of enlightened Orthodoxy, but the problem cannot be solved, in Israel, any more than in the democratic Diaspora, by holding on to both horns of the dilemma. There are certain definite consequences that follow from accepting a democratic system and the democratic spirit for the conduct of a modern state, and one is that theocratically oriented law must be revolutionized. It is no accident that the Orthodox movements are political parties, as well as religious sects.

But the Orthodox will not readily abandon *halakhah* in so far as it applies to civil law. Their religious doctrines are all-embracing, and they must, if they are true to their beliefs, apply them consistently. The trial of some army personnel who were brought up on charges by the Chief Chaplain for having eaten leavened bread during Passover gives us an inkling of the kind of legislation which could and probably would be developed in an Orthodox Jewish state.

The non-Orthodox parties are organized primarily for political purposes, but the religious overtones are unmistakable. Mapam is far from neutral in its religious attitudes, being avowedly atheistic and desirous of eliminating ecclesiasticism from Jewish life. In a positive vein, however, Mapam and all other left-wing parties seek to rework the tradition so that it can function as an ideological influence in the life of the people. None of the non-Orthodox parties, however, is bothered by the problem of *halakhah,* since they have all accepted representative government. For them, *halakhic* regulations are only one of many sources from which they draw in legislating for modern Israel.

7

Considering the importance of religion to Jewish life, there has been a remarkable paucity of theological and religio-philosophical deliberation in Israel. Until a few years ago there had been practically none; in recent years there have been a few noteworthy contributions, but in the main these have been made by thinkers, like Julius Gutmann, Martin Buber, and Hugo Bergmann, who have been continuing work that had germinated in Germany and other European countries. In his years in Israel, Buber has indeed developed his religious sociology of the Jewish people, to say nothing of deepening his conception of the encounter between man and God. His prolific and profound writing has brought him international renown. Yet he has failed signally to influence the Israelis. His religious philosophy is scarcely pondered beyond the circle of his students, except for his ethical views as a leader in the Ihud group. And in that capacity he has met with vigorous opposition. Yet Buber should have appealed to many people in Israel. He is non-Orthodox, being far removed from a traditionalist position in ritual. His vigorous championing of subjective integrity in religon should have won him a much wider hearing, if not, indeed, a larger group of disciples. Yet he has not captured the imagination of the Jewish community of Israel.

There are, I believe, two basic reasons for Buber's strange role in Israel—strange, that is, when contrasted with his world-wide fame. The first is his highly subjective metaphysics. The I-Thou relationship requires a tremendous leap beyond possibilities of verification. I cite just one example among many that could be culled from Buber's writings: "The person who makes a decision knows that his deciding is no self-delusion; the person who has acted knows that he was and is in the hand of God. The unity of the contraries is the mystery at the innermost core of the dialogue."[20] The question, to which Buber supplies no satisfactory answer, is how one knows when one is confronted with God. Conscience has played many tricks in the history of religion. However dissatisfied many Israelis are with traditional religious conceptions, they are equally opposed to the subjectivism of Buber.

Perhaps more important as an explanation of his lack of

influence on the Israelis is Buber's very liberalism in matters of ritual and folkway. The opponents of Orthodoxy abhor the rigidity and the authoritarianism of the Orthodox in these matters, but they are at one with the latter in making their point of departure the practices and customs of Jewish group life. Neither the Orthodox nor the non-Orthodox can sympathize with Buber when he speaks of his philosophy as dealing with "the faith of Judaism," and not with the religion of Israel. He employs "religion" to denote "cult, ritual and moral-religious standards,"[21] while "faith" refers to the way in which the image of God grows among men. In spite of Buber's great concern with Jewish peoplehood, in spite of his recognition of its need for social forms and institutions, he starts his religious philosophy from a metaphysical jumping-off point that fails to attract men and women who want to base the forms of their life on rational motivation and who seek new forms to fit an essentially naturalistic, if still incoherent, conception of the universe.

The theological and philosophical speculation that does take place in Israel shows the impact of Orthodoxy on liberal thinkers. That impact is manifest in their inability to conceive of religion in terms of the naturalistic position which is their basic philosophy in other areas of life. A number of writers for *B'terem*, an influential serious-minded Israel journal (which in the past few years has had an article on problems of religion in almost every issue) demonstrate what seems to be generally characteristic of Israel's thinking on religion.

Menaham Haran finds that our generation is living without God, and consequently without religion—certainly without meaningful religion. As he states, all Jewish customs and practices which have been stamped with the religious seal, "stand upon the fundamental faith that God watches over the world, that He chose Israel to be a special bearer of His influence and that, therefore, He placed upon it special duties and restrictions. If you uproot from the latter this basic faith, they become both superfluous and meaningless."[22] This assumption that the Jewish way of life stands or falls on certain theological dogmas, such as God's providence and the election of Israel, is characteristic of the Orthodox defense of tradition. Haran remains close to the Orthodox position also in declaring, "As long as customs are secular, they belong to the category of the voluntary; from the moment they become sanctified by religion, they become decrees."[23] Choice, pluralism, voluntarism—these, for Orthodoxy, are irreligious attitudes. Religion alone, says Haran, can provide the soul-satisfying answers that men seek to life's problems, but his conception of religion is absolutistic.

Yet Orthodoxy does not satisfy Haran:

> We of the modern epoch are largely a generation without God. The God in whose existence our ancestors believed and before whom they walked is no more. At most, His hold over us lasts till adolescence. It is a fact that we do not even seek Him, not primarily because it is comfortable for us without Him, but mainly because it is not possible, with our own resources alone, to escape the encirclement of skepticism. Of might it be that our period marks a return to the fundamental *Weltanschauung* of idolatry, which sees in the cosmos only blind laws and eternal forces, laws and forces to which the gods themselves are bound? But even if this be so—it would apparently be a case of idolatry without any gods.[24]

Haran's position is that of a thinker who has lost his ancestral faith but who feels that this faith which he can no longer accept is the only one worth having. Call it part of the "failure of nerve," the sense of cosmic loneliness, the ex-

istential situation, or what you will—thinkers of this type
find it difficult to accept the possibility of there being room
within the purview of religion for tentative judgments, for
beliefs not founded on faith in supernatural intervention in
nature and the affairs of men, and for voluntarism in ritual.
It is difficult to analyze why men like Haran, who are
too sophisticated intellectually to accept Orthodoxy, cannot think their way through to a naturalistically oriented
position. I suggest above that, in a sense, they may never
have left Orthodoxy. It may be that they are driven by an
urge for certainty but are too intellectually honest to accept
the Orthodox position. Or perhaps they are prone to think
in rigid categories. Religion, by definition, must begin "with
theological axioms and cannot end with them."[25] Therefore, a reasoned religion is an intellectual impossibility.

Whatever the explanation may be, it is clear that this
non-Orthodox position can serve only a critical function.
It cannot, of itself, contribute to a positive philosophy of
religion that can serve to inspire the large number of non-
Orthodox Jews in Israel. That philosophy will be formulated only when a more objective appreciation of the nature
of religion as a human, and not merely a Jewish, phenomenon has been reached. For the present, at least, the folk
aspects of contemporary Jewish religion are evolving and
are occupying the attention of the Israelis. When a folk
"style" has been achieved, perhaps in keeping with the
halutziyut approach, the Israelis will begin to delve more
deeply into the meaning of their group life and into the
problems of human destiny that have engaged the humble
and the great of all generations. Then there may arise religious geniuses who will not only criticize the general lack
of philosophical depth, but who will release the pent-up
religious energies of the Israel adventure.

8

Nowhere can the treatment of religion by Israelis be better observed than in their approach to worship. We have already noted Benari's "secularist" substitute for Bible reading before Friday night supper. But even those who still want to preserve the formal worship of the synagogue fail to understand the tremendous problems that stand in the way of revitalizing the prayer service.

Israel synagogues, while frequently crowded, attract only a small portion of the Jewish community. The service, barring a few minor variations, is that which is familiar to Orthodox Diaspora Jewry. About the only change which is urged among Orthodox leaders is an increase of decorum. Recently, however, there have been other voices calling for some reform of the service. Jacob Hertz, in the course of his remarks on the need for religious reform, makes the radical suggestion (for Israel religionists) that "if prayers do not express the feelings of the worshiper, what can we expect of him? How can we expect, for example, that the idea of good and bad angels traveling back and forth in the world will be acceptable to the mind of our youths? And another question which I dare to raise: Are there still many among us who pray honestly for the return of the sacrificial system?"[26] Hertz goes on to urge the revision of the prayers to fit the needs of the present generation. He does this while calling for changes in other practices, such as the abolition of the *Sefirah* period and its restrictions, the addition to Tisheah Beav of the experiences of the past two decades, and the abandonment of the idea of rebuilding the Temple until our form of worship becomes so universal in character that the rebuilt Temple could indeed become "a house of worship for all peoples." This last suggestion indicates how far-reaching Hertz's revision of the service is intended to be. Despite this radicalism—these remarks are radical for anyone like Hertz, who belongs to the religious moshav, Sdeh Yaakov —his whole approach is vitiated by his failure to see the total context in which reform in worship can alone take place. Elsewhere in his essay Hertz states, "On Sabbath and holidays, we cannot consider the convenience of the community. Rather must the community be educated to observe properly both Sabbaths and holidays."[27] Hertz is opposed to compulsion, but he would divest these days of any secular activity like sports. How this is to be accomplished without compulsion he does not say. What he implies, therefore, is that the reform of worship can take place only in a community which accepts Orthodox standards *as a point of departure*. For this reason he urges the Orthodox kibbutzim to take the lead in transforming the service, although reluctantly he admits that they, too, seem to hesitate. What is lacking in Hertz's presentation is an explanation of how it is possible for the Orthodox to remain Orthodox and at the same time introduce basic reforms into their ritual practices and form of worship.

A more philosophical treatment is accorded worship by J. L. Benor. "According to our concept, the infinite God requires no prayers from us. Prayer for us is not an end, but a means, and not a means to propitiate God but to satisfy the demands of our religious sensitivity, when there are such demands—with the condition that it must not be compulsory."[28] Since men differ in their religious feelings in terms of experience and intellectual capacities, and since different hours are available to them for daily worship, they cannot be satisfied by a single form of service, held at regular times. They can, in fact, find spiritual satisfaction in an Orthodox, even a Hassidic synagogue—or in no synagogue at all. Benor states that what is needed is a synagogue service that can "arouse feelings of awe and esthetic beauty . . . and involve the worshiper in a fashion that gives him an opportunity of self-satisfaction."[29]

On the basis of this attitude, Benor makes the following suggestions. First, the service should be elastic. Second, the synagogue building should be beautiful, capable of evoking a worshipful mood. Third, the service should be orderly. Fourth, he recommends changes in the prayers themselves; all Aramaic passages should be eliminated or translated into Hebrew, repetitions should be eliminated, prayers for the sacrificial system should be shortened or dropped. Fifth, community singing should be encouraged. Sixth, additional music, even by non-Jewish composers, should be included, with accompaniment (using records, if necessary). Seventh, short sermons should be preached. Eighth, children's services should be organized.

Undoubtedly, there is merit to Benor's specific recommendations. They would, in all likelihood, make it possible for many more Israel Jews to attend the synagogue. Whether one can cure so simply the spiritual malaise of a generation that has largely lost the power to pray is another question. Benor never pursues the alternative which he mentions, namely that for the religious person (as he understands him) a synagogue may not even be needed. I question whether a synagogue of the type outlined by Benor could, under existing conditions in Israel, become more than a curiosity. And what about the prayers themselves? After describing the need for cultivating spiritual sensitivity, the best that Benor can contribute is a shortened service. Are not the contents as well as the length of the prayers of the essence? It is surprising that a reformer like Benor still thinks of the service in Orthodox terms.

Other writers have stressed the individual and subjective nature of prayer and have tried to show the need for encouraging individual self-expression. Just how this is to be developed—where and when, and on the basis of what criteria—is never touched upon. Worship in Israel is very much in a state of distress.* For even the most minute experimental changes are still in the stage of scattered comment and discussion; there is hardly anything being done to bring about reform in practice. Perhaps the most vital steps forward are being taken by the Hebrew poets who have put into verse the feelings and aspirations which may some day form the liturgy of a revised Israel service.

Despite the apparent paucity of profound religious thinking and courageous efforts at change, the situation of religion in Israel is potentially more fertile than almost anywhere else in the world. In Israel we are witnessing a new stage in the evolution of Jewish religion, one which I would call a naturalist stage. To my mind there is no more exciting adventure of the human spirit than the effort of Jews in Israel to spiritualize their group life without compromising their conviction that there may be no conscious force outside of nature upon whom their fate rests. They may, as l believe, overestimate the extent of their independence of religion, but that can be historically explained. It is to be hoped that wisdom will bring about greater insight into the nature of religion so that some of the creativity now coming to the surface may help shape the future of Jewish religion in Israel.

---

*Shortly after this passage was written, a small group of pioneers established a non-Orthodox synagogue in Haifa. It is too early to predict the impact of this group, but this may well be the first serious step in the organization of non-Orthodox Jewish religion in Israel.

The success of the whole venture will depend in large measure on the ability of the Jewish community in Israel to conceive of the Jewish people as transcending the State of Israel and as possessing the ability to enrich the life of the individual Jew without recourse to coercive power of any kind. Jewish religion is primarily a group concern, but unless the group is so constituted as to satisfy the fundamental spiritual needs of its most sensitive members, its religion will have failed in its central purpose. There are many sensitive souls in Israel, and in their grappling with the problems of Jewish life they may well fashion a Jewish religion that will once again exercise a profound influence upon world civilization. However, if we judge correctly the desire of mankind for religious freedom, it may be asserted with confidence that Israel cannot long afford to temporize with religious authoritarianism by perpetuating the official connection between the Orthodox rabbinate and the state. That tie between the religious Right and the secular government is the key issue in a war which is already being waged on a small scale. But the major battles lie ahead. Whether or not Israel will benefit from the outcome remains to be seen.

7

JEWISH RELIGION IN THE UNITED STATES

THE CENTRAL PROBLEM FACING JEWISH religion in America is the creation of a community to sustain it and to fructify it. In saying this I do not lose sight of the fact that the main function of any religion is to raise the sights of man to the heavens of spirituality. Religion should direct the mind of man to those values essential for world peace and social justice. Through Jewish religion Jews should learn to live their lives in accordance with the prayer found in the morning service of the traditional prayer book, "At all times let a man revere God in private as in public, acknowledge the truth, and speak the truth in his heart." To speak, then, of community organization as a "central problem" in religion might seem to substitute a secular interest for a religious one. But in the light of the foregoing discussion, the reader should understand what this remark implies. Jewish religion can hardly function or survive without a living body. Conceptions of Jewish religion and Jewish religious doctrines can be preserved in other cultures or in the pages of reference books, but the religion of the Jewish people can exist only in a living community.

Up to the present time the term Jewish community has been loosely used to refer to the activities of the myriads of Jewish organizations which have cropped up during the three hundred years Jews have lived in the United States. The frequent references to the "Jewish community" in sermons, newspapers, magazines, and books create the impression that a well integrated organization of Jews, satisfying all their social, cultural, and welfare needs, functions on the American scene. Nothing could be further from the truth. Not a single effort of the several that have been made has succeeded in drawing Jews of all shades of opinion into a united community organization.

There are some American Jews who consider the "over-organized anarchy" that prevails among Jewish organizations to be desirable. They contend that the free environment of the United States should not be the scene of organized minority groups because these might tend to become "cultural ghettos." They assert further that any attempt to organize a Jewish community would inhibit the free functioning of individual Jews and Jewish groups whose thinking did not accord with the "official" policy of an organized community. This view, however well-intentioned, not only is illogical but exhibits a lack of faith in the democratic potentialities of Judaism, of the Jewish people, and of American civilization.

1

There is no point in discussing American Jewish religion as if it could grow in a vacuum. Jewish religion in this country has become what it is largely as a result of the pressures of the American environment, and if plans are to be drawn up for its future development they must take into account the climate of American life.

A century and a half of American independence had passed before anyone articulated a fact of American life that has steadily been becoming one of the ideals of democracy—the fact of the pluralistic make-up of American society. Horace Kallen, who has been the leading philosopher of cultural pluralism, speaks of our culture as an "orchestration" of the various traditions brought here by generations of immigrants. The American people is compared to an orchestra composed of many members, each playing a different instrument; the resulting music is a harmonious blending of the sounds of all the various instruments. To understand the importance of cultural pluralism, one must realize that until its articulation the dominant interpretation of American life was that of the "melting pot." According to this theory, America was composed of many different cultures, all of which were expected to amalgamate into a new alloy, Americanism, losing their individuality in the process. Kallen's hope has been to see a society develop in which the contributors to its culture would retain whatever distinctiveness was compatible with the welfare of all the citizens and was inherently worthwhile. The growth of this kind of society calls for free cultural exchange among people who respect each other's differences and who are prepared to sacrifice the security of a cultural ghetto for the more hazardous but more spiritually satisfying arena of inter-cultural challenge. Neither cultural totalitarianism nor iso-lationism is compatible with cultural pluralism.

Not all pluralism, however, is compatible with American democracy. No proponent of cultural pluralism envisages a duplication, on the American scene, of the kind of national minority status which plagued Eastern Europe. No one wants, for the sake of pluralism, to perpetuate here a variety of rival nationalisms. Whatever ethnic or religious cultures are encouraged, in the American scheme of things, must be supplementary to the common American experience of all. After this is said, however, it is still a problem of some magnitude to define the exact character of the supplementary cultural groups.

A good beginning to such an analysis has been made by W. Lloyd Warner and Leo Srole in their study of the ethnic groups in a small New England community. Their findings indicate that immigrant ethnic groups, whether stemming from countries in which their own nationalities had domi-nant political status (the French, Poles, etc.) or from coun-tries where they had no formal position (the Jews), would upon "moving into Yankee City and finding themselves . . . a minority . . . turn to re-create that church which in other times and circumstances had served to keep alive the na-tional group identity. With certain significant exceptions, each established a church following a pattern which had served it for hundreds of years as its first formal institution in Yankee City. The church was the first line of defense behind which these immigrants could organize themselves and with which they could preserve their group, i.e., system, identity."[1] Thus the Irish would organize a Catholic church, the Greeks a Greek Orthodox church, the Jews a synagogue, and the Norwegians a Lutheran church.

It was not the sole purpose of the founders of these religious institutions to establish houses of worship. They had broader interests which encompassed the cultural values of their ethnic heritage.

> "Since . . . the church subsystem is the repository of the sacred values as well as of the national attitudes of the original society, and since these were assertive aspects of the ethnic personality, it was inevitable that the first formally organized structure of the ethnic community system in Yankee City should be the church. . . . Subsequent structures which appeared in the community system reflected the fact that the changing personalities in the group were mixtures of ethnic and American elements. These later structures, for example, the association, had no direct antecedents in the society of the homeland. The church structure alone linked the community with the national social system. The association and schools which later emerged in the ethnic community were structural fences newly contrived to keep the ethnic individual articulated to the church and the community while keeping him from straying too far out into the Yankee City social system."[2]

The church, then, helped preserve ethnic characteristics; in order to accomplish this objective, it had to become more than a house of worship.

The work of Warner and Srole documents the organic relation that exists between religions and ethnic groups. The best-known example, of course, is the Catholic group, many of whom are organized in ethnic churches. The Irish, the Italians, and the French Canadians, all have their own communities centered in a Catholic church. In each case, the particular variety of Catholicism possesses certain unique values associated solely with the national life of the ethnic groups.

That the strongest religious units in the United States are those with an ethnic basis is a valuable hint to anyone interested in religious survival. Considerable further study would be needed before any firm conclusions could be drawn. However, it would seem to follow from the picture painted by Warner and Srole that a religion which seeks to survive must establish some sort of community life transcending sacrament and worship. There is no evidence that a purely secular ethnic group has much chance for survival in the United States; nor does it appear that the urge to continue ethnic traditions beyond a generation or two is a compelling motive, unless those traditions are associated with religious ideals and practices. It should be added that a religious orientation is no guarantee of survival; all that the study has established is that it slows the process of group disintegration. Whether or not the religion itself has survival power is, in my opinion, a matter of creative planning.

In his provocative study of the religious scene in the United States, Will Herberg[3] combines the melting pot and cultural pluralism theories into a "triple melting pot" theory of American society. It is his view that ethnic distinctions gradually give way through their absorption into the dominant American religious groups—Protestant, Catholic, Jewish. These three historic religions constitute more and more the pluralistic culture of America.

Ethnicism plays a much smaller role in Herberg's view than in that of Warner and Srole, which, as we have seen, held that religion can delay but not prevent ethnic assimilation. What is not made clear in either study, however, and what is vital from the standpoint of our concern for the future of Jewish religion in America is the unique nature of Jewish ethnicism. The Jewish group is *sui generis* in that its ethnic characteristics not only are involved in the group religion but are essential features of it. There are, of course, local habits and folkways which Jews acquired in various European stopping-off places and which they brought with them to the United States. These will probably eventually disappear under the pressure of the American environment. But that which is commonly recognized as Jewish culture by all segments of the Jewish group—the religious folkways and rituals, the Hebrew language as the language of study and of the synagogue, the concern for and participation in the life of Eretz Yisrael—these are sufficiently "different" from the trans-ethnic characteristics of Christianity to continue to mark the Jews as a group apart—as an ethnic as well as religious entity, as religion is understood in the American idiom of Sunday churches. This uniqueness gives American Judaism a better than even chance to survive in America as a minority culture provided that Jewry deals intelligently with the doctrinal issues that confront all American religions in the current scientific atmosphere and with the problem of polity that is inherent in the nature of the Jewish group.

2

The plight of the American churches and of the religions they are designed to teach results from the impact of a free environment. Voluntarism, which often has to be maintained against the will of reactionary religious leadership, subjects the once cohesive traditions of the various immigrant ethnic groups to open criticism and evaluation and to constant comparison with the traditions of others. Under these circumstances, uniformity gives way to variety and ethnic unity either to dissolution or to some conscious effort at reorganization. This is the pattern of American life today, within which Jewish religion must function.

Contrary to popular opinion, the uniformity of the traditional East European Jewish communities had already begun to break down before the large influx of immigrants to this country at the end of the nineteenth century. The myth that all Jews who came to the United States from Eastern Europe were "pious and observant, loyal conformists to the *Shulhan Arukh,* dedicated to Torah and to the service of the Creator" has been exploded by Herbert Parzen.[4] There were, on the contrary, revolutionaries of varying shades, secular territorialists and Zionists, and "enlightened" religionists. The modern Jewish types were already to be found in this country by 1900, and the further atomization of the Jewish community since then has been merely a continuation of a process that had begun with the first exposure of Jews to the Enlightenment. The American Jewish community today consists of almost every conceivable sect, while Judaism has been subject to countless interpretations.

The separation of church and state in America has contributed greatly to highlighting doctrinal, as opposed to group, religion, and has eaten into the very marrow of Jewish religion. A similar, if not identical, challenge, faced the Jews of Western Europe during the Emancipation period. They were then required either to renounce their rights of citizenship or to tear up the national roots of their religion. The Reform movement chose the second alternative. In the United States, the tradition against an established church has forced all the historic religions to place great emphasis on doctrine. Not that the Christian sects have ever abandoned their assumption, however vaguely defined, that American polity and Christian religion are somehow related; for them it is simply a question of how to work Christianity adequately and democratically into the American political framework. Jewish religion in the United States has been affected by this Christian mind-set to a greater degree than most Jews realize. Whereas, in every previous Jewish community, religion was a vital and integrated part of the communal whole, in the United States it is a matter of personal choice. Any effort to bring religion into internal Jewish communal affairs is looked upon as an attempt to impose something on the community—even if that effort is made by a nonsectarian group like the Synagogue Council, in which all varieties of religionists are represented. There is, in other words, a clearly defined tendency in Jewish communal affairs, as there is, in theory, in the wider American community, to confine religion to the house of worship and the home.

On the other hand, the synagogue and the rabbinical associations have done their share to misrepresent the role of religion in Jewish life. Jewish religious leaders, being unwilling to acknowledge that the American synagogue, organizationally, is a copy of the American church rather than of the historic synagogue, have sought to extend the hegemony of their institutions over broad areas of Jewish communal life. But Jewish group religion, being by its very nature bound up with the entire folk, cannot be confined to the four walls of the synagogue. The synagogue of old, unlike the American synagogue, was the Jewish community; the synagogue building was the locale of all community activities. But the various communities were far more uniform doctrinally than is the case today. The pre-Enlightenment Jews may have had differences of opinion, but their behavior followed a set regimen. Religion today, being both in theory and in practice a matter of personal choice, differences of opinion in all religious matters abound. Naturally, then, the "neutral" activities of the Jewish community require a "neutral" agency. Most of the charitable activities of American Jewry are conducted outside the synagogue, though *tzedekah*, or charity, is one of the basic ideals of Jewish religion. It is none the less religious when conducted by a "secular" agency than when sponsored by a synagogue, yet the synagogues, missing the point, have been trying to restore such nonsectarian activities to their original base. Thereby they misdirect their energies. They ought instead to be concentrating on overcoming the needless competition and disunity in their own ranks. Understanding and cooperation—and this does not mean ideological agreement—among the segments of religious Jewry are prerequisites to the ultimate harmonization of religious and secular Jewish interests.

There have been a number of feeble attempts at coordinated action within organized religious Jewry. It is to be hope, of course, that some of these efforts, still under way, will succeed. The Synagogue Council, to take one instance, is still functioning despite the understanding among its constituents that decisions on matters involving religious principles require unanimity. To date it has failed to bring about much in the way of coordination or united action, but its continued existence at least testifies to the fact that the three major religious divisions of American Jewry are still talking to one another. Among the rabbinical bodies, in recent years, there has been talk of unification of the Reform and Conservative associations, and at one point a segment of the Orthodox indicated a willingness to join in the publication of a single professional journal for rabbis of all denominations. Several years ago, the Conservative Rabbinical Assembly voted to invite the Reform and Orthodox clergy to work with them toward the establishment of uniform marriage and divorce procedures for the entire Jewish community. The proposal was never implemented, but the fact that it could have been passed by an important rabbinical association was a straw in the wind. The organization, in May 1955, of the Reconstructionist Fellowship of Congregations, designed to embrace like-minded synagogues in all three divisions, may some day be looked back upon as as a decisive step in the realignment and organizational unification at least of religious Jewry.

I do not propose to give here a history of such efforts. I think it sufficient for our purposes to indicate the issues at stake in all proposals for the unification of religious Jewry. What is possible? What is desirable? And what is wise? These are the key questions. They are frequently undifferentiated in the minds of American Jews. For example, it might be both desirable and wise to have community-wide standards for Jewish marriage and divorce, but it is patently impossible under present circumstances even to hope for such a development. In matters of ritual, it is neither possible, desirable, nor wise to try to impose uniformity.

Any approach to coordination or unification among religious Jews based on a *halakhic* approach is doomed, and rightly so, to failure. I have discussed this matter at some length elsewhere.[5] Here I want to add only that the American democratic tradition will make it impossible for a Jewish community to impose standards—let alone laws—on its members even when these standards are widely accepted. The voluntarism of Jewish life will always enable dissenters to dissociate themselves from the prevailing opinion of the community. As we have seen, in Israel, matters of religious belief and ritual have largely become private concerns. How can we expect an American Jewish community, which possesses no political instruments to exert more of a force for

uniformity than does the State of Israel? Do we, in any case,
want uniformity?

3

The attitude toward the rabbi and the attitude of the
rabbi are crucial for the future of Jewish religion. Whether
in Israel or in the United States, the function of the rabbi
has to be readjusted to reality. The reality of which I speak
is that spiritual religion must be taught; it can never be
imposed. Only when rabbis see themselves as teachers, and
laymen view them in that light shall we have some chance
of building a Jewish religion worthy of its great past.

What would be involved in transforming the role of the
rabbinate into that, essentially, of a specialized group of
educators? First of all, it would remove from the rabbi the
aura of the legislator of values, standards, and practices. A
teacher's job is to stimulate his student to think and act
for himself. He can describe what is done, help students to
evaluate what they experience, and perhaps suggests patterns
of thinking and behavior that may be advantageous to their
growth as persons. A teacher does not dictate behavior. The
main responsibility of a teaching rabbinate would be to set
in motion among the laity forces leading to creativity and
to critical appraisal of the tradition. It seems to me that this
would be a far more worthwhile purpose for rabbis to set for
themselves than the futile attempt to force the "ignorant
layman" into the mold of an ecclesiastically conceived
Jewish life in which he has no vital concern.

It is utter nonsense for religious Jewry to look to the
rabbinate to legislate changes in Jewish religion. Even if
rabbis could agree on the steps to be taken (in itself an
impossibility), the laity would be no less divided than they
are now in their attitude toward rabbinical decisions. Israel

and American Jewry can, and should, learn from each other in regard to the role of the rabbinate as initiators and legislators of ritual or doctrinal change. In Israel, where conditions are ripe for forward steps, and where the charge of a lack of rabbinical authority cannot legitimately be made, there has been not a single noteworthy *halakhic* decision rendered, since the establishment of the State, which would in any way indicate that the rabbinate is aware of the depth of the problem facing *halakhah*. There is a stubborn insistence on maintaining both the possibility of reestablishing the traditional system of Jewish law which covered civil, criminal, and ritual affairs, and the desirability of restoring this essentially theocratic and ecclesiastic manner of legislation. Scant attention is paid to the contradictions between the *halakhic* system and that of democracy to which lip service is given. It may be that the failure of the Israeli rabbinate to pursue more diligently a program of change in *halakhah* is due mainly to their realization that the populace as a whole is not prepared to heed their edicts. The majority of Israel's Jews are no more Orthodox than their brothers elsewhere in the world. Unless the Orthodox are able to gain political control, all the efforts to restore *halakhah* to its former position in Jewish life must fail.

American Jews can expect even less in the way of legislative authority from their own spiritual leaders—less, that is, if they want their rabbis to act as legislators, telling them how to live observant and spiritual Jewish lives. There is not the slightest possibility of the American rabbinate's ever being able to dictate the norms of Jewish life; the very Jews who today urge their rabbis to liberalize Jewish religion would resist any effort of the rabbinate to attempt such dictation. The case of lay people who want action from the rabbis is an example of confusing a noble purpose with a means which has not been properly assessed. The purpose of rendering Jewish religious life meaningful and inspiring is one to which no Jew will take exception, but that purpose would be impossible to achieve were the responsibility to be placed solely in the hands of the rabbinate.

On the other hand, the Israelis, particularly the Orthodox, should learn the lesson of Jewish religion in a democratic political setting. They ought to face squarely the following issues:

1. Is law divine or human? Is the revealed tradition to be taken seriously as God's word or as an effort of our people to interpret the divine in their own experience?
2. Is law, even religious law, to be of and by the people, as well as for them? Should the responsibility rest with the electorate or with a group of experts?
3. Should ritual come within the purview of law, or should it become more and more a matter of personal reaction and creativity? Are people's diets, their manner of spending their days of rest and relaxation, and the way in which they conduct their funerals to be circumscribed by communal law, or should these practices be left, within the limits of health and reason, to the individual?

The experience of American Jewry has, of course, emphasized the human origins of and responsibility for law and the progressive emergence of areas of individual choice. Among the latter is the realm of religious belief and practice. Inevitably, the close tie between Jewish religious beliefs, ritual practice, and law had to be weakened in a democratic state. As a result, the rabbinate can no longer control those areas of life which the Orthodox rabbinate would like to see under their sole aegis. It would seem to me, however, that this is a small price to pay for the freedoms of democracy. The Israelis would do well to understand that the weakness of American rabbis in enforcing their will (or the will of Jewish religion, in whose name they speak) has nothing to do with their abilities; but it has everything to do with the climate of opinion and behavior in a free environment.

As teacher the rabbi would have to overcome the vicious attitude, too prevalent among rabbis, toward the "ignorant layman." The overwhelming majority of American Jews are, it is true, grossly uninformed about many facets of Judaism. This, however, should not disqualify them from having a say about the major issues in Jewish religion. To state, for example, that the expert in *Yoreh Deah* is better qualified to discuss the merits of *kashrut* than the student of anthropology, who may know few of the specifics of *kashrut,* is to miss the fundamental fact that behavior patterns must always be judged on their present relevance and impact. The anthropologist, if he is true to his calling, will want, of course, to hear what the *halakhic* expert has to say, but he has a right to judge the testimony in terms of his own reasoning. The same right is the due of every Jewish layman. This right is the hazard but at the same time the very essence of the democratic method of arriving at truth, or, at least at group decision which tries to approximate truth. The "ignorant layman" is almost always an expert in something, even if it be only in knowledge of himself or his children. It is precisely *his* personality and *his* needs with which Jewish religion is supposed to be concerned. The rabbi, then, in helping to establish a creative relation between the tradition and his congregants, has much to learn from the latter. A teacher who lacked this humility before his students could never hope to succeed.

A good teacher has far fewer answers than he has questions in regard to the mysteries of existence. Most rabbis are too reluctant to admit their spiritual doubts. In religion this is fatal; it can only lead to the kind of smugness and complacency which have driven from the synagogue some of our most sensitive men and women.

None of this precludes the rabbi's courageously assuming other functions, as the necessity arises. He may be called upon to speak forthrightly in behalf of Jewish traditions and values, on which he ought not to compromise. He may have to stand for democratic principles when other members of the community are prepared to knuckle under to authoritarian pressure. He may sometimes be required to adjudicate disputes. His judgment may be sought in important matters of policy. Many such situations arise in the career of the average rabbi; they indicate that the community views him in many different lights. All the more reason for the rabbi to evaluate the Jewish scene for himself and to adopt the role most calculated to advance the cause of a creative, vigorous Judaism.

A simple conclusion which would seem to follow from what I have said is that if greatness is to be achieved by Jewish religion in the United States, it must flow from the give and take of Jews in all walks of life who want to take advantage of this heritage to enhance the quality of their lives. Such a process would have to involve a much greater study of the tradition than is now engaged in. If the purpose of such study were to help Jews to face life and not simply to master a fund of knowledge, the disposition to examine the treasures of the Jewish spirit would, I am certain, be much greater. There is a thirst for knowledge among Jews, but they want that knowledge to lead to action and not merely to inform them of how other Jews, past or present, have behaved. If our rabbis understood their function as teachers, they would spend most of their time trying to discover what bothers their congregations and then in trying to set in motion a cooperative search for solutions.

When the problems of Jewish religion come to be viewed as those of human beings looking to find in their tradition answers to the elusive questions of existence, we may possibly be in a position to create some better form of community than now exists in Jewish religious ranks. Religion in a new key demands emphasis on questions rather than answers. Indeed the finest type of spiritual kinship may be found between people who want to share their resources in meeting a common problem. Religion ought to be treated primarily as a search. Only thus can it really unite people. Once the emphasis is placed on presumed satisfactory answers, there cannot fail to be disunity. We mortals are not privileged to inherit the Truth; at best, we catch a glimpse of it. But, like the perception of a familiar face which disappears immediately in a crowd, even that glimpse is uncertain. We can never be sure that our perception was correct. Jewish religious unity must be primarily a feeling of empathy, a participation in the hunger for knowledge and truth of fellow Jews as they try to understand their tradition and its implications for themselves and for mankind. Organizational unity which is not founded on basic fellowship can hardly be of any spiritual value. To help create this understanding among Jews of all types of religious outlook should be the exalted mission not only of the rabbis but of all who serve the Jewish community professionally.

Obviously, however, the rabbinate* operates in a larger communal setting. Rabbis cannot by themselves succeed as

---

*What I say about the rabbinate applies to other Jewish civil servants as well. If I have concentrated on the rabbis it is because I know them and their problems best.

teachers without a properly organized unit in which their teaching has relevance. We shall discuss later some of the broader questions of Jewish community organization as they bear on Jewish religion. Now, however, we examine some of the proposals being put forth for the future of American Jewish religion.

4

The voluntarism of American Jewish life, coupled with the intellectual interaction between Jews and non-Jews, must be reckoned with. It is inevitable that some Jews be caught and swept along by the winds of doctrine that are blowing about the house of Israel. But the adoption of ideas originating in non-Jewish sources, while it is a natural reaction, is not the only possible reaction for Jews who want to be fully integrated into American life. While eschewing the extreme views of the timid and the chauvinistic Jews who condemn all outside influences as exercising *a priori,* an assimilatory effect—views, incidentally, which are far from the truth, as all who are aware of the non-Jewish influences on Saadia Gaon, Maimonides, and the Zionist theoreticians of our own day can testify—we must evaluate these influences in terms of their possible effect on Jewish religion. Simply because Jews, like all peoples, have to live in a particular environment is no reason for them not to be selective about it.

Of especial interest is the Protestant theological influence on Jewish thinkers who have come to see the future of Jewish religion in terms of specific theological presuppositions. I cite the theologies of Will Herberg and Emil Fackenheim. I make no attempt in this study to offer a complete analysis of their thinking; I want only to indicate by reference to their approach the inadequacy of any theological solution to the problems of Jewish religion.[6]

Herberg, who cites Niebuhr, Barth, Buber, and Rosenzweig as the theologians who have most profoundly affected his thinking, conceives of Judaism as a special kind of culture supernaturally bestowed upon the Jewish people and constituting a responsibility which the people as such cannot relinquish. Individual Jews, the inauthentic ones, may escape, but not the "chosen people." The Jew, by definition, is one who accepts the covenant; however, an individual born a Jew remains a Jew even if he does not assume the burden of Jewish life, for in accordance with a Rabbinic principle, Herberg believes that a Jew, however much he may sin, is still a Jew. Nevertheless, the covenant itself, the divine election of the Jewish people, is not dependent upon the decision of individual Jews.

> We miss the entire meaning of the covenant as understood in biblical-rabbinic thought if we imagine it as something that depends for its power and reality upon the voluntary adherence of the individual Jew. The covenant, in biblical-rabbinic faith, is not a private act of agreement and affiliation; it is not a contract that becomes valid only when the individual Jew signs it. Indeed, the individual Jew would not be a Jew at all in any intelligible sense were he not *already* under the covenant. The covenant is an objective supernatural fact; it is God's act of creating and maintaining Israel for his purposes in history.[7]

Herberg is trying to answer two questions at one and the same time. The first is the mystery of the continued survival and identity of the Jewish people, a people which has apparently transcended time and space, and which seems to persist as an identifiable entity despite the numerous forms that it has assumed and assumes today in countries throughout the world. The second question is the mystery of the continued survival and identity of Judaism, a civilization which has persisted in the midst of countless types of environment. My chief objection to Herberg's view on the nature and destiny of the Jewish people and its civilization is, as already outlined, my opposition to its supernaturalism and to its insistence that only a supernaturalist position does justice to the facts of the Jewish situation. Regarding his opinion about the future of American Jewish religion, I challenge the feasibility of Herberg's monistic, and indeed mechanistic, solution. It is altogether unlikely that Jewish unity, survival, or spiritual creativity can be assured by theological uniformity or necessity, for the achievement of uniformity appears to be impossible in a democratic society. To criticize his position on the grounds of feasibility or realism, Herberg might respond, in no criticism, for the covenant, after all, makes no concessions to the ephemeral fashions of modern life. Its validity cannot be tested by man since it is not of this world. But in reply to Herberg, realism need not be equated with shallow perception or with opportunism. The pluralism of American culture is a profound creation of the human spirit and stands in direct opposition to monistic systems of thought. Similarly, the wide disagreement as to the meaning of Jewish life should lead one to suspect that no single theory encompasses a final answer and that the ultimate, theological truth about Jewish religion is indeed to be found in the "end of days." To reckon with and acknowledge the truths in the many theologies and secularist philosophies of Judaism is not only realistic but probably affords a more accurate insight than Herberg's simple formula into the mystery of Jewish identity. Jewish identity and survival are inextricably involved in and determined by the human predicament of the Jewish people, and the answer to the mystery of Jewish identity is to be sought not in metaphysical assumptions but in the common history, experiences, and aspirations of Jews throughout the world. It is true that just as the ego of the individual transcends the phases of growth and activity of body and mind, so Jewish identity transcends the Jewish group in particular times and places. But Jewish identity cannot be understood apart from its relation to the corporate and earthly experience of the Jewish people.

Herberg would be the last to claim exclusive possession of the truth. All that he asserts is that his reading of biblical-Rabbinic religion is legitimate, and that only this version of Jewish religion is authentic or desirable. But even with this reservation his view lacks conviction for those who look upon Jewish religion as the life-blood of a living people; from such a perspective, the correctness of Herberg's understanding of traditional Judaism is beside the point. To cite an analogy, no American will deny that the original Constitution sanctioned slavery. This does not mean that the present generation must restore the institution in order to merit being called American. No more is the swallowing of a Jewish theology of ancient or hallowed vintage a prerequisite to authenticity in Jewish life. Herberg's theology, however valuable it is as a corrective to views which ignore the Jewish people's obligation to understand its ancestral theology, is hardly calculated either to unite Jewry or to serve as a satisfying answer to the spiritual problems of naturalist-minded Jews.

In his search for an answer to the question, "What is a Jew?," Fackenheim proposes a definition that is identical with Herberg's: "A Jew is anyone who by his descent is subject to Jewish fate ('the covenant') ; whether he responds to Jewish fate with Jewish faith (whether he is 'obedient' or 'stiff-necked') does not affect, though it is related to, his Jewishness."[8]

Fackenheim will have none of the variety of rationalism that prevailed in nineteenth-century and in much of twentieth-century thought.

> The rationalists . . . saw in Judaism the assertions that man is free, though morally obligated; that God represents moral law; that the messianic age is to be brought about by human effort. But they conveniently forgot the rabbinic assertions concerning the *yetzer ha-ra'* (the evil inclination), an inclination so strong that only God in the world-to-come can uproot it. They forgot that God is represented not only as moral law (which may be understood in naturalistic terms), but also as love, forgiving to just and unjust alike (which cannot be so understood).* They forgot that while on the one hand the Messiah is said to arrive when men repent—when the world has become good enough to make his coming *possible*—he is on the other hand said to come when the world will be so wicked as to make it *necessary*. They stressed the midrashim asserting Israel's election as the result of its free choice, but ignored those that saw it as a supernaturally imposed fate.[9]

> "*Judaism*," continues Fackenheim in criticism of the rationalists, "*is to be understood, not as an evolution of ideas in the direction of a pure rationalism, but as confrontation of finite human existence with the infinite.*"[10]

Kierkegaard's influence, which Fackenheim readily acknowledges, is apparent.

---

*Why love is any less natural than moral law is something that Fackenheim fails to explain. It is just such recourse, however, to essentially false distinctions between natural and supernatural manifestations which confer upon philosophies like those of Fackenheim and Herberg whatever plausibility they may seem to have.

There are other elements in Fackenheim's theology worth exploring, but this is enough to show the direction in which this approach would lead. There is justification in tradition for Fackenheim's thesis that many of the great ideas of the Jewish religious heritage arise dialectically "in and from the basic relationship of finite to Infinite."[11] Fackenheim can also find plenty of support in Buber's conception of Jewish religion as a dialogical relationship between man and God and Israel and God.

However, the same criticism that Fackenheim levels against the rationalists can be turned against him, namely the ignoring of other, naturalistic developments in the tradition and certainly in the interpretation of the tradition. When the rabbis put into the mouth of God the sentiment that He would prefer that His people followed His Torah rather than be preoccupied with Him, they were expressing, in their own way, their aversion to theological speculation and their preference for making life on earth just and worthwhile. Moreover, as Milton Steinberg commented, "while there is in Judaism something akin to what Rabbi Fackenheim discerns, it appears inconstantly, indecisively, hardly ever in the form and never in the idiom he employs. Whatever then may or ought to be the role of tension between the Absolute and the individual, it can scarcely be said to be what Rabbi Fackenheim finds it, the key clue to an understanding of Judaism."[12]

Jewish religion cast in the theological mold of a Herberg or a Fackenheim would become a doctrine having no relation to the ways Jews behave or think. True, if all Jews could accept the metaphysical tension under which Herberg and Fackenheim would have them live their lives, if they could see as inevitable the tragic paradox in man's sinning even when he would do good, the Jews would probably become a "holy people," holy, that is, in their recognition of "the tragic sense of life." But it is altogether conceivable that such a metaphysical system, even if we were to accept all its premises, would in no way be superior to a "rational" Jewish religion, in which the great gap between ideals and their realization is acknowledged but in which there is a concentration on bridging that gap rather than a preoccupation with trying to explain its significance dialectically and metaphysically.

In all candidness, however, it must be admitted that the aversion that some of us have to theological solutions to a human problem is also based on a practical consideration. Wherever human reason is involved—and what human problem can be solved without it?—the possibility of error and difference of opinion is always present. No group problem is solved by intellectualization alone. The theories that men devise must be tested. How, except by assent, is one to build a Jewish religion based upon belief in a supernaturally imposed covenant? Once one begins to test the contents of that covenant, it loses its absolute character and becomes subject to all the buffeting around in the arena of intellectual and practical life from which the theologians try to protect it. Herberg, Fackenheim, and the other thinkers who have taken many of the insights of Protestant theology and applied them to the study of Judaism, have performed a service by revealing some of the unplumbed depths of the human situation and of our tradition, but they cannot be said to have revealed a Jewish religion around which all Jews can rally and to which every Jew, whether metaphysically equipped or not, can contribute.

5

Religion as a group phenomenon can hardly be planned

with exactitude. The direction of group life, its social forms, its economic and political structure, its aspirations—all these can be selected and planned from previous experience and from the examples of other groups. But collective religion, that which renders life worthwhile for the group, is itself the culmination of the group's development. Just as the God of personal religion must exist somehow in the experience of the individual before conceptualization is possible, so the group religion must grow to maturity, must exist, before it can be articulated. This fact about religion in no way absolves the individual from formulating his own ideas as to what path his group ought to follow or from establishing for himself a satisfactory religious philosophy. But humility, if not understanding, should prevent anyone from describing his group's religion solely in terms of his own doctrinal approach.

Though the future of Jewish religion in the United States cannot be blueprinted, it is possible to suggest some steps that might at least create the conditions essential for a new religious development among American Jews. Such steps would have to begin with a realistic appraisal of the American environment and the present state of Jewish religion.

Planning presupposes a general optimism. Yet there is no guarantee that the Jewish people in the United States will survive. Since survival is not, or should not be, an end in itself, the Jewish will to live may wane. But at the present rate of intermarriage it would take many generations for American Jewry to disappear, and "while there's life, there's hope." Actually, the vitality of American Jewry has never been stronger than it is now, and planning for its future should take into account existing assets.

In speaking of Jewish religion, our first point of concen-

tration must be the Jewish people. Its character, framed
partially by the heritage of previous generations, will determine the Jewish religion of the future. In this regard, we
should heed the warning of Ernst Simon that the organized
efforts of Jews in the United States to survive as a people
must not obscure the need to make over the religious purposes of their group survival. As Simon writes, "Certain
forms of life may serve in the Diaspora as life-keepers for a
menaced social minority with a strong will of self-assertion.
That has nothing to do with religion, with a living belief
in God and His revelation, but it may work for a while as a
substitute. In my humble opinion, it will not work for too
long."[13] Without subscribing to Simon's conception of religion, we can agree that religion and group organization
are not identical, and that only where the latter is imbued
with spiritual and ethical purpose will religion evolve. As
now constituted, American Jewry is dissipating its inherited
spiritual capital by an overconcentration on various forms
of partial Judaism. Unless American Jews do something to
channel all their divergent ideologies into a single stream
of Jewish life, American Jewry will produce sectarian religious doctrines unrelated to a thriving, creative community. Those doctrines will have little survival power.
Existentialist Judaism, supernaturalist Judaism, naturalist
Judaism—all these can freshen Jewish life and serve a creative purpose provided that there is a Jewish community to
absorb their insights. If these doctrines are made the be-all
and end-all of Jewish religion, they cannot but contribute
to the dissolution of Jewish life and ultimately to their own
demise as life-giving forces.

American Jewry must develop for itself a polity that will
reckon with American cultural pluralism and the folk basis
of Jewish religion. The American scene is hospitable to

ethnic survival only on a religious basis, whereas Jewish religion has flowered most when it has been the heart of a united community with many and catholic interests. Judaism is the clearest example of an ethnic religious culture. Its chances for further growth in the United States are therefore very great, if the Jews will it. But this growth calls for a pooling of resources, a sharing of personal, cultural, and educational facilities, and the creation of many more opportunities for shared experience and communal policy. A Jewish community united solely for defense or for public relations is hardly likely to produce religious values.

Here I pause to answer critics who charge the proponents of Jewish community organization with seeking to create a monolithic structure which is out of keeping with the democratic spirit. Their constant refrain is that such community planning is a return to the "authoritarianism" of East European Jewish communities, with the consequent suppression of minority opinion. The simplest way to refute this argument is to point out that every seriously considered plan for American Jewish community organization has assumed three basic democratic principles:

1. The Jewish community must be voluntary in character. Every Jew must have the right to affiliate or to abstain from affiliation, or to resign.
2. Plans for community organization must be based on democratic control, including full minority rights of expression or dissent.
3. Only constitutionally determined areas of interest would become subject to communal control. By and large these areas would be matters of utmost concern to the survival of the Jewish group.

The two other main types of criticism of community organization do not hold up any better under scrutiny. The assertion that as a religion Judaism has no need for polity bespeaks, as we have seen, ignorance of the nature of religion and of Judaism. The thesis, enunciated most prominently by Oscar Handlin, that the failure of previous attempts at over-all community organization proves its impossibility and undesirability, overlooks two considerations that should occur to the historian above all.

First, owing to the opposition of certain groups no plan for Jewish community organization has ever really been given a chance to succeed. Historically, however, opposition to a particular social plan always has the chance of being overcome at some future time. The American Jewish Committee, presumably open-minded as it is, may some day be convinced it has been wrong.

Second, failures of the past should not per se deter us from future efforts. History is replete with examples of failures that spurred men to renewed and eventually successful striving toward worthwhile goals. Nothing in the history of attempts to organize an American Jewish community warrants the conclusion that such a community, democratically conceived, is either undesirable or impossible of achievement.

It is hardly necessary to elaborate these points. There is simply no basis for assuming that the effort of Jews to enhance their spiritual life by forming a free and voluntary organization within the framework of American society is undemocratic. Quite the contrary, just as Protestant efforts to effectuate unity among their churches is a necessary reaction to the separation of church and state, so is a Jewish drive toward community essential to Jewish survival in a free, mobile culture.

While the particular form of the American Jewish community must evolve from trial and error, Jews cannot afford to wait for the "final" product; they must experiment with means of unifying their activities in some organic fashion. As far as Jewish religion is concerned, the rabbinate and the religious laity would perform a service for Jewish life if they would work toward making explicit the religious qualities—and, more specifically, the Jewish religious qualities—inherent in many activities currently being pursued outside the synagogue. Religious leaders ought at least not to make the mistake of defining Jewish religion in institutional terms. They will have to help Jews raise the sights of their communal activities to the religious purposes they originally served, which ought to become the basis of the Jewish contribution to American cultural pluralism.

6

The prevailing view among religious Jews is that the synagogue is the basic unit around which an American Jewish community can and should be built. A clear and forthright presentation of the view has been made by Robert Gordis. In a paper delivered before a recent convention of the Rabbinical Assembly, Dr. Gordis argued that it is idle to expect all Jews to join in a program for Jewish life which would be of any consequence. He pointed out that the community councils, for example, are at best able to develop cooperation in noncontroversial charitable enterprises and anti-defamation activities. Therefore, those Jews who view Judaism organically should voluntarily join together in a union of synagogues. The resultant community would be characterized by "the free association not of those Jews who accept one or another element of Jewish life, or even none, but the willing union of those Jews who accept all the basic elements of Judaism as an organic unity."[14] These basic elements, ten in number, are the unity of Israel as a people, the centrality of Jewish religion, the creative role of Eretz Yisrael, the survival of American Jewry, the role of American Jews as an integral element of the American people, the ethical duty and destiny of Israel, the right of all Jews to fellowship with the people of Israel, the acceptance as participants in one or another phase of Jewish life of those unable to assent to its full program, cooperation between the organic Jewish community and those Jews remaining outside its scope, and the central role of Jewish education.

There is much to be said for Gordis's thesis. It accepts the fact that any American Jewish community will have to be voluntary; it attempts to build around the synagogue, which is undoubtedly the strongest institution in American Jewish life; and it develops a conception of the synagogue's function which reckons with the nature of Judaism as more than a creedal religion. During the discussion on his paper, Gordis took account of the charge that the religious forces in Jewry are today divisive influences. He responded that the same applies to the secular groups and that therefore at least those who see Judaism whole should make an effort to unite.

Gordis acknowledges the sad failure of the Synagogue Council, which is logically the embodiment of his theory. The right of veto by Reform, Conservative, and Orthodox representatives has rendered the Council incapable of acting on any religious issue where "matters of principle" are at stake. More significant, it is not likely that any union of synagogues can make an appreciable difference in the quality of Jewish religion, for problems of worship, ritual, ethics, and theology are not subject to resolution by votes, even in a council of synagogues. It is still in individual homes and synagogues that religious creativity must flower. It is hard to see on what kind of religious platform, other than the present innocuous one of the Synagogue Council, Reform, Conservative, and Orthodox Jews could stand united. The only advantages that can flow from such a union are the respect that accrues to the tradition as a whole and the arousing of the religious sensibilities of the congregational members. However, such respect can be and has been won in broader community organizations involving nonsynagogue Jews. Why, then, the assumption that more is to be gained by isolating the "organic" Jews?

Gordis does not seem to realize the tremendous amount of work that remains to be done before a program of organic Judaism can be built around the synagogue. I need only mention the shallow religiosity of those who, by virtue of having joined a synagogue, are labeled as religious Jews. Given this kind of membership, even an organic Judaism based on the ten principles outlined by Gordis is likely to be nothing more than a slogan, devoid of content and built largely on organizational, rather than ideological, commitment. The real job of American Jewry, preceding or running concomitantly with organizational unification, is the deepening of Jewish education. Of course, Gordis includes this as one of his ten principles, but, again, what is to be gained by separating "organic" Jews from "nonorganic" Jews, when it is precisely the give and take between them that is essential to creative thinking? Does Gordis seriously maintain that "religious" Jewry has already developed an educational philosophy which meets the spiritual needs of Jews as they grapple with life? Will "organic" Jews formulate a better educational program without the cooperation of "secularist" Jews than with it? Gordis would reply that his plan does not read out cooperation between his organic community and nonorganic Jewry. But if so, would not the same approach apply to cooperation on relations with Israel (with, let us say, the American Jewish Committee or the Jewish Labor Committee), on defense against anti-Semitism, and so on down the line. In the meantime, within the organic community, differences of opinion on religious, educational, and cultural matters would very largely prevent even a unified school system.

The point is that a creative Jewish community must be built step by step; it must involve all Jews who are ready to cooperate with one another in any or all of the areas which Gordis mentions. It would be well if men, like Gordis, who take an organic view of Judaism would use their influence on all Jews with whom they come into contact and try to transmit that understanding to them. This would be a far greater contribution to the organization of Jewish life than trying to build a Jewish community on the foundation of the synagogue. The assumption that the synagogue has a monopoly on religiosity is a gratuitous one. The lack of spirituality, the perfunctory character of worship, the self-glorification of some rabbis, the undemocratic procedures, the snobbery, the complacency—these are only a few of the characteristics that make all too many synagogues no more fit vehicles for an organic Judaism than many secular organizations; yet Gordis, though he places the secular organizations in the category of "sinners," invites their cooperation with the organic community.

Blueprints such as the one drawn up by Gordis have, of course, educational value. They indicate the possibilities, they set desirable goals, they establish criteria, and they stimulate discussion. Thus the Gordis plan, the similar plan of Henry Hurwitz,[15] and others that are brought forward from time to time should be argued pro and con until the issues are clear. This is the only way—the slow process of interaction and education—to bring into being a community with spiritual and cultural depth. I need not add that efforts at creating a Jewish community should proceed apace with study. We need not wait for a completely literate Jewry before we proceed to bring Jews together.

7

If we must be satisfied with piecemeal organization for a long time to come, we must nevertheless be prepared to take first steps. Such a step toward Jewish unity can be taken through a joint effort to build first-rate common schools for children of religious and nonreligious parents. The establishment of such schools must become part of the program of the local bureaus of Jewish education. So far they have succeeded in bringing the Reform, Conservative, and Orthodox synagogues together for the purpose of raising educational standards, but they have left each group completely free to conduct its own type of schools. By continuing to train their children in Jewish schools whose sectarianism is pure and unadulterated, American Jews make sure that their children will grow up without really appreciating Judaism in all its variety.

Critics of a specific proposal like the communalization of Jewish education object that it disregards the place of ideology in the shaping of curricula. How can one conceive of Jewish religious education without a commitment by the school and the teachers to a particular version of Jewish religion? I do not believe in the possibility or the desirability of a completely "objective" curriculum. Teachers must have a point of view. I do suggest that it is more desirable to confront children with the pluralism which pervades Jewish life than to narrow their perspective unrealistically in the classroom.

One example of this approach should suffice to make

the point clear. Teacher A presents a lesson on the Shabbat
by outlining its observance, from candlelighting to *havdalah*.
She presents an enthusiastic, glowing account of the day,
interspersing prayer, melody, and story to make the tradition come alive for the children. Sincere? Undoubtedly.
Beautiful? Yes. Exciting? If the teacher has the personality
to get her feelings across, she can be very effective. Realistic?
No. For only a handful of the students in the average Hebrew
school class see the Shabbat in its fullness. The rest can
only wonder what all this has to do with their lives. Or
they may ask why their parents have denied them such
beauty. Or, as frequently occurs, they may view the entire
lesson as ancient history.

Teacher B asks the students what their families do on
Shabbat. One student says his mother lights candles; another says his father plays golf; another tells of a weekly
visit to grandma and grandpa for a festive meal; another
adds that everything is the same as on other days, except
that his father sleeps later. The question then arises as to
how to account for these differences. The teacher carries
the lesson over to the next class session; as homework each
student is to find out how his grandparents observed the
day. Most likely the answers will fall into a more uniform
pattern, but differences will still be observable. Starting thus
realistically, it is possible for the teacher to explore the
meaning of the Shabbat and to account for the many experiences and varieties of points of view that make up contemporary Jewish life. As in the classroom of Teacher A,
there will be considerable disagreement, but here the atmosphere is likely to be one of inquiry into the making of
a tradition. In the hands of a sympathetic teacher, the many
complex problems which parents and fellow students have
had to face in shaping their lives become understandable.

Children will disagree with one another, but, as I have witnessed on numerous occasions, opinions about the tradition will change in the direction of greater appreciation of its beauty and relevance.

Education ordinarily proceeds slowly, with many contradictions and stumbling blocks. The methods of teachers and the reactions of students are not always so clear-cut or well-formulated as I have indicated. Parents may resent the teacher's "prying" into their family life, and students may be reticent when it comes to discussing their parents. But the principle that the classroom must be as true to life as possible, not in the sense of justifying the status quo but of initiating the educational process with the child's own experience, has been proved to be a valid one.

Admittedly, this philosophy of education assumes a pluralistic approach to the teaching of Jewish religion. It places a premium on free inquiry and criticism. But is not this the essence of democratic education? Surely, the Jewish school, which avowedly wants to contribute its share to American democracy, must have faith in the ability of children to think for themselves and in the ability of Jewish tradition to hold its own in their minds and hearts.

The evolutionary approach to Jewish communal organization calls for a willingness to make basic changes in Jewish education. If the Synagogue Council would do nothing else but bring Orthodox, Conservative, and Reform Jews together in community-wide classes, it would perform an invaluable function in Jewish life. It is in the classroom that Jews with conflicting views may learn to appreciate their common heritage and become more tolerant of each other's positions. At present the institutions of Orthodoxy, Reform, and Conservatism are strengthening themselves within their own ranks but are building barriers between

one another. Educational isolationalism in Jewish life is
the surest road to complete sectarianism. No one should
ask Jews to renounce their convictions; let them worship
as they please and behave as they please. But they cannot
afford to make the understanding of the Jewish tradition a
sectarian affair. Jewish education, on the adult no less than
on the child's level, must become the responsibility of all
Jews interested in preserving Jewish life.

8

These modest proposals are simple to pen but by no
means easy to carry out. The path to Jewish community,
the prerequisite for a revitalized Jewish religion, is strewn
with the obstacles of vested interests, intellectual obtuseness,
and personality conflicts. All talk of Jewish religion, however, is idle chatter, unless it is predicated upon an all-out
effort—an American counterpart to the building of Jewish
life in the State of Israel.

Such a community would by no means preclude the continued cultivation of the different approaches to Jewish
life that are now current. Indeed, to be successful as a
voluntary enterprise—which, as has been said, it must be in
a democratic environment—a united Jewish community
would have not only to countenance but to encourage the
freest expression of belief and action among its members.
Where "community" action would be decided on in a manner binding on all members of the Jewish group, the decision
would have to be reached in accordance with a generally
accepted plan. Those who feel that a voluntarily organized
group has never any right to speak on behalf of its members ought never to join any group. Occasionally, all of us
must find ourselves in a minority, but we must learn to

accept that status in good humor and with a sense of discipline so long as the group permits us freedom of dissent.

The vitality of American Judaism depends also on the ability of American Jews to recapture the sense of the relevance of Jewish religion to their everyday life as American citizens. There should be some bearing of Jewish religion upon Jewish participation in American civilization. Unless religion can be so related to everyday problems, it has no future. For American Jews, this means a conscious effort to throw the searchlight of Jewish experience on American civilization both in an appreciative and, where necessary, in a critical way. What I am advocating is not a Jewish vote or a Jewish labor movement; my plea is for Jews to study their tradition in terms of its relevance to American life and, more specifically, to the role of Jews in American life. For example, if the Jewish festivals are to have meaning to American Jews, they cannot be merely a reminder of what Jewish farmers are doing in Israel at the particular moment. Neither can the ideals that inhere in each of the holidays be made vital to the American Jew if they fail to be connected in his mind with his daily experience.

Americanism, the civilization of the United States, is not a monotone culture. It has its bright spots and shadows, its ethically valid and invalid features. Jews, like all other citizens, must be selective in their partaking of the American heritage. Also, as free citizens of a free and still evolving civilization, they have an obligation to contribute the best in them to that civilization. It is time for Jews, who are here to stay, to cease being apologetic about the at-homeness of their Judaism in America. Whatever in Judaism is incompatible with the highest expression of the democratic spirit should and will cease to exist, and those elements in the Jewish religion that enhance the quality of American life deserve the devoted backing of American Jewry. Truth can triumph only when those who can contribute to its revelation teach what they believe and are prepared to test the validity of their teaching in the crucible of experience.

If Jews want an agenda for Jewish religious contributions to American civilization, they might explore, by way of example, the implications for the welfare state of the biblical, Rabbinic, and modern Zionist ideologies, the bearing of the tradition on race relations (particularly on current Jewish attitudes toward Negroes), the Jewish emphasis on education and its possible lessons for the problems of American education. In some instances the Jewish tradition is crystal-clear. Where it is, it only remains for Jews to appropriate the attitude—if they agree with it—and make it part of their contemporary way of life. If the tradition has nothing to say, or if it is indecisive, then modern Jews will have to create a tradition of their own and add it to their Oral Law. The saying in *Ethics of the Fathers* that everything is to be found in the Torah is only an opinion; Jews should be realistic enough to know that new dimensions must be achieved by the Jewish religion.

If the ideal of religio-cultural pluralism is to be realized, it can only be done by the earnest efforts of the various religio-cultural groups in the United States to harmonize their traditions with the common democratic heritage. This, as must be emphasized again and again, is a two-way process. All groups must examine their own ways of life in the light of the democratic spirit; they must renounce dogmatism and pretensions at exclusive possession of truth. Each group has the right to try to convert the rest of the world to its own doctrines and practices, but it must recognize that its tradition is not the only path to salvation. Self-criticism, however, should be but the prelude to critical appraisals of the American scene. The right of the National Council of the Churches of Christ in America, the Rabbinical Assembly of America, the Central Conference of American Rabbis, and similar groups to criticize some of the social evils of American capitalism is the legitimate and necessary counterpart of the limitations in power which each of these organizations must accept in a democratic environment.

American Jews cannot hope to duplicate here the direct control and responsibility for the total economic, social, and political set-up of the Jews in Israel. But neither must they sit with their hands folded and assume no responsibility for the character of American civilization. They are implicated in American democracy; their religion, therefore, must play an active role in its growth or else atrophy as a useless appendage to the body of American life.

9

The recognition of the need for Jewish unity and for the development of a religion revelant to American life is only part of a sociologically oriented approach to Jewish religion. A major effort is needed, akin to the trial-and-error method of the non-Orthodox Jews in Israel, to refashion the ceremonials and worship services of Jewish religion.

It is no secret that home ceremonials and public worship among Jews are at a low ebb. Whatever vitality Jewish life has is expressed in cultural, educational, and philanthropic activities. The synagogue and the Jewish home face a serious crisis, which cannot be camouflaged by the current widespread synagogue building campaigns and increases in membership. The synagogue as an institution is still the chief medium through which the American Jew affiliates himself with Jewish life, but the synagogue as a spiritual force touches only a small proportion of the Jewish population. One would assume that a condition of this kind would galvanize religious leadership into courageous and far-reaching action. The rabbinate has long been aware of the fact that synagogue attendance is on the wane, originally perhaps for economic reasons, now for other, more serious, ones. The late Friday evening service was American Jewry's most creative response to the challenge, and there is no question that in many communities this step has helped to preserve organized worship. By this time, however, the late Friday service should be recognized for what it is—a stop-gap measure. The service depends for its success or failure on the popularity of the rabbi; anyone who has attended a service of this kind knows that the worship portion lacks warmth and vitality. People come to "hear the rabbi." This represents a revolution in Jewish religion, for the synagogue used to be a place where Jews came to worship—regardless of the quality of the cantor's voice or the spell-binding abilities of the rabbi. As a matter of fact, the rabbi used to preach only rarely; his function was chiefly to interpret the Law and to teach.

In the modern American synagogue, prayer seems to be entirely perfunctory. Nevertheless many Jews rise up in arms whenever a change in a prayer or in synagogue procedure is proposed. The objections often come from people who do not know the meaning of the Hebrew prayers and who do not frequent the synagogue. One might infer from their attitude that the emotionalism with which they react is motivated either by guilt feelings or by a fear of the magical potency of the traditional ritual.

The problem of synagogue worship transcends the synagogue itself; it embraces the whole spiritual orientation of the modern Jew. Prayer as our forefathers experienced it is becoming increasingly unimportant to men and women trained in a scientific universe of discourse. Even the theologically oriented Jewish intellectuals who subscribe to the idea of a supernaturally imposed covenant are not naive enough to believe that God hears their prayers and consciously responds to them. But this is exactly what our ancestors believed and what made their praying an experience full of deep feeling. Lacking that belief, the modern worshiper must find an entirely different rationale for the recitation of the traditional prayers. If we are to judge by actual conversations with Reform, Orthodox, and Conservative synagogue attenders, prayer among Jews today is motivated by duty and habit, by a desire to associate with fellow Jews, by a need for relaxation and meditation, by a love for the traditional forms, by the need to cleanse the soul—and only rarely by a yearning to commune with God. The soul has been removed from Jewish collective worship.

If Jews were honest with themselves, they would admit that the reason for the paucity of synagogue worshipers and the lack of feeling among those who do pray regularly is not a perverse refusal to open their hearts to the beauty of the traditional and modern forms of worship. Only the blind can fail to see that a revolution of the same magnitude as the ancient change from sacrificial worship to prayer is taking place. No one can predict what the ultimate outcome of this revolution will be but Jews ought to prepare themselves to accept the consequences of the scientific world outlook.

It will not avail them to await word from on high as to the next step in worship. American Jews ought to learn from the experience of Israel's non-Orthodox Jews. They ought, in particular, to take heart and not to fear that by altering this or that prayer or by experimenting with synagogue procedure they may further assimilation or weaken

the chances for Jewish survival. On the contrary, by allowing the synagogue to remain in its status quo, they are divest-
ing it of its function of spiritual leadership.

Congregations which are prepared to act should tackle the
problem of public prayer in the spirit suggested in Chapter 4. They must find out what worshipers really think about
the services and what keeps those who do not attend away.
They should experiment with various types of prayers and
services, investigating the possibility that study, directed to
the clarification of ethical and spiritual values, might be the
fulcrum on which modern worship could rest. Traditional
Jewish worship recognized religious study as prayer; selections from biblical and Rabbinic literature were included
in the prayer book. Surely it is worth following this clue
from tradition; it might lead to some conclusion as to the
extent to which study constitutes a valid form of worship
for those who have irretrievably surrendered belief in the
supernatural. It would be idle to speculate on the outcome
of experimentation of this kind. Religious inspiration cannot be prepared in a test tube, and a single devout personality may do more to inspire the hearts of men than
all the planning of lay and rabbinical commissions. But since
we cannot afford to wait for the arrival of such an inspired
leader, we can only struggle along with our own limited
powers and try to prepare the ground for our religious
growth. There is no tried and true method for strengthening
the synagogue and public worship; there is only the certainty
that ignoring the plight of worship means its gradual dis-
appearance from Jewish life—or what is more likely, the
gradual estrangement of Jews from Jewish religion.

The approach suggested here for dealing with the problem of prayer ought to be applied to the home rituals of
Jewish religion—the Passover seder, Sabbath kiddush, hav-

dalah, etc. Commissions of laymen, rabbis, artists, group workers, and others who might have some insight into the value of ritual should be set up to create reinterpretations or new content for traditional rituals. What Israel's Jews have done with the *haggadah* should be attempted here on a much greater scale than is the case now. The many young Jewish couples who are striving to give their children a Jewish upbringing through the medium of the synagogue want a Jewish religion that commends itself to their intelligence and their aesthetic sense. They are not looking for easy ways out, as their more conservative critics charge; they want an adequate rationale for the rituals they are asked to practice, and they want to derive some inherent satisfaction from the rituals themselves. Those Jews, to cite just one example, to whom the traditional *haggadah* makes no sense or is uninspiring—even when they understand its meaning—should be provided with a home service which does justice both to the tradition and to their need for spiritual edification.* It is nonsense to assume that the compelling ideal of freedom which the epic of the Exodus first gave to the world has been drained dry of all its power of inspiration. Reactionary religion can go to its grave hugging to its breast all the hallowed heirlooms, but a living religion will go forth in search of new treasure, armed with a faith in its own potentialities for discovery.

We are told that the true way of life had to be revealed on Mt. Sinai, because man's unaided intelligence could not

---

*There are now thousands of Jewish families who have introduced the Seder into their homes as a result of the publication by the Jewish Reconstructionist Foundation of *The New Haggadah,* which, for the first time, gives American Jews something of the meaning of Passover as it relates to the problem of freedom in Jewish and human existence. But this effort is only a beginning. Other haggadot, highlighting different themes and reckoning with the varied backgrounds which Jews have, should be prepared.

with sufficient rapidity have arrived at the Truth; it is hard
to understand why God should have been in such a hurry.
For it is quite clear that even revelation has not opened
the mind of man to the "Truth." Perhaps revelation comes
only to those who storm the heavens to get it and have
enough strength to bear up under its spiritual impact.
Moses, apparently, fought for the knowledge he needed to
lead his people out of slavery, and he had the courage to
undertake the terrible burden he was asked to shoulder.
His followers did not. The Bible tells us, "And all the
people perceived the thunderings, and the lightnings, and
the voice of the horn, and mountain smoking; and when
the people saw it, they trembled, and stood afar off. And
they said unto Moses: 'Speak thou with us, and we will
hear, but let not God speak with us, lest we die.' " Evidently the Israelites of Moses' day lacked the fortitude of
their leader. They were afraid to listen to the divine
imperative.

The hope of American Judaism is the Jews who are asking questions and demanding forthright answers. The new
revelation, if and when it comes, will be the reward of their
efforts to wrestle with the problems of human life and to
find answers in their existence as Jews. Perhaps Jewish
religious leaders ought to lift their eyes from the hallowed
tomes of the Written and Oral Law and look at the masses
of Jews standing at the foot of a new Sinai. They might
then be moved to mingle with them, to encourage them in
their efforts to scale the heights and to comfort them when
they fail. Perhaps if the leaders would thus concern themselves with the needs of Jews rather than with those of the
Book, there would arise one whose compelling voice will
reach to the peak of the mountain and cause it once
again to erupt into inspiring flame.

8

THE END OF THE MATTER

IF THIS BOOK HAS ACCOMPLISHED ITS purpose it will have cautioned the reader against loose usage of the term religion, and it will also have led him to a new awareness of the role religion still has to play in human life—helping man to find his way through the complex labyrinth of his ever growing knowledge to the ultimate objective of making himself more human. There may be other accretions to this objective, and there may be different paths through the labyrinth. Some men prefer to travel along an intellectual road, mapping their path according to a doctrine of whose validity they are convinced. These are the men whose religion, deeply personal at its outset, must be taught to others before it can change the course of society. There are other men who find the achievement of the goal of human life to be a cooperative project for mankind as a whole and its subdivisions. For them doctrinal formulation and assent are the end product, rather than the starting point of religion. These are the men who see religion as a group phenomenon.

The two paths are not altogether separate. They often cross, and at times they converge. In a completely harmonious society they would be identical—but probably the scenery along the way would be very dull. I for one see no reason to hope for a final and complete answer to life's perplexities. Some of the most interesting questions in the Talmud end with *teku*—the question will remain unanswered until the *Tishbite* (Elijah the Prophet) comes to answer it. Meanwhile, however, the group religions of mankind must be made as hospitable as possible to individual men with their varying needs and as receptive as possible to their honest criticism and evaluations of the traditional viewpoints.

Applied to the Jewish group and its tradition, this approach makes clear that a *sine qua non* for the future of Jewish religion, far more important than the universal acceptance by Jews of a single, all-embracing theology, is a mutual respect that will help them live with their differences and enable them, as did the controversies between the House of Hillel and the House of Shammai, to serve the cause of God. Nothing but good can come from such mutual respect, as it will lead Jews to try to understand one another's needs and honor one another's point of view.

In my discussion of religion in Israel and the United States I have said little about the relation between the two Jewish communities. It should be evident, however, that the lessons each has for the other can be effective only if both are living entities. "Torah shall go forth from Zion," but it will not be heard by American Jews unless they are spiritually attuned to receive it and organizationally equipped to make use of the new lessons. Furthermore, the future character of the Jewish people depends on the ties that will bind Israel and American Jewry. If the Jews of Israel are to remain part of the Jewish people, then they will have to affirm their transnational bond with Jews throughout the world. World Jewry will have to develop a form of international organization that will serve as a spiritual cement.

To the timid souls who shudder at the mere thought of an international body of Jews, let it be forthrightly stated that its purpose would be revolutionary. It would be an effort on the part of the Jewish people to assist humanity in the achievement of its unification. To unify mankind, it is essential to renounce in dramatic terms the chauvinstic patriotism of all state nationalism and to affirm the prior loyalty of all men to God and to the universal values which all nationalisms should, but unfortunately do not, embody. This is the avowed purpose of the ecumenical movement in world Protestantism, and it is the ultimate justification for a world Jewry. Conceived of as spiritual peoplehood, Jewish nationalism has a deeply religious purpose, to enable Jews to become better human beings by virtue of their belonging to the Jewish people. It is this religious conception of Jewish life which entitles them to pray with conviction. "How happy are we! How goodly is our portion, how pleasant our lot, and how beautiful our heritage."

NOTES

INTRODUCTION

1. See e.g., Homer W. Smith, *Man and His Gods*, Little, Brown, Boston, 1952, Chap. I.
2. Mordecai M. Kaplan, "What Is Judaism?," *Menorah Journal*, Oct. 1915.

CHAPTER ONE

1. Max C. Otto, *Science and the Moral Life*, New American Library (Mentor), New York, 1949, p. 27. Ernst Cassirer is among those who reject the theory that fear motivated all early religions; see his *Essay on Man*, Yale University Press, New Haven, 1944, p. 85. See also Winston L. King, *Introduction to Religion*, Harper, New York, 1954, pp. 17-19.
2. Morris R. Cohen, *The Faith of a Liberal*, Holt, New York, 1946, p. 354.
3. Harold J. Laski, in *I Believe*, ed. by Clifton Fadiman, Simon and Schuster, New York, 1939, p. 148.
4. Morris R. Cohen, *op cit.*, p. 52.
5. Irving Kristol, "God and the Psychoanalysts," *Commentary*, Nov. 1949.
6. Emil Brunner, *Christianity and Civilization*, Scribner, New York, vol. 1, p. v.
7. William Barrett, in the symposium "Religion and the Intellectuals" (IV), *Partisan Review*, May-June 1950.
8. See e.g. Tillich's essay "Formative Power," in *The Protestant Era*, University of Chicago Press, Chicago, 1948.
9. See e.g. *Man Is Not Alone*, Jewish Publication Society, Phila., 1951; *God in Search of Man*, Farrar, Straus and Cudahy, New York, 1955.
10. Lionel Ruby, *The Art of Making Sense*, Lippincott, Phila., 1954, p. 53.
11. Ernst Cassirer, *The Problem of Knowledge*, Yale Uuniversity Press, New Haven, 1950, p. 305.
12. Joseph Albo, *Sefer Ha-'Ikkarim*, Jewish Publication Society, Phila., 1946, vol. 4, p. 65.

CHAPTER TWO

1. George Gaylord Simpson, *The Meaning of Evolution*, Yale University Press, New Haven, 1950, p. 5.
2. Morris R. Cohen, *The Faith of a Liberal*, Holt, New York, 1946, p. 341.
3. Horace M. Kallen, *The Liberal Spirit*, Cornell University Press, Ithaca, 1948, p. 104.
4. Morris R. Cohen, *A Dreamer's Journey*, Free Press, Chicago, 1949.
5. Erich Fromm, *Psychoanalysis and Religion*, Yale University Press, New Haven, 1950, p. 21.

6. V. I. Lenin, *Religion*, International Publishers, New York, 1933, p. 32.
7. Morris R. Cohen, *Reflections of a Wondering Jew*, Beacon, Boston, 1950, p. 157.
8. Victor Serge, *Russia Twenty Years After*, Hillman-Curl, New York, 1937, p. 131.
9. Alfred North Whitehead, *Religion in the Making*, Macmillan, New York, 1926, p. 16.
10. Peter A. Bertocci, *Introduction to the Philosophy of Religion*, Prentice-Hall, New York, 1955, pp. 210-216.
11. Erich Fromm, *Man for Himself*, Rinehart, New York, 1947, p. 7.
12. Hans Kohn, *The Idea of Nationalism*, Macmillan, New York, 1944.
13. Salo Baron, *Modern Nationalism and Religion*, Harper, New York, 1947.
14. Maurice Samuel, *The Great Hatred*, Knopf, New York, 1940.
15. An interesting documentation of the recognition by Protestants of their need for community is to be found in *Brooklyn Protestantism 1930-1945*, Brooklyn Church and Mission Federation, Brooklyn, 1946.
16. *History of the Communist Party of the Soviet Union*, ed. by a Commission of the Central Committee of the Communist Party of the Soviet Union, International Publishers, New York, 1931, p. 353.
17. *Ibid.*, p. 355.
18. José Ortega y Gasset, *Concord and Liberty*, Norton, New York, 1946, p. 2.

CHAPTER THREE

1. Joseph Albo, *Sefer Ha-'Ikkarim*, Jewish Publication Society, Philadelphia, 1946, vol. 3, p. 206.
2. George La Piana, "Doctrinal Background of Moral Theology," in *Moral Principles of Action: Man's Ethical Imperative*, ed. by Ruth Nanda Anshen, Harper, New York, 1952, pp. 380-381.
3. *The Wisdom of Laotse*, trans. and ed. by Lin Yutang, Modern Library, New York, 1948, pp.45-46.
4. *Ibid.*, p. 95.
5. *Ibid.*, p. 45.
6. *Ibid.*, p. 63. The sacrificial straw dogs were puppets thrown away after the sacrifice.
7. *Ibid.*, p. 63.
8. *Ibid.*, p. 64.
9. *Ibid.*, p. 65.
10. George Foot Moore, *History of Religions*, Scribner, New York, 1937, vol. 1, p. 52.
11. *Ibid.*, p. 55.
12. *The Wisdom of Laotse*, p. 68.
13. See Bertrand Russell, *A History of Western Philosophy*, Simon and Schuster, New York, 1945, p. 578.
14. Milton Steinberg, "The Common Sense of Religious Faith, Part III—The Nature of Religious Faith," *The Reconstructionist*, March 21, 1947.
15. Samuel Alexander, *Space, Time and Deity*, Macmillan, London, 1927, vol. 2, p. 347.

16. Quoted in John M. McCarthy, *The Naturalism of Samuel Alexander,* King's Crown, New York, 1948, p. 84.
17. McCarthy, *The Naturalism of Samuel Alexander,* pp. 86-87.
18. Quoted in *Readings in Philosophy,* ed. by Philip P. Wiener, Scribner, New York, 1953, p. 575.
19. Alexander, *op. cit.,* vol. 2, p. 413.
20. Alfred North Whitehead, *Religion in the Making,* Macmillan, New York, 1926, p. 90.
21. Alfred North Whitehead, *Process and Reality,* Macmillan, New York, 1929, p. 392.
22. *Ibid.,* p. 374.
23. Whitehead, *Religion in the Making,* p. 104.
24. *Ibid.,* p. 95.
25. *Ibid.,* p. 98.
26. *Ibid.,* p. 99.
27. *Ibid.,* pp. 119-120.
28. See Sterling P. Lamprecht, *Our Philosophical Traditions,* Appleton-Century-Crofts, New York, 1955, p. 477, note; Lamprecht's brief but lucid exposition of Whitehead's philosophy (pp. 476-486) is recommended to the reader.
29. John Dewey, *A Common Faith,* Yale University Press, New Haven, 1934, p. 50.
30. *Ibid.,* p. 48.
31. *Ibid.,* p. 51.
32. *Ibid.*
33. A. J. Ayer, *Language, Truth and Logic,* Dover, New York, 1950, p. 115. My criticism of Ayer should not lead the reader to minimize my indebtedness to logical positivism. The positivists have performed a valuable service in clearing the muddy waters of metaphysics and theology.

CHAPTER FOUR

1. Moses Maimonides, *The Guide for the Perplexed,* trans. by M. Friedlander, Dutton, New York, Chap. 58.
2. Gershon G. Scholem, *Major Trends in Jewish Mysticism,* Shocken, New York, 1946, p. 11.
3. Eugene Kohn, *Proceedings of the Rabbinical Assembly of America,* New York, 1949, p. 430.
4. Santayana puts it this way: "What men attribute to God is nothing but the ideal they value and grope for in themselves, the commandments, mythically said to come from the Most High, flow in fact from common reason and local experience" (*The Life of Reason: Reason in Society,* Scribner, New York, 1930, p. 188).
5. Susanne K. Langer, *Philosophy in a New Key,* New American Library Mentor), New York, 1949, p. 29.
6. *Ibid.,* pp. 39-40.
7. See Robert Ulich, *The Human Career,* Harper, New York, 1955, for a fine treatment of self-transcendence.

8. Max C. Otto, *Science and the Moral Life,* New American Library (Mentor), New York, 1949, p. 166.

CHAPTER FIVE

1. Will Herberg, *Judaism and Modern Man,* Jewish Publication Society, Phila., 1951, p. 271.
2. *Ibid.,* p. 270.
3. *Ibid.,* p. 271.
4. *Ibid.,* p. 273. Sholem Asch in *One Destiny* (Putnam, New York, 1945) actually interprets the doctrine of chosenness in this sense of the suffering servant.
5. Theodor Herzl, *The Jewish State,* American Zionist Emergency Council, New York, 1946, pp. 153-154.
6. Ruth Benedict and Gene Weltfish, *The Races of Mankind* (Public Affairs Pamphlet No. 85), Public Affairs Committee, New York, 1943, pp. 12-13.
7. Mordecai M. Kaplan, *The Future of the American Jew,* Macmillan, New York, 1948, p. 72.

CHAPTER SIX

1. See Anson Phelps Stokes, *Church and State in the United States* (Harper, New York, 1950), Leo Pfeffer, *Church, State and Freedom* (Beacon, Boston, 1954), and other standard texts on the church and state issue in the United States.
2. This and the next quotation are from Chester Inwald, "Sabbath, Sunday and State," *The Jewish Horizon,* Sept. 1949. See also the further documentation supplied by Samuel Abrahams, "Sunday Laws and the Courts," *The Jewish Horizon,* Feb. 1956.
3. From a speech by Sh. Z. Shragai at the tenth convention of Hapoel Hamizrachi, published in *Sheluhot, Kislev* 5610 (1950).
4. *Mishneh Torah, Hilkhot Melakkim,* 1:4.
5. *Hatzofeh,* 19 *Shebat,* 5607 (1948).
6. *South African Jewish Times,* July 1, 1949.
7. Martin Buber, *Paths in Utopia,* Macmillan, New York, 1950, p. 142.
8. Ernst Simon, "Tomorrow's Jew in the Making," *Commentary,* July 1948.
9. A. D. Gordon, *Selected Writings,* ed. by Frances Burnce, League for Labor Palestine, New York, p. 13.
10. From an address by David Ben Gurion delivered at Ein Harod, published in *The Jewish Frontier,* June 1950.
11. This passage and the five following quotations are from N. Benari, "Giving a Form to Our Holidays" in a summary of a symposium of the cultural committees of the kibbutzim and moshavim in the Gilboa region, held at Ein Harod, Feb. 24, 1944, published by the Palestine Contacts of the Habonim Movement.
12. Zeev Bloch, "The Sociological Origins of the Festivals," in the summary cited in the preceding footnote.

13. Yeshaya Leibowitz, "The Sabbath and Modern Technology," in *Iggeret Lagolah*.
14. "The Sabbath in the State," *B'terem*, June 1, 1951. Many of Leibowitz's talks and essays on the subject of the adjustment of *halakkah* to the demands of the modern state are to be found in his *Torah Umitzvot Bazeman Hazeh, Massada*, Tel Aviv, 1954.
15. "The Crisis of Religion in the State," *B'terem*, April 15, 1952.
16. *Ibid.*
17. "The Crisis of Religion in the State," *B'terem*, April 1, 1952.
18. Moshe Zvi Neriah, "The Laws of the Sabbath and the Practices of the State," *B'terem*, Feb. 16, 1952.
19. "The Laws of the Sabbath and the Practices of the State," *B'terem*, Mar. 1, 1952.
20. Martin Buber, *Israel and the World*, Schocken, New York, 1948, p. 17.
21. *Ibid.*, p. 13.
22. Menaham Haran, "A Generation without God," *B'terem*, Jan. 1, 1952
23. *Ibid.*
24. *Ibid.*
25. *Ibid.*
26. Jacob Hertz, "The Necessity for Religious Reform," *B'terem*, Nov. 1, 1952.
27. *Ibid.*
28. J. L. Benor, "What Is Progressive Judaism?," *B'terem*, Dec. 1, 1951.
29. *Ibid.*

CHAPTER SEVEN

1. W. Lloyd Warner and Leo Srole, *The Social Systems of American Ethnic Groups*, Yale University Press, New Haven, 1945, p. 160.
2. *Ibid.*, pp. 161-162.
3. Will Herberg, *Protestant—Catholic—Jew*, Doubleday, New York, 1955.
4. Herbert Parzen, "Is the American Environment Responsible?," *The Reconstructionist*, Feb. 10, 1950.
5. Jack J. Cohen, "The End of Halakkah?," *Conservative Judaism*, Jan. 1952.
6. Readers interested in more thorough treatments of Herberg's existentialism are referred to Harold Weisberg, *"Escape from Reason," The Reconstructionist*, Dec. 1, 1950; Eugene Kohn, "The Menace of Existentinist Religion," *The Reconstructionist*, Jan. 11, 1952; Meir Ben-Horin, "Herberg vs. Dewey," *The Reconstructionist*, Feb. 6, 1953.
7. Herberg, *Judaism and Modern Man*, p. 271.
8. Emil L. Fackenheim, "Can We Believe in Judaism Religiously?," *Commentary*, Dec. 1948.
9. *Ibid.*
10. *Ibid.*
11. *Ibid.*
12. Milton Steinberg, "Theological Problems of the Hour," *Proceedings of the Rabbinical Assembly of America*, New York, 1949.

13. Ernst Simon, "On the State of Judaism in the State of Israel," *The Jewish Layman*, Nov.-Dec. 1948.
14. *Proceedings o the Rabbinical Assembly of America*, New York, 1949, p. 324.
15. Henry Hurwitz, "Toward a Noble Community," *Menorah Journal*, Autumn 1948.

Index

Index

A

Abraham, 69, 74

Absolute, the, and search for, 80-82, 124, 137, 138, 255

after-life. *See* other-worldliness

agnostics, 16

Albo, Joseph, 30, 81

Alexander, Samuel, 96-101, 103, 111, 112
Space, Time and Deity, 101

altruism, 135-36

American Jewish Committee, 260, 264

American Philosophical Association, 10

analogy, language of, 95

animism, 60, 142

anthropomorphic God. *See* God

"anti-religious," "irreligious," and "nonreligious," 9, *note,* 31

approach to religion, 120-62

Aquinas. *See* Thomas Aquinas

Aristotle, 41, 74-75, 87, 102, 128, 129

asceticism, 52

aspects, doctrinal and social, of religion, 5, 41

assimilation of Jews, 176, 250

atheism, 6, 62, 87, 140

atomic weapons, 160

Augustine, 12

authoritarianism, 45, 46, 232, 259

Ayer, A. J., 115

B

Baron, Salo, 54

Barth, Karl, 251

behavior, evaluating, 132

Benari, N., 211-16, 228

Ben Gurion, David, 209

Benor, J. L., 229-30

bereavement, 156

Bergmann, Hugo, 223

Bible, the, 9, 68, 84, 87, 88, 200

Bloch, Zeev, 217-18

brotherhood, 53

Brunner, Emil, 13

Buber, Martin, 199, 223-25, 251, 255

Buddhism, 13, 20, 51, 129, *note*

C

Cassirer, Ernest, 29

categorical imperatives, 114

categorization of religion, 20

Catholics. *See* Roman Catholics

Cause, First. *See* Prime Mover

Central Conference of American Rabbis, 271

certainty, search for, 80-82. *see* also Absolute

challenges, modern, to Jewish life, 170-71

children and religion, 139-42

Chosen People (Covenant), 165, 172, 226, 251, 256, 273

Christianity, 13, 20, 42, 51, 55, 57, 58, 68, 71, 166, 168, 174, 182, 183, 188, 240-41